THE STORY OF SYRIA

THE STORY OF SYRIA

by

Ghayth Armanazi

[handwritten inscription: To Nadia + Thereza with best wishes]

G

GILGAMESH
PUBLISHING LTD

The Story of Syria

Published by Gilgamesh Publishing in 2017
Email: info@gilgamesh-publishing.co.uk
www.gilgamesh-publishing.co.uk

ISBN 978-1-908531-52-0

Photographics credits:

The author would like to thank the following for providing some of the photography
reprinted here: Mai El Guindi, Talal Akilli, Bashar Al Azmeh

CIP Data: A catalogue for this book is
available from the British Library

Dedicated to the memory of Ali Armanazi and Najib Armanazi.

One gave his life and the other devoted his career to the country they loved.

ACKNOWLEDGEMENTS

There are many I would wish to thank for their support and encouragement during the writing of the book. I owe a debt of gratitude to several of my family and closest friends for their assistance and advice throughout that time As far as professional help is concerned, I would like to name in particular Max Scott who first broached the idea for the book and, through Gilgamesh Publishing, provided the necessary incentive and support in the various stages of pre-publication. I especially appreciated the very light touch he displayed in the structure and format of the book allowing me a freedom that I suspect is rare among publishers dealing with new authors. Also central to the project was the work put in by Sophie Bradford, whose editing skills I will always admire, despite some vigorous exchanges over a few points of disagreement! I always was aware of her love for Syria, and her commitment to the book was a clear product of that passion.

Ghayth Armanazi

CONTENTS

Foreword	8
Author's Introduction	9
At the Beginning	13
The Aborting of Faisal's Syrian Kingdom	33
1920-1946: The Struggle for Independence	49
The Early Years of Independence	76
1949-58: The 'Revolving Door' of Coups and Counter-Coups	88
The Rise And Fall of the United Arab Republic	113
1961-63: The Last Hurrah of the Old Political Class	128
A Fractured Baath Turns on Itself	144
Hafez Assad: The 'Eternal Commander' With the Iron Grip	171
2000-2011: From Reform to Firestorm	233
Epilogue	258

FOREWORD

As the continuing civil war takes its terrible toll on its citizens and its heritage, there is no shortage of books about Syria. Much of that writing is ill informed and superficial and with no proper understanding of history.

But in this well researched and eloquent book the author has with detail and judgement placed contemporary events in their proper historical context. He does so with the insight of both scholar and diplomat. His account of the ascent of Hafez al Assad and his son provides a perceptive illumination of the policies and priorities of the present administration in Syria.

In this period of frustrated efforts for a settlement which would restore stability to Syria, Ghayth Armanazi's concluding epilogue reminds the reader of the country's historical achievements and its peoples resilience and asserts that these could be a foundation for the future. Some may find this optimistic but if Syria is ever to recover from its present crisis optimism will be required.

Menzies Campbell
The Rt. Hon Lord Campbell of
Pittenweem CH CBE PC QC
House of Lords

AUTHOR'S INTRODUCTION

The following pages are not the product of meticulous and dry academic research, and some readers could conceivably point to omissions or disputed accounts. I make no apology for a work I always intended to be a personal take on Syrian history, born out of a strong bond of attachment to the country and drawing on private experience and family ties to Syria's past and politics.

In writing this book I had one principal mission in mind: to introduce the country of my birth to the general reader. Such a reader has been subjected in the past few years to a deluge of headlines and broadcasts that depict a land in the grip of an unfathomable conflict whose graphic horrors have, with time, lost much of their power to shock. I hope that I will succeed in planting in readers' minds another 'reality' that places Syria where it should belong. It is a country that has been at the centre of the World, both geographically and culturally. It has absorbed a lot from that World, and gave in turn much that has enriched and shaped that World going back to the very beginnings of settled communal and agricultural life. In modern times Syria has been a central and leading force in the formation of an Arab movement of enlightenment and political and social advancement, being the flag-bearer for colonial emancipation and secular nationalism that has been an inspiration to other countries seeking independence in the post Second World War era.

Of course, that historical reality sits very uncomfortably with today's tragic descent into the abyss of ethnic and sectarian conflict, The breed of leaders currently in (nominal) charge of the country have tragically betrayed the legacy of those who had raised the flag of Syrian independence seventy years ago. A vast chasm exists between that early generation of leaders, who, with the most meagre of resources and with little by way of political or military clout, faced down the colonial masters of that era and achieved full and unfettered independence, and those who claim today to be Syria's overlords. Apart from the incomparable death, destruction and destitution over which the latter 'reign' they have meekly surrendered any remnants of Syrian independence, handing out parcels of the country's sovereignty to a myriad of local warlords and to regional and international state and non-state actors coveting territory. These are 'victories' that brings to mind the words of the Roman orator and historian Tacitus: 'they have created a wasteland, and they call it peace'.

Almost a hundred years ago and with all the absolute power it possessed over a conquered country, France could not impose its colonial dream off splitting Syria into what it believed to be ethno-sectarian components. Those very 'minority' communities themselves refused to be split off from the nascent Syrian state and worked alongside the 'majority' in resisting foreign rule and clinging to the notion of a free and united Syria. How ironically and egregiously different from today when by their own hands many Syrians, whether 'loyalist' or 'opposition', are manifestly engaged in carving out and demographically 'cleaning' territories to make way for the creation of a Syria of 'statelets' as dreamt of by the colonialists of yesteryear! Worse still, foreign armies, already imbued with deep sectarian and ethnic hatreds, are being brought in by the thousands to consolidate the breakup of Syria.

It is ironical to note that exactly one hundred years ago two imperial powers carved up Syria according to what became known as the Sykes-Picot Agreement. At the time of writing, a hundred years on, latter-day imperial powers, namely the United State and Russia are engaged in intensive talks for a new carve-up: perhaps a Kelly-Lavrov Agreement?

Yet, amid all that is so apocalyptic there are striking examples of an indomitable Syrian spirit emerging from the depths of despair. Examples such as that of Syrian doctors in Aleppo and elsewhere who have decided to remain amid the rubble, caring for the victims of merciless bombings in half-destroyed makeshift hospitals. Worthy of special admiration are the dedicated teams of rescuers who risk life and limb, rushing through indiscriminate air raids, in the search for survivors beneath the remnants of shattered buildings. Incredibly, those on the ground in Syria testify to a remarkable grass-roots resilience among besieged and starved communities and to a will not only to live, but also to provide locally administered social and educational services and a semblance of normality, in defiance of the surrounding horrors. Among the millions of Syrians who have had to seek refuge in neighbouring countries as well as further afield in Europe, examples abound of Syrians facing up to the unbearable circumstances of their exile, many by invoking the entrenched legacy of the Syrian mercantile spirit and establishing successful enterprises. It is to be hoped that they, and the many educated and professional talents that have been forced out of the country, will return to rebuild a new Syria that is not only free of the current brutal war, but also of its authors: tyranny, oppression and terror.

Ghayth Armanazi
September 2016

CHAPTER ONE

At the Beginning

She has looked upon the dry bones of a thousand empires and will see the tombs of a thousand more before she dies. Though another claims the name, Damascus is by right the eternal city.

— Mark Twain

The Arabs called it *Al Sham or Bilad Al Sham*. The origin is probably the Arabic word *shamal* (north), meaning the area north of the Arabian desert, famed since ancient times for its pleasant climate, green pastures, orchards and mountains – in sharp contrast to the bleak and unforgiving terrain and harsher temperatures that mark the bulk of Arabia proper. Indeed, the Prophet Muhammad, who in early life engaged in trading excursions that reached the outskirts of Damascus, is quoted as saying that he refused to enter the city itself, 'not wanting to experience Paradise before ascending to Heaven.'

The name Syria, as used by the rest of the world from ancient times until today, has a more complex genealogy and covers a territory that shrank and expanded at different historical periods. The ancient Greeks called the country *Syroi*, a name thought to derive from Assyria, the empire whose territory stretched from Mesopotamia to the shores of the eastern Mediterranean. In classical Roman times Syria denoted almost all the territory north of Arabia until Asia Minor, taking in parts of modern-day Iraq. In more recent times, Syria became more or less commensurate with the geographic term the Levant, which in turn was often interchangeable with Greater Syria, encompassing Lebanon, Jordan and Palestine, in addition to the modern state of Syria. This fluidity in identifying the area of Syria has significance beyond the academic and etymological. As we shall see in later chapters, the very lack of geo-national certitude has always influenced the course of Syrian history, producing strong socio-political tensions and undercurrents affecting the stability of the whole Levantine region.

Certainly beyond dispute, regardless of its precise configuration and boundaries, is that Syria has a historical pedigree second to none. Over twelve thousand years ago it was a primary centre of Neolithic culture where humanity first developed the techniques of agriculture and the breeding of cattle herds. Archaeological finds provide evidence of an ancient culture rivalling any in a neighbourhood known as the 'cradle of civilisation.' Discoveries over recent decades have established the importance of the kingdom of Ebla, founded around 3500 BC, with its massive, priceless library, centred on the region of Idlib, in north-western Syria. The thousands of tablets forming that library depict a prosperous state trading with Sumer, Assyria and Akkad, as well as Asia Minor, and receiving gifts from Egypt's pharaohs. The language of Ebla is transcribed in one of the oldest forms of Semitic writing. Rivalling Ebla was the equally ancient kingdom of Mari in the north-east of the country. From the middle of the twenty-fourth century BC, until the middle of the twenty-second century BC, Syria came under the dominance of the Akkadian Empire of Mesopotamia, an era which saw the decline of both Ebla and Mari. Towards the end of the twenty-first century BC, most of Syria fell to a people called the Amorites, who established a number of city-states and maintained control for two centuries. In 1809 BC, an Amorite king called Shamsi-Adad swept from northern Syria to take over the Assyrian Empire from the Akkadian King Erishum II, ensuring Amorite domination over the whole of the Levant and Mesopotamia, in addition to large areas of Asia Minor. The most famous of the Amorite kings, Hammurabi – the first ruler to establish a codified system of law – came to power in 1792 bc. He is known to have established Babylon as a major city and to have declared himself its king. Under his rule the Babylonian Empire began to take shape. During that period a rival empire known as Yamhad emerged in *Halab* (Aleppo). Tablets uncovered in Mari describe Yamhad as the mightiest state in the Near East. The state of Ugarit on the Syrian Mediterranean coast also rose during that time and gave the world its renowned alphabet derived from its Ugaritic language (related to the Canaanite family of languages).

Over the course of the following centuries Syria witnessed the ebb and flow of many more empires competing for mastery of the region. They included the Hittite, Egyptian and Assyrian empires, with the last gaining supremacy towards the end of the eleventh century BC, when it reached the Syrian coastline and even into Cyprus. By the end of that century the Assyrian grip started to recede amid the expansion of the power of Aramean tribes. Originating from the desert, the Arameans established states around cities such as Damascus and Hama. Henceforth the name *Aram* became synonymous with most of geographical Syria. Aram-Damascus grew into a major regional power, and Aramaic was to develop into the *lingua franca* of the eastern Mediterranean, surviving well into the post-classical era and providing Jesus Christ with his mother tongue. Meanwhile, the thirteenth century BC on the Syrian coast, a seafaring civilisation known as Phoenicia spread its influence through pioneering trade links all across the Mediterranean and establishing colonies as far west as Spain. Their most famous outpost, Carthage, was created in the ninth century BC and was to become an empire in its own right (later destroyed by its bitter rival, Rome).

Back in Syria a resurgent neo-Assyrian Empire engulfed the country once again, reasserting its regional dominance at the expense of the Arameans, and bringing the independence of Damascus to an end in 732 BC. Despite their conquest of Aram, the Assyrians retained Aramaic as the *lingua franca* of all their domains. They were finally defeated around 605 BC and replaced by the Chaldeans, whose capital was in Babylon. This brought Syria under the Chaldean yoke – until 539 BC, when the neo-Babylonians were crushed by a rampant Persian Empire sweeping west towards the Mediterranean, seizing Syria and declaring it their fifth province. However, again in recognition of Syria's cultural influence, Aramaic was recognised as the official tongue of the Persian Empire.

A new historical age began for Syria around 330 BC. It was to leave deep and lasting marks on the country's cultural evolution. Alexander the Great of Macedonia seized Syria from the retreating Persians and inaugurated the Hellenistic period that lasted until 64 BC. It was the Greeks who ultimately gave the name to the region which formed part of the Seleucid Empire inherited on the death of Alexander. Indeed, the

Greeks applied the name *Syroi* to all of the former Assyria, combining both Mesopotamia and modern-day Syria. The Arameans to the west and the Assyrians to the east were both referred to as Syrian or Syriac. That usage continued well into the Roman period, which began in 64 BC when the Roman legate, Pompey, abolished the Seleucid Empire and created the province of Syria, with its capital in Antioch. Under the Emperor Augustus, Syria enjoyed a period of significant prosperity, and was acknowledged as one of the principle provinces of the new empire, governed by a legate of consular rank answering directly to the emperor himself. Antioch became the third most important city in the empire after Rome and Alexandria, while Damascus, Palmyra and other urban centres grew and flourished. Syria's prosperity was linked not only to its role as an entrepôt of special importance in the trade between east and west, bringing in luxury items from India and China, but also to its wealth in grain, wine and agricultural produce that supplied the markets of Rome. The cities of Syria, where the inhabitants spoke Greek in addition to the native Aramaic, benefitted greatly from the favoured position of their province. Damascus, for example, witnessed much infrastructural growth as well as the building of monuments such as the Temple of Jupiter, later to be transformed into the great Umayyad Mosque.

Syrian influence was to be felt in Rome itself with the coming to power of a string of Roman emperors of Syrian origin, the most famous of whom being Philip the Arab, who ruled from AD 244 to 249 AD. During that same century the power of the kingdom of Palmyra in central Syria grew well beyond the country, with its ruler, Zenobia, laying claim to the title Queen of the East. Eventually, however, she was to overreach herself by challenging Rome directly. She was defeated in battle in 272

AD, captured and paraded as a prisoner through Rome, where she ended her life.

The Emperor Constantine proclaimed Christianity as the official religion of the Roman Empire in 313 AD; yet Syria had already been the centre from which Christianity spread, with the famous conversion of St. Paul 'on the road to Damascus' in the middle of the first century. Many of the most ancient Christian sites were located in Syria, and no area in the Mediterranean contains as great a wealth of churches and monastic remnants from that period. The country also became a vortex for early theological debates, often very fractious, about the new religion, causing rifts within early Christianity over such issues as the nature of Christ. This gave rise in the later period of Byzantine Roman rule to sharply defined schisms represented by distinct trends like Monophysitism and Nestorianism, which set many Syrians against the prevailing orthodoxy in Constantinople. A weakened Byzantine Empire, compromised both by internal Syrian religious dissent into its territories from Persia, was ill prepared for the eruption northwards of Arab tribes driven by the overpowering fervour of a new belief.

The Islamic-Arab conquest of Syria was a profoundly significant turning point, not only in that country's history, but also in the history of the vast region that was to form one of the greatest empires known to mankind. Before invading Syria in 832 AD, a few years after the death of the Prophet Muhammad, the newly established Islamic Caliphate in Medina was considered no more than a local cult that posed little danger to the regional superpowers of Byzantium and Persia. It must have been a shock to both powers when Damascus fell so readily to this charge of desert tribesmen, following the crushing defeat they had inflicted on the Byzantine army at the celebrated battle of Yarmouk in 636 AD. Led by the great Arab general Khaled Ibn Al Walid, these improbable conquerors swept through Syria and Iraq, eventually destroying the Persian Empire and pushing Byzantium back into Asia Minor. It was in Syria that the Arab conquest transformed itself; from a revolt largely by religiously motivated Bedouin tribes into a state in the making, with all necessary attributes of administration and governance. This was demonstrated by the very light touch of the conquering Arab regiments. They blended with the indigenous populations and allowed them largely to run their own communities, thereby benefitting from their long historical experience of a multitude of previous powers, by now including the Canaanite, Hellenistic, Roman and Aramean civilisations.

The process of 'Syrianising' the Islamic-Arab invasion reached its zenith when the first Umayyad caliph, Muawiyah, chose Damascus to be the capital of his empire. Muawiyah succeeded to the caliphate after a bitter and bloody struggle with the fourth caliph, Ali (who fell prey to an assassin), and his followers. Under Muawiyah and his immediate successors, Damascus and Syria became the centre of the world, commanding an empire that stretched from Central Asia to Spain. It was Muawiyah who established for the first time in the caliphate the practice of dynastic rule, with his son Yazid succeeding him as caliph and commander of the faithful. Yazid is noted as having been the ruler who finally crushed the insurgency by the followers of Ali at the battle of Kerbala in AD 680. The battle, which resulted in the killing of Ali's son, Hussein, proved to be of defining historical importance as it cemented the schism in Islam between Sunnism (meaning 'mainstream' orthodoxy) and Shiism (meaning 'partisans,' in reference to Ali).

Under the caliphs Abd Al Malik Ibn Marwan and his son Al Walid (685-705 AD). a massive programme of building projects added to the splendour of Umayyad Syria. Two of the most illustrious and lasting of the monuments of that age are the Alaqsa Mosque in Jerusalem and the magnificent Umayyad Mosque of Damascus, built around the foundations of an original Graeco-Roman temple that had later been converted to a church. Eventually the Umayyad state began to show signs of weakness and decline, finally giving way to a new dynasty, the Abbasids, who marched on Damascus from Iraq and put an end to Umayyad rule in the Muslim east in AD 750. However, the Umayyad line continued for a further five hundred years in areas of North Africa, and particularly in the great civilisation that was to flourish in Andalusian Spain. Echoes of Umayyad Syria were to remain in much of the art, music and architecture of Andalusia, and of course in the Spanish language itself.

The long era of the Abbasid Caliphate (ending officially in 1258) saw an early surge of advancement and vigour, with the creation of Baghdad and the spread of learning and science under the great Caliph Harun al Rashid. However, the Abbasids soon fell prey to strong societal and ethnic pressures, which eroded the Arab identity of the Islamic Caliphate and allowed strong Persian influences to permeate the body politic of that state. This ultimately resulted in the growth of a mixed Arab-Persian elite and a loosening of the hold of the capital, Baghdad, on the provincial regions. In Syria local governors and military commanders established autonomous and sometimes independent entities that even rivalled the central caliphate in power. Invasions by Turkish nomads were also of great historical significance. Indeed the Seljuqs exercised hegemony over the Abbasids and obtained from them the 'right' to rule most of Syria well into the twelfth century.

The vulnerability of the Arab-Muslim heartland was thrown into sharp focus by the challenge that came from the west in the shape of the crusaders. The empire readily descended into contested loyalties, division and fragmentation. Syria, especially its coastline, was at first little able to resist the foreign invaders, who captured Jerusalem in 1099 (massacring its Muslim and Jewish populations in the process). The crusaders established various proto-colonial fortress kingdoms along Syria's western axis, and it took some time for the local centres of power to react to the mounting threat. The response finally began in Aleppo, where the ruling Zengid dynasty had established a powerful realm (only nominally answerable to the Seljuks and the Abbasid caliph). Nur ad-Din Zengi was the leader who first successfully summoned a unified Muslim force from both Aleppo and Damascus and began the retaliation against the crusader presence that had proliferated along the Syrian coast. Nur ad-Din was able to counter that presence and regain some territory, but it was his nephew Saladin who was to achieve the great victories, including the restoration of Jerusalem to Muslim rule in 1187.

Saladin assumed the leadership of the resistance on his uncle's death in 1176, having already established his fame as a great military commander. Acting on behalf of the Abbasid Caliphate he had crushed a rival caliphate, the Fatimid Shiite dynasty, which had gained control of Egypt. With Damascus as his base he established the Ayyubid dynasty (named after his family) and united all of Syria under his rule, while extending his domain to include Egypt. He formed an alliance to combat the Franks – or *Al Faranjah*, the name by which the invading crusaders were known to the indigenous population. This was the first time since the beginning of the crusades, nearly a hundred years previously, that a Muslim commander (of Kurdish origin) could claim the near total allegiance of the forces resisting the 'infidel' enemy. Saladin used this power to great effect. In 1187 he lured the crusaders into battle at Hattin, south of Damascus, and defeated them comprehensively. That encounter, and the resultant liberation of Jerusalem, has gone down in Arab and Muslim lore as a great defining moment. It raised the spirit of the contemporary forces of Islam and continued to resonate for many generations to come. Saladin's tomb, located in Damascus, is an enduring shrine that powered the Syrians' resolve as they encountered new enemies and invaders. This is especially true for the modern era with the struggle for independence and the wars over Palestine (which were seen to bear a resemblance to the fight against the crusaders a thousand years earlier). It was the memory of Saladin and his heroic achievements which served as strong ideological inspiration for the forces of nationalism that emerged in the twentieth century.

Yet Saladin was not able to achieve a total victory over the crusaders, who were to maintain a substantial presence on the Syrian coast well into the thirteenth century. By that time Ayyubid rule was fading, to be replaced by that of the Mamelukes. These were professional soldiers of Turkish and Central Asian extraction, originally brought as slaves (*mamluq* in Arabic means 'he who is owned') to serve the Abbasid Caliphate, but who rose to become *de facto* rulers themselves. From its base in Cairo this emerging power managed to galvanise resistance to the devastating Mongol invasion of Syria. The Mongols were defeated at the celebrated battle of Ain Jalout in southern Syria, making way for the expansion of Mameluke power throughout the region. Under the Sultan Al Malek Al Zaher Baibars, these conquerors went on to confront the remaining redoubts of the crusaders, finally eliminating their presence in Syria and launching an era of Mameluke governance that embraced both Egypt and Syria.

Mameluke rule lasted for over a hundred years, beginning with a long period of stability and prosperity. However, towards the end of the fourteenth century, Syria suffered a series of civil wars that weakened the hold of the rulers. In 1400 a new Mongol invasion, under Tamerlane, seized and sacked both Damascus and Aleppo, massacring their inhabitants and dealing a further blow to the tottering Mameluke realm which was soon to meet its ultimate demise. That came with the movement south of a power that had established a strong presence in Asia Minor and managed, in 1453, to achieve a historically momentous task: the capture of Byzantine Constantinople and the destruction of an empire that had lasted for over a thousand years. Fighting under the banner of Islam, the Ottoman Turks presented themselves as the ultimate 'defenders of the faith' on the back of a victory that had eluded even the most successful of preceding Islamic powers. With such a reputation behind them the challenge of conquering Syria, and then Egypt, was hardly going to be daunting. Led by the Sultan Salim I (Salim the Conqueror as he came to be known) they easily overcame the Mameluke army that assembled against them near Aleppo in 1516. Shortly afterwards the garrison of Damascus withdrew, allowing Salim free entrance into that iconic city. Indeed Damascus was to benefit from the largesse bestowed upon it by the successor to Salim, Sulaiman the Magnificent (known among Muslims as Sulaiman the Law-giver), whose long reign (1520-66) was marked by impressive building works, such as the beautiful mosque in central Damascus named after him, and important administrative reforms. Crucially, the country was no longer riven by the divisive and disruptive rule of the Mamelukes. There was general acknowledgement of the unifying authority of the Ottoman Sultanate, which assumed – in later claiming the caliphate – spiritual and temporal power over a vast expanse of territory, encompassing Syria-Mesopotamia, Arabia, Egypt and most of North Africa, as well as much of eastern and southern Europe.

In the early period of Ottoman rule Syria grew in prosperity. Its geographical location meant it became a crucial staging post for the annual Muslim pilgrimage to Mecca – a role that would render many economic and commercial rewards. Further north, Aleppo became an important hub of the Silk Route, and the centre of a flourishing trade that stretched from western Europe to China. Some of the earliest European consulates, housing Venetian, British and French emissaries, were established in that city, which led to a substantial foreign presence in the Levant. The immigrants benefitted from a series of 'capitulation' treaties signed between the Ottomans and European powers, giving the citizens of the latter certain privileges and immunities in carrying out their trading activities. Turkish rule remained largely loose in nature, allowing local governors (usually with the title of Pasha) a great deal of autonomy. Moreover, although the Ottoman Empire inherited the role of Muslim Caliphate, it was generally not heavy-handed in dealing with minority religions and sects. Rather, under the 'millet' system, these were left to handle their own spiritual, cultural and family law affairs. The Christians especially thrived under these arrangements and were able to play an increasingly profitable role as intermediaries, often enjoying privileged access to the ascending powers of Europe.

By the eighteenth century the Golden Age of the Ottoman world had begun its steady decline. This would affect the fortunes of Syria, as well as most other provinces of the empire, and coincided with the growth of trade routes to Asia that bypassed Syria, either via the seas to the south or along roads to the north of the country. The first half of the nineteenth century saw the early signs of the crumbling of Ottoman rule, with the rise in Egypt of a virtually independent and defiant governorate ruled over by Muhammad Ali Pasha, a reforming leader who aspired to bring Egypt into the modern European age. His son, Ibrahim Pasha, launched an expedition into Syria in 1831, expelling the Turks from the country and briefly introducing his father's reformist agenda to the governance he personally established in the country. However, nine years later, and with Britain's Foreign Secretary, Lord Palmerston, leading the powerful opposition to Muhammad Ali's dream of taking over the Ottoman Sultanate, Ibrahim was forced out of his Syrian domain and Ottoman rule restored. The propping up of the Ottoman dynasty was to be a firm article of British foreign policy for many years to come, especially against the Russian threat, even though by then the Ottoman Empire had been labelled 'the sick man of Europe.'

The restoration of Ottoman rule in Syria did not herald a return to stability. The empire's hold had been much weakened by the long standoff with Muhammad Ali. Furthermore, eager to compete for the imperial rewards that the ailing Ottoman Empire might deliver, Western powers were making inroads into its social and sectarian fabric, especially in Syria and Lebanon. As a consequence tensions rose among communities that had hitherto succeeded in maintaining a positive *modus vivendi*. A wave of inter-confessional violence hit Lebanon in 1860, which pit Druze against Maronite and soon spread to the very heart of Damascus, where many Christians were massacred before order was restored. The emir, Abdul Qader al Jazairi, who in earlier years had led the revolt in Algeria against the French and chose exile in Damascus after it was crushed, is credited with having calmed the rioting while providing sanctuary for many Christians. Events in Lebanon had already prompted France to land troops on the coast, giving vivid expression to the imperial manoeuvrings that were to blight the region for decades to come.

In tandem with the visible cracks in the power and prestige of the Ottoman Sultanate, from the middle of the nineteenth century there started to grow in Syria the stirrings of a national consciousness that looked at a future separate from Turkey, or at least with a strong regime of home rule. Foreign educational and religious missions had been spreading in cities such as Beirut and Aleppo and brought about the diffusion among some elites of Western-inspired Enlightenment ideas. This was especially the case with the Christian population. An important landmark was the establishment in 1866 in Beirut of the Syrian Protestant College (later to be named the American University of Beirut) by American missionaries. Soon after, in 1875, a French Catholic institution, the *Université Saint-Joseph*, was founded, drawing much of its student base from the Maronite community in the country. Smaller centres of missionary education sprang up over the decades to come (such as Broumana High School in Mount Lebanon founded by the Quakers). However their appeal was largely confined to the Christian communities. It was much later in the century before they could attract, for example, students from the majority Muslim population.

Given this trend in education it was not surprising that the forerunners of what came to be called the Arab Awakening were mainly Christian. Through the propagation of a Syrian or Arab identity they sought a future free from the shackles of a Muslim Ottoman Empire, which, in their eyes, could never aspire to be inclusive. Two names – both Christian and from Lebanon – stand out as pioneers of the rising new spirit: Nassif Yazigi, a poet, writer and civic preacher who extolled the beauty of the Arabic language and addressed both Christians and Muslims, reminding them of their common Arab heritage, and Butrus Bustani, another renowned writer and teacher, who, following the sectarian killings in 1860 in Lebanon and Damascus, founded the publication *Nafir Sourya* (the Clarion of Syria) in Beirut. It was the first political journal to be published in the country as a medium for national and religious reconciliation and for promoting ideas of scientific knowledge and modernity. These men were examples of the first stirrings of a patriotic and inclusive approach to a new concept of citizenship – one embracing all Syrians. Both Yazigi and Bustani were instrumental in the founding of the Society of Arts and Science, again dominated by Christians. In 1857 the Syrian Scientific Society was formed with members from all denominations drawn from the social and intellectual elites of the country. It could be said that this society was the cornerstone upon which were built the foundations of the Arab national movement. Ibrahim Yazigi, son of Nassif, was one of its most active members. He wrote a widely read poem evoking the spirit of Arabism and denouncing sectarian hostility. More radically he called on Syrians to unite against Turkish oppression.

In response to the challenges at home and the pressures from abroad the Ottoman rulers reluctantly accepted the need for a drastic reform of the structure of the state. In 1864, as part of a series of reforms begun some years earlier known as *tanzimat* (reorganisation), they promulgated a law dividing Syria into two provinces, while maintaining for Mount Lebanon a special autonomous regime. The reforms were intended to provide a more modern and regulated administration for the

Ottoman Empire, which was seeing its writ eroding as a result of insurrections in its European domains and the encroaching on its sovereignty in Arab lands by the European powers. Yet they also gave rise to a questioning among Syria's new educated generation (imbued with the legacy of Yazigi and Bustani) of the very foundations of three and a half centuries of autocratic Ottoman rule. The reform process was further spurred on by demands within the Ottoman establishment itself for constitutional change. This resulted in the proclaiming of a constitution by Abdul Hamid II in 1876, the year he took over as sultan.

The hopes raised by the new constitution, with its many liberal ideas and checks on the power of the ruler, and by his reputation as a reformer which Abdul Hamid had carefully nurtured, were soon to be dashed as he used the pretext of a war with Russia in 1877 to suspend this same constitution. With the signing of the Treaty of Berlin in 1878 (when Britain's strong intervention overturned the earlier Treaty of San Stefano imposed on Turkey by the victorious Russians), Turkey was forced to loosen its hold on what remained of its territory in Europe. However, its Arab domains remained largely unaffected. The brief conflict with Russia resulted in the termination of the nascent programme of constitutional reform, and the introduction of a long period of tyranny associated with the much-detested reign of Abdul Hamid. Increasingly the instruments of oppression and censorship were applied, and those Syrians who had started to believe in a freer future, and who saw those beliefs destroyed, started to turn to a subversive mode of activity. Secret societies sprung up and pamphlets were distributed calling for an end to despotism and preaching civil and political freedom. These agitators benefitted from the impact of increasingly centralised rule from Istanbul, in variance to that of earlier times with local and regional autonomy. From Syria also spread the still embryonic ideas of Arab unity and nationalism, which Syrians (including Lebanese) carried with them into other Arab lands. This was especially the case in Egypt where there was much tolerance under the 'khedives' (officially viceroys of the Ottoman sultan but in reality semi-independent rulers, who, by the end of the century, were firmly under the British imperial thumb). The celebrated Egyptian newspaper *Al-Ahram* (The Pyramids) was, for example, founded during that period by two publishers from Lebanon, the Takla brothers. Towards the end of the nineteenth century these same ideas, which until then were almost exclusively borne by the Christians and students of Western educational institutions, began to permeate more deeply into the psyche of Muslim society.

A leading figure in the annals of the early struggle for Arab emancipation was Abdul Rahman al Kawakibi. Born in Aleppo in 1849 to a Muslim family, he studied at the leading Muslim college of the time, known for its tradition of humanistic education. His reformist leanings and outspoken denunciation of tyrannical rule were to lead to a spell in prison. Upon his release in 1898, he decided to seek refuge in Egypt, where he knew he could write and promote his views much more freely. It was there that he wrote his seminal work, *Taba'i al Istabdad* (The Nature of Despotism), which delved deeply into the societal and cultural elements that lead to tyranny, and broke new ground by associating despotism with the patriarchal family structure. A daring venture into the heartland of sacrosanct orthodoxy, it spread widely and served as a blueprint for the new generation of freedom-seeking Arab activists. Kawakibi's career, cut short by his mysterious death at the age of fifty-four, served to pass on the torch of liberal nationalism from the hitherto almost exclusive hands of Christian Syrians to the mainstream Muslim community. The doctrine adopted by Kawakibi and his entourage was, however, still largely confined to an elite class, and adherents were subject to the harshest of measures by the secret police of Sultan Abdul Hamid, whose name by that time had become synonymous with tyranny at its worst.

In 1908 the Young Turks staged their palace coup, acting under the umbrella of the Committee of Union and Progress (CUP), they compelled a dramatic climb-down by the sultan, inaugurating a return to constitutional rule. This was initially well received by those Syrians who had been agitating for national and individual rights. The reinstatement of the Ottoman constitution of 1876 was greeted with jubilation across the empire, with Turks, Arabs and other communities seeing in it the promise of a brighter future for all. Before long, however, and after gaining nearly full control of the affairs of the empire – having deposed Abdul Hamid in 1909 and appointed a docile sultan (Mehmet V) in his place – the CUP soon revealed its true face: that of Turkish nationalism. A scarcely concealed policy of what became known as 'Turkification' was applied at all levels of power and decision-making, including, for example, having only three Arabs among the forty-member senate appointed by the sultan. This soon provoked angry responses from Syrians who felt that the Ottoman Empire was sinking into almost pure and xenophobic Turkish despotism. Cries of protest started to be heard from many Syrian activists, with the slogan '*la markaziyah*' (decentralisation) echoing among leading voices ('independence' was seen as too dangerous a demand to make openly). Societies that had recently grown in influence, having profited from the brief era of political openness, such as *Al Ikha Al Arabi* (Arab Brotherhood) were soon suppressed, some of them going underground.

The policies of the CUP served, ironically, to give strong impetus to an Arab movement, which, although founded many years earlier, had never had nationalism as a central demand. Indeed, most Syrians remained loyal to the deep-rooted attraction of an inclusive Muslim Caliphate, albeit one that was in need of fundamental reform. With the Young Turks increasingly seen as shutting down that option by excluding non-Turks from sharing in its destiny, many prominent Syrians joined groups such as *Al Muntada Al Adabi* (The Literary Club) in Istanbul and the Ottoman Decentralisation Party in Cairo, which asserted Arab rights. Other Syrians preferred to organise clandestinely within secret societies with more radical Arab separatism as their motive.

Special mention must be made of one particular secret society, *Jamiat Al Fatat Al Arabiya* (The Society of Young Arabs), which took the Young Turks as its model. Founded in Paris in 1911 by just seven young Syrians (all Muslim) it openly called for complete Arab independence from Turkey. Its influence and membership grew rapidly (but all the time secretly) back in Syria, especially within urban centres like Beirut and Damascus. The call in the streets, however, remained for decentralised governance, and agitation manifested itself in growing demonstrations, public meetings and even strikes that provoked repressive measures from the Turkish CUP regime. In early 1913 various activists discussed the possibility of holding a congress that could officially unite and spell out Arab demands. A meeting was held in Paris in June that same year with twenty-four participants – these were almost exclusively Syrian, and divided equally between Muslims and Christians. Six days of deliberations, with an Arab audience that numbered two hundred, produced a moderately worded set of demands that avoided reference to independence while emphasising the need for autonomy, the recognition of Arabic as an official language, power-sharing and political rights within a restructured Ottoman state. Despite its relatively conciliatory tone, the Paris conference is seen through the prism of modern Arab history as a key milestone in the march towards freedom from Turkish domination.

At first the Turkish authorities adopted a mild approach to the event in Paris. The CUP even sent their party secretary to Paris to negotiate with the leading participants, and invited a delegation to Istanbul for further discussions regarding the demands proclaimed by the Arab Congress. But initial concessions proved to be ephemeral. A return to repressive rule saw Syrians once again lose faith in a deal with the CUP and resort to sometimes open, sometimes secretive action on the ground. An example of the latter was the formation in early 1914 of *Al Ahd* (The Covenant), composed almost entirely of Arab officers in the Ottoman army, in particular Iraqis. This society was organised in a similar fashion to *Al Fatat* – indeed it could be described as the secret military branch of the Arab movement. These societies became the foremost exemplars of the underground activity that helped sow the seeds of the Arab revolt against Turkish rule in the years following the outbreak of the First World War.

CHAPTER TWO

The Aborting of Faisal's Syrian Kingdom

We members of this Congress as representatives of the Syrian nation proclaim unanimously the independence of our country Syria within its national boundaries ... and we have chosen His Excellency Emir Faisal, the son of His Majesty King Hussein, ... as Constitutional King over Syria with the title of His Majesty Faisal I.

Resolution adopted by the Syrian congress in Damascus,
7 March 1920

O n the eve of the outbreak of the First World War events in Syria and beyond foretold a seismic transformation in the destiny of the Ottoman Empire and the nations under its sway. In Syria in particular the Arab movement for independence was gathering pace, with the two secret societies, *Al Fatat* and *Al Ahd*, gaining influence among the educated class, both Muslim and

Christian. Within the Ottoman state, the structure the Young Turks had organised within the CUP had strengthened their grip on power, with the sultan and his entourage being pushed to the sidelines. On the international level a Turkish-German alliance was solidifying, a process that had begun many years earlier, with the Ottoman army heavily dependent on German training and even on high-ranking German officers holding key positions within it. The capitals of what were to become the Entente Allies in the impending showdown, particularly London, were seething in their attitude to Istanbul and its alliance with Berlin. Their anger was directed in particular at the Young Turk putschists whom they saw as betraying a long history of trust and support without which the Ottoman 'sick man of Europe' could hardly have survived. By the time Turkey officially entered the war – on the side of the Central Powers, in November 1914 – planning was already underway to counter the threat of a Muslim enemy acting as the caliphate and claiming to represent all of the World of Islam. It was a claim that rang alarm bells within British and French governing circles who were hoping to rely heavily on troops originating from their vast Muslim domains in the battle to be waged. Britain was especially worried about the impact of the call to Muslims to join in a holy *jihad* in defence of the caliphate on its Indian military recruits largely drawn from the Muslim communities of the subcontinent. A further concern was the potential risk to Britain's position in Egypt, a key strategic asset, which was already feeling the pressure of a restive Muslim population. It was no accident that, in the first few weeks of its entry into the war, Turkey saw the opportunity to strike a decisive blow against Britain by launching a military campaign across the Sinai Peninsula.

Largely in reaction to the Turkish threat, British planners started to look at co-opting the Ottoman Islamic appeal, hence their approach to no other than the descendant of the Prophet Muhammad himself: the Hashemite Grand Sharif Hussein of Mecca. While owing nominal allegiance to the sultan in Istanbul, Hussein could become the source of a rival pan-Islamic allegiance should he be persuaded to join the Allied cause. Thus, over the years 1915-16 a series of secret letters (totalling ten) was exchanged between the British high commissioner in Cairo, Sir Arthur Henry McMahon, and Sharif Hussein. Of deep historical importance, this correspondence is also of lasting resonance, especially as it serves, in the minds of Arabs, to underpin an image of 'perfidious Albion.' As such, the contents of the letters have undergone considerable analysis, and the subject of what was or was not promised to the Arabs has received many interpretations. What matters is that the Arabs, at least those of the Hejaz (western Arabia) and the tribes closely associated with Hussein, believed that Britain promised to secure the independence of an Arab realm, incorporating Arabia, Syria and Mesopotamia, under the kingship of Sharif Hussein. The correspondence contained a number of ambiguities over exact boundaries, with McMahon introducing qualifications and reservations over the fate of southern Syria (Palestine) and the western coastal strip of that country (from Tyre to Alexandretta). Yet the general thrust of the message delivered by the British envoy, acting, as he insisted, upon instructions from London, was that if the Arabs were to throw in their lot with the Allies, then in any post-war settlement Britain would steadfastly stand by its solemn commitments to them.

While McMahon was busy reassuring Sharif Hussein of Britain's good faith, his government had already entered into secret talks with France and Tsarist Russia to decide on the future of the territories of the Ottoman Empire should Turkey be defeated (as was envisaged). The initial understanding was that Russia would seize for itself the region of the Bosphorus, while France staked its 'historical' claim to Syria, and Britain to an area stretching from southern Syria (Palestine) eastward to include Mesopotamia, thus ensuring a land route to India. Later to become known (or notorious) as the Sykes-Picot agreement – in reference to Sir Mark Sykes and Georges Picot, respectively the British and French delegates officially charged with drafting the accord – it has gone down in history as an iconic example of imperial deceit and duplicity. Notwithstanding the rumours that started to circulate in relation to the backroom deal, Sharif Hussein and his followers seemed content to follow through on the plans for a revolt to be coordinated with a British military campaign launched from Egypt. Preparations had already included contact between Hussein and the underground national movement in Syria. Hussein's son, Emir (Prince) Faisal, made a number of trips to Syria in 1915 and discussed the possibility of an uprising with members of the *Al Fatat* and *Al Ahd* societies, becoming a sworn member of both in the process. The two societies became aware of Sharif Hussein's correspondence with the British, and drew up a common protocol to be submitted via Faisal to his father, and through the latter to Britain, containing the demand for the complete independence of the Arab lands of western Asia.

The year 1915 also saw Syrian nationalists experience the full horror of retaliation against what the Turks concluded were subversive activities against state security. Dozens of leading advocates of emancipation, mostly civic leaders, writers and intellectuals drawn from all communities – Muslim and Christian – were arraigned before military tribunals sentenced to death and executed in groups. (among them the uncle of this author, Ali Armanazi). The final and biggest batch went to the gallows on 6 May 1916, a day annually commemorated in Syria and Lebanon as Martyrs' Day. Because of these acts and other measures of brutal repression, the Governor of Syria (and one of the most powerful figures in the Turkish government), Jamal Pasha, earned the sobriquet 'The Butcher.'

It was at this moment of the deepest possible resentment towards Turkish rule that the Arab Revolt was finally launched in Mecca on 10 June 1916 with attacks on the Turkish garrisons in the city. Other attacks developed in other towns of the Hejaz, and by September almost all had fallen to the rebels. In Syria, the Turkish authorities acted with increased ferocity. Jamal Pasha ordered wholesale arrests of suspected supporters of the revolt and many would have died had Prince Faisal not warned the Turkish governor that the Turkish officers taken prisoner by his forces would be killed if those dissidents in Turkish custody were harmed. The warning seemed to have an effect and the prisoners were soon released – although kept under close supervision. By that time the Syrian population was also suffering a severe famine. A wave of emigration began to destinations such as the American continents.

It took several months for the revolt in the Arabian south to make any headway northward and it was not until 1917 that the first important victory was achieved. On 6 July the Arab forces captured the port of Aqaba on the Red Sea. They were aided by T. E. Lawrence, who had been seconded by the British to liaise between General Allenby, the overall commander of the Allied campaign, and Emir Faisal. Meanwhile, Allenby's forces were making good progress in Palestine and entered Jerusalem on 9 December. Earlier, in November, a potentially critical bombshell had struck the Arab camp. The revolution in Russia resulted in the public revealing of the – until then only rumoured – secret agreements between the Tsarist regime, Britain and France over the division of the spoils of a defeated Ottoman Empire. Seeing a great opportunity to turn the tables on the Allies, Jamal Pasha communicated the texts of the agreements to Faisal in letters via a secret emissary. The letters were accompanied by a proposal for a separate Arab-Turkish peace agreement. Obviously disturbed, Faisal sent on the evidence of suspected British duplicity to his father, Sharif Hussein, in Mecca. The latter, still trustful of the word of His Majesty's Government, simply passed on the letters from Jamal Pasha to the British high commissioner in Egypt, Sir Reginald Wingate. There followed a further spate of correspondence, attempting to reassure the Arabs of Britain's good faith. One message praised King Hussein for having 'loyally' passed on the letters received from Jamal Pasha and confirmed once again that the British government stood by the unity and freedom of the Arabs once liberated from Turkish oppression.

Having momentarily overcome the 'misunderstanding' surrounding secret agreements, the British and Arab forces advanced on the grand prize of Damascus on two axes. It was important for Faisal, backed by T. E. Lawrence, that the Arab forces be seen to enter Damascus before those of the British in order to enhance the legitimacy of an independent Arab realm, particularly in the face of ominous French declarations regarding historic claims to all of Syria. Thus it was that the Arab army entered Damascus on 1 October 1918, just ahead of an Australian Light Horse Brigade (which, despite having arrived first at the entrance to the city, held back from entering it until the Arab units had joined them). The flag of Arab Liberation, adopted by King Hussein, had already been hoisted over the town hall the day before, following a hurried withdrawal from the city by remnants of the Turkish garrison. Scenes of jubilation greeted the new conquerors, and Faisal, riding a magnificent Arabian steed, made his entrance into Damascus on 3 October. A temporary Arab administration was set up and it indeed seemed that a new dawn of Arab freedom had arrived. However, no time was lost by those who wielded the real power against the Turks in disabusing their Arab ally of any ideas above his station. Arriving in Damascus on the same day with fresh instructions from London to curb the ambitions of the prince (as well, it seems, as those of T.E. Lawrence who was seen by British officials to have gone native), General Allenby quickly called a meeting with Faisal. He reminded him of the fact that he was in overall command of what would remain, until the end of the war, Occupied Enemy Territory. Allenby conceded that Faisal may establish his own administration in areas of 'inner Syria,' to include the south-to-north cities of Damascus, Homs, Hama and Aleppo. However, areas to the west, including the coast and the cities of Beirut and Tripoli, remained outside the Arab autonomous zone and were handed over to French administration (in accordance with the former secret but now officially acknowledged Sykes-Picot agreement). The flag of the Arab Revolt, which had briefly flown in Beirut, was hastily pulled down and Faisal's representative in that city shorn of all authority. It was the first of many indications that Britain's promises to the Arabs weighed far less than its relationship with its Entente partner, France, which was already complaining loudly about Faisal being a British stooge and Lawrence a devious agent out to undermine France's position in Syria.

On 5 October 1918 Emir Faisal announced the establishment of an Arab Military Government for Syria – a step agreed with Allenby. He addressed the people of Syria, promising them a constitutional government that would recognise all citizens as equal in rights and the benefit of justice be they Muslim, Christian or Jew. Meanwhile the military campaign against the fleeing Turks continued apace and by 25 October Homs, Hama and Aleppo fell to the combined Arab-British force. An armistice was signed on 30 October in which the Turks surrendered their forces in Arabia, Syria and Mesopotamia. Almost exactly four hundred years after the decisive Ottoman victory at the plain of Marj Dabeq in northern Syria, which ushered in the conquest of Syria, and on the same site, the final surrender of the Turkish army took place. The irony was not lost on those with a historical perspective. Nor was the victory achieved against the Turks without some hidden forebodings among many Syrians – feelings only to be strengthened by subsequent developments. In time they would start to wonder whether they had simply substituted one conqueror for another – and this time one not averse to considering its triumph a historical watershed whereby the Christian West could finally lay to rest the ghost of past crusader defeats in Syria and the Holy Lands.

Initially Syrian hopes remained strong that, as they approached the start of negotiations for a general post-war peace settlement, the European powers would live up to the promises made to their Arab allies. These hopes where given a boost when the text of an Anglo-French Declaration was revealed on 8 November 1918. It stated *inter alia* that 'the object aimed at by France and Great Britain [in pursuing the war against Turkey] is the complete and definite emancipation of the peoples so long oppressed by the Turks and the establishment of national governments and administrations deriving their authority from the initiative and free choice of the indigenous populations ...' Speaking in Aleppo a few days later the ever-trusting Prince Faisal read out an Arabic translation of the declaration and called it 'one of the great declarations of history … [and a reflection of] noble and humanitarian sentiments.' He thanked both Britain and France very warmly 'for their great help and support' in assuring the success of the Arab Revolt. Faisal used the occasion once again to stress the importance of Arab unity, saying that it should transcend any other identity – Muslim, Christian or Jewish, who should all be equal before the law: a very radical and enlightened notion for the time, when such a doctrine must have sounded strange to a society still steeped in the traditions of tribal, religious and sectarian bonds of loyalty.

The mood of optimism (unfortunately soon to be rendered obsolete) did not only draw its strength from a naive belief in the intentions of the Entente but was also inspired by principles announced by Woodrow Wilson. The American president's famous Fourteen Points were intended to govern, and ensure peace for, the post-war world. Arabs were particularly heartened by Wilson's reference to the principle of self-determination for the people liberated from imperialism as a result of the conflict. A further fillip to their aspirations came when Faisal was invited to attend the Versailles Peace Conference. He was received in Paris by the president of France and decorated with the *Grand Croix de la Légion d'honneur* before going on to London. However, unbeknown to Faisal and before his arrival in Britain, a series of crucial meetings had taken place in London between the British prime minister, Lloyd George, and the French premier, Georges Clemenceau, during which the Syrian Question, as it was to become known, was discussed in detail. Most importantly, this led to a review of the Sykes-Picot agreement and significant modifications to the map underpinning the accord. The new understanding regarding that map reflected the dominance of Britain as an occupying power in the region. It allowed her to claim the oil-rich district of Mosul as part of the zone of British-controlled Mesopotamia (previously allocated to the area of French-controlled Syria with which it had strong historical and socioeconomic links). The weeks and months that followed saw Faisal pursuing tirelessly, whether at home or in Europe, the implementation of what he and his father – now referred to as King Hussein – regarded as the promises given to the Hashemites in return for their having joined the cause of the Allies. Faisal attended meetings in both France and Britain (some occurring – especially when it came to the French – in circumstances that smacked of deliberate humiliation), which resulted in conflicting messages and ambiguous commitments. The biggest deceptions appeared to emanate from the mandarins of the British Foreign Office, who, while writing to Faisal in fulsome prose about Britain 'living up to its promises,' continued horse-trading with their French counterparts. Although history records that at some stages in their discussions over Syria at the margins of the Paris Peace Conference Lloyd George argued strongly that an Arab kingdom, at least in Syria's interior, was a *sine qua non* of any final agreement, the French premier managed to get the last word (outfoxing Lloyd George in the eyes of some contemporary observers) and never committed to underwriting Britain's promises to Hussein or Faisal. Indeed Britain had already conceded the principle that the French would be given the mandate over the whole of Syria. (The handing over of 'mandates' was the formula adopted by the Peace Conference for the governance of territories liberated from Turkey. Temporary control was assigned to a Great Power with the responsibility of guiding and mentoring a given country until it became capable of independent self-government.) Further, by announcing that its forces would soon be withdrawing from Syria, Britain signalled to the French that a march on Damascus would not face opposition from any British military presence.

The double-dealing over Syria by Britain and France was confirmed when they pulled out of a tripartite commission delegated by the Peace Conference to travel to the country to ascertain the wishes of the people regarding their future. Only the American section of the commission eventually left to carry out the duty with which it was charged. The King-Crane Commission, as it came to be known (after its two heads, Dr. Henry King and Charles Crane), travelled to Syria in the summer of 1919 and toured the whole country (which then was still considered to include both Palestine and Lebanon), seeking the feelings and opinions of leaders of the various communities. It issued its final recommendations in August of that year, including the following salient points:

> That Syria should remain unified, and any mandate limiting its independence should be for a limited period and be administered by a single mandatory power.

> Concerning Lebanon the recommendations stated the following: 'As a predominantly Christian country ... Lebanon would be in a position to exert a stronger and more helpful influence if she were within the Syrian State, feeling its problems and needs, and sharing all its life, instead of outside it, absorbed simply in her own narrow concerns. For the sake of the larger interests, both of Lebanon and of Syria, then the unity of Syria is to be urged. It is certain that many of the more thoughtful Lebanese themselves hold this view.'

> Regarding Palestine the commission also argued the case for its inclusion within the broader Syrian state. It was critical of the Zionist demand for a Jewish

state in Palestine founded on the British 'promise' as expressed by the Balfour Declaration of 1917. (This had stated that 'a national home for the Jewish people is not equivalent to making Palestine into a Jewish State; nor can the erection of such a Jewish State be accomplished without the gravest trespass upon the civil and religious rights of existing non-Jewish communities in Palestine.')

That 'Emir Faisal be made head of the new united Syrian State.'

The King-Crane Commission's recommendations were ignored by the Paris Peace Conference. Furthermore, the hope that at least the United States under President Wilson would stand by the findings of its chosen delegates was soon to be dissipated as that country, disillusioned with the return to the scheming and machinations of European imperial politics by Paris and London, effectively withdrew from the wrangling over the post-war settlement. With failing health and soon to lose power President Wilson was no match for the seasoned Machiavellians Lloyd George and Clemenceau. Faisal made desperate appeals to his British 'friends' and attempted to placate the growing voraciousness of the French, who, meanwhile, felt the weakening of Britain and the United States in their resistance to French ambitions in Syria. Notwithstanding these efforts, the future of his position, as well as that of the fragile state centred on Damascus of which he was head, seemed set on a perilous course. Matters were complicated further for Faisal as his room for manoeuvre in reaching any compromise with the French was becoming increasingly narrowed by a surge of national and popular opinion and the growth of new Syrian political parties that rejected any watering down of the demand for full independence within a unified state. By the end of 1919 it had become abundantly clear that Syria was being abandoned to its fate. The British could do very little to continue to protect their ally and protégé Faisal, having decided years earlier that their solemn pledges to the Hashemites could never supplant the priority of their ties to the French.

As all other options started to close, and confrontation appeared inevitable, a despairing Faisal was carried along by the domestic public mood, which took the form of a unilateral declaration of independence. On 6 March 1920 the General Syrian Congress met in Damascus and a day later defiantly issued a historical resolution proclaiming the full independence of Syria within its 'natural boundaries' (including Palestine and rejecting the Zionist claims for a Jewish national home in that land). The congress also announced that it had chosen Faisal to be king of Syria with the title His Majesty King Faisal the First. It resolved the end of the occupying military government installed by the Allies, with its powers falling to a Syrian constitutional monarchy. Lebanon was to be given autonomous status within the new monarchy. The congress called for the independence of Iraq and for a political and economic union between the two countries. The next day, 8 March (which for decades remained a Syrian national holiday), the resolutions adopted by the congress were read aloud from the balcony of the town hall in Damascus as the newly proclaimed King Faisal rode on horseback among the cheering crowds to the loud booms of ceremonial canon.

The resolutions of the Syrian Congress were met with rejection by both Britain and, inevitably, France. The latter protested loudly, especially at the inclusion of Lebanon within the proclaimed state. At the behest of the French a hastily convened meeting of Lebanese Christian notables led to the proclamation on 22 March of the independence of Lebanon as a countermeasure to the decisions taken in Damascus earlier that month. To illustrate further the chasm between the decisions being taken by Syrians and those being adopted over their heads by the Allied powers, the Allied Supreme Council convened in April in San Remo, Italy, to set out the future of the Ottoman territories once and for all. The result was that France, through a mandate, was officially given charge of Syria's destiny. Lloyd George himself would write in later years that the mandate system was 'a substitute for old Imperialism.'

In Damascus and across Syria the news from San Remo of impending French rule was greeted with mass demonstrations and protests. Yet the now 'King' Faisal still clung to his belief in British assurances, conveyed by Allenby and others, that the granting of the mandate to France did not contradict the principle of an independent Syrian state. In a speech delivered in Damascus at the end of May 1920 he called on the populace not to despair, for 'no sentence of death has been passed upon us and such a sentence will never be passed.' At the same time he called for readiness and patience and for unity and courage in the face of adversity. He stressed that independence was not a gift but had to be won, and announced the issuance of a government loan that would finance the building of a national army. Events moved at a rapid pace from then on, with a French mobilisation of forces in Lebanon signalling an almost inevitable showdown with the regime in Damascus. Matters came to a head in early July when the British urged Faisal to travel to Europe once more to present his case to the Allies, and especially France. But Faisal was refused permission to depart from Beirut by the commander of the French forces, General Gouraud, who was also the appointed high commissioner, under the mandate, for Syria and Lebanon. An ultimatum was then sent to Damascus by Gouraud on 14 July listing a number of demands, including the acceptance of the French mandate, the demobilisation of the Syrian army and the punishment of those who had demonstrated enmity to France. A deadline of three days was set for their acceptance. News of the ultimatum immediately sparked a popular uprising in Syria, which only grew when reports spread that Faisal and his cabinet, acting under *force majeure* having lost hope of any intervention by their erstwhile protectors, particularly Britain, had accepted the ultimatum and disbanded the army.

Syria's capitulation to French demands could not save Faisal's government. Citing the late arrival of the response from Damascus, and raising even higher the ceiling of conditions to be met, the die was cast and the French forces began their advance eastward. Troops hastily assembled from remnants of the disbanded Syrian army and other volunteers, led by the minister of defence, Youssef Al Azmah, met the invading French battalions at the village of Maysalun, just east of the Lebanese mountains. There was only one possible outcome: the makeshift collection of Syrian fighters, highly spirited but lacking in organisation and equipment, stood no chance against the overwhelming strength of a modern, mechanised and armoured force. The result was a crushing defeat for the Syrians and the death of their commander. From that day on the names of Maysalun and Azmah (whose statue stands in the centre of a main Damascene square) have stood as immortal emblems of Syria's national pride and its resistance to colonial conquest. General Gouraud triumphantly entered Damascus on 24 April 1920 and headed straight to the tomb of Saladin. There it is said he alluded to the legacy of the defeat the warrior had inflicted on the crusaders by announcing: 'Saladin, we have returned.' King Faisal and his cabinet had by then left the city and a few days later, faced with an expulsion order from Gouraud, Faisal left Syria through Deraa into Palestine, where he looked to the British for refuge. (Later, the British were to compensate Faisal for their failure to stand by him in his hour of need by awarding him the crown of Iraq.)

Alongside the Balfour Declaration nothing has left a deeper, more lasting stain on the reputation of Britain among Arabs than the perceived betrayal of its commitments, first to Sharif Husain and later to his son Faisal. The latter's Syrian Kingdom, representing the first flourish of a promised Arab national renaissance, was seen as being cruelly sacrificed at the altar of imperial gluttony. No epitaph to that episode in British history can rise above the eloquence of Winston Churchill, who, speaking in 1921, stated:

> General Gouraud marched an army against Damascus, routed the Arabs, seized the city and is now in occupation of the four towns I have mentioned [Damascus, Aleppo, Homs and Hama] as well as the whole of Syria … it was extremely painful to British opinion, and to British officers particularly who had served the Arabs, to see those who had been our comrades such a little time before, and our Allies, and who looked to us for protection and to see their wrongs righted, to look on while they were thrashed and trampled down and their cities taken against the spirit of the treaties, if not against the letter, by the French; and that has been a deep source of pain to politicians and to the military men who have been concerned. However, we have these strong ties with the French and they have to prevail, and we were not able to do anything to help the Arabs in the matter …

CHAPTER THREE

1920-1946: The Struggle for Independence

Tender Salutations from the source of Barada along with tears that will not dry, O Damascus ... the horrors that have befallen you incredible as they appear are nonetheless true ... Bombs we are told have fallen on the landmarks of History raining destruction and fire ... France has experience of the blood of revolutionaries and she knows it is the Light and the Truth ... There is a door leading to Red Liberty and all blood-soaked hands knock on it ... The Almighty shall reward you, O people of Damascus ... and the glories of the East start at Damascus.

From 'Ode to Damascus' by the Egyptian poet Ahmad Shawqi (known as the Arab Poet Laureate), written in 1925 on the occasion of the fierce bombardment suffered by the city at the hands of the French.

The period of French rule in Syria was one of almost continuous tension and protest punctuated by stretches of armed rebellion. From the start the French authorities scarcely hid from the Syrians the fact that the mandate was little more than a facade behind which the traditions of unreconstructed, old-fashioned colonialism reigned supreme. Immediately they declared the dismissal of the government appointed by Faisal and the appointment of a cabinet composed of known 'friends' of France – or at least those with no nationalist affiliations. To add insult to injury they imposed on the cabinet a sum of two hundred thousand gold dinars as reparations to be paid to the French in compensation for 'hostile anti-French actions' preceding the invasion and overthrow of Faisal's erstwhile state. They further demanded of the government the resolute pursuit and punishment of any active remnants of the nationalist era, and made it clear that any police, gendarmerie or military forces would remain under the direct control of the French commander-in-chief. The newly appointed prime minister, Ala al-Din Droubi, sounded hollow when assuring Syrians that the mandate authorities would rule with a light touch. In fact the jails were soon to be filled with suspected agitators and many nationalist leaders (a large number of whom had gone into exile) were sentenced to death and had their properties confiscated. The response from the nationalists was almost immediate: on 21 August 1920 Droubi was assassinated in a village just outside Damascus, visibly illustrating the strength of feeling against the imperial rule being imposed by the French under the guise of the mandate. At the same time, in the north, a hero of the resistance, Ibrahim Hanano, was continuing a fierce guerrilla campaign which had begun in 1919 against the French forces stationed west of Aleppo. Hanano had been receiving help from the Turkish commander Mustapha Kemal (later to be known as Ataturk), who was also locked in battle against the French. He was eventually defeated in 1922, partly because by then the Turks and the French had reached a final settlement. Having fled to Palestine, Hanano was arrested by the British and turned over to the French authorities in Syria, where he was put on trial. However, realising the level of public outrage that would ensue from any conviction, the French felt it wiser to release him. In the years that followed, and until his death in 1935, Hanano remained a leading figure in the developing nationalist movement buoyed by the reputation he had gained in that early chapter in the resistance.

Another hero of that early period of resistance was Sheikh Saleh Al Ali, a scion of an influential Alawite dynasty. He rallied to the Arab revolt and the state in Damascus declared by Emir Faisal but soon found himself in tactical alliance with Mustapha Kemal's Turks in opposition to the French occupation of the Syrian coastland. Ali refused to recognise the French seizure of the Alawite heartland and led a rebellion in the name of all Syrians, joining forces on occasion with that being waged to the east under Ibrahim Hanano. The French suffered heavy losses in a number of armed encounters but eventually succeeded in crushing Ali's insurgency. Ali then went into hiding, and, having been sentenced to death *in absentia*, only emerged after a general amnesty. He remained a reclusive figure and did not appear in public again until much later, as an honoured guest at a parade celebrating Syria's independence in 1946.

Ominously, and in keeping with the age-old principle of divide and rule, the French soon embarked on a policy of breaking Syria up into several separate statelets. On 1 September 1920, General Gouraud announced the creation of Greater Lebanon, which added to the recognised Mount Lebanon region additional swathes of the coast, as well as the plains at the foothills of the Ante-Lebanon mountain range where a largely Muslim population felt close affinity to the Syrian interior. On 8 September a further decree ordained the separation of a 'state' of Aleppo from the rest of Syria, and fifteen days later an Alawite 'state' was created on Syria's north-western coast. Later, in March 1921, a similar independent regime was established for the Druze Mountain in southern Syria. Thus the planned dismemberment of what was already a truncated Syria was put into effect (Britain having sliced off Palestine and Transjordan as part of its share of the inherited Ottoman estate). Damascus became the capital of the State of Damascus. As a further blow to Syrian national ambitions the district of Alexandretta, comprising Syria's ancient capital, Antioch, was created as a distinct entity with special privileges for the Turkish section of the population in accordance with an agreement between France and Turkey signed in Ankara in October 1921.

Moves by the French to entrench their strategy of ethnic and sectarian territorial and administrative separation were met with an immediate backlash. Protests erupted all over the country and the demand for Syrian unity became the rallying call behind all manifestations of political and national sentiment for years to come. An initial success was to be achieved in December 1924 when union was declared between the states of Aleppo and Damascus. Meanwhile a protracted state of resistance to the French occupation as a whole began to take shape. General Gouraud himself was the target of an assassination attempt in June 1921, leading to a brutal crackdown against nationalist strongholds, and the summary arrests of numerous suspected ringleaders. In April 1922, on the occasion of a visit to Damascus by Charles Crane, co-author of the King-Crane Commission report which, a few years earlier, had borne witness to the legitimacy of Syrian national aspirations, a flurry of popular activity and protest engulfed Damascus and many other parts of Syria. The French army bore down heavily on the protesters and several arrests were made among the nationalist leadership. That in turn led to an escalation of the disturbances, culminating in a general strike in Damascus and the declaration of martial law. Eventually the French were forced to release the political leaders they had imprisoned on the island of Arwad off the Syrian coast.

Persistent and loud demands for Syrian unity and independence found expression not only within the country but also among many Syrians who had sought refuge abroad – particularly in Egypt, where leading voices of the resistance to French rule organised themselves into the Syrian-Palestinian Congress. Other Syrian expatriates, even many in France, were eager to express solidarity with their brethren at home, and reports about the continuing unrest in Syria appeared in many newspapers and journals of the time. Neither General Gouraud nor his successor, General Weygand (later of World War II fame), were able to quell the spreading disturbances. By the time the third high commissioner, General Sarrail, took over in 1925 the French army, in the words of Sarrail himself, 'had buried five thousand dead troops.'

Yet worse was to greet Sarrail in that fateful year of 1925. Soon after his arrival in Beirut in January the new viceroy received a delegation from Damascus and Aleppo. The delegates presented a number of demands, including:

> The unification of Syrian territory to include the Alawite and Druze mountains, the governorate of Alexandretta and the areas annexed to Lebanon.
>
> The convening of a constituent assembly to draft a constitution for the country establishing a parliament

with full legislative authority and to which the government of the country would be answerable.

The ending of military rule and of the interference of (French) advisers in the running of the country's affairs.

Respect for individual liberties.

The standardisation of the legal system, ending the role of foreign courts, and recognition of Arabic as the sole official language.

Although the French high commissioner appeared at first attentive and responsive to these demands, he seemed unable to convince his own government of the need to reconsider their stubborn approach to the tinderbox of Syrian national grievances. Meanwhile a spark came from the area of the Druze Mountain. The French 'adviser' to the local administration had been creating enmity with his high-handed attitude and the local population was becoming increasingly restive at being subjected to arbitrary and intrusive administrative control in contradiction to the stated promise of self-rule. A delegation representing the Druze community was formed with the intention of submitting its demands to the new high commissioner in Beirut. General Sarrail, however, refused to meet the delegation and threatened its members with exile if they did not return forthwith whence they came. There followed a series of incidents and gathering protests leading to the arrest of a number of Druze leaders. One of them, however, Sultan Pasha Al Atrash, eluded arrest and, having assembled a fighting force from his loyal supporters, set a trap for a column of French troops deployed to capture him. The encounter, known as the Battle of Al Mazraa, was a resounding defeat for the French, who suffered heavy casualties and lost much equipment and ammunition which fell into the hands of the Druze fighters. Sarrail's first reaction was near panic: he cabled Paris for reinforcements and attempted to placate the rebels by releasing the leaders he had earlier arrested.

The Druze rebellion soon spread, gaining momentum and evolving into a pan-Syrian insurgency. Many volunteers from Damascus and other cities journeyed to the Druze Mountain to join its fighters. The newly formed pro-independence party, the People's Party, was at the forefront of the process of mobilisation and agitation in support of the armed struggle, and the French reacted with strong measures of repression against the leaders and officers of the group. Battles started to rage in the environs of Damascus, in particular the areas of the Ghouta – the lush, orchard-rich fields that provided the city's green surroundings. A new French commander, General Gamelin (also to feature later in the catastrophic World War II Battle of France), was hurriedly placed in charge of the Armies of the Orient – the name given to the forces under French command in Syria and Lebanon. Yet Gamelin found that forcing his way through to the centre of the rebellion in the Druze Mountain was no easy task. Meanwhile Hama had risen and was subjected to a severe bombardment. But worse was to befall Damascus in October 1925. The city was extensively shelled and heavily damaged, leading to outrage and protests that spread throughout the world, including in sections of the French press. By then the rebels, now officially proclaiming themselves the Syrian National Revolution with Sultan Pasha Al Atrash as their commander, had issued a call to arms to the Syrian people. Their objectives, announced by Atrash, echoed the demands presented to General Sarrail by nationalist leaders earlier that year. They centred, once again, on the unity and independence of Syria across all its geographical territory, on the withdrawal of the forces of occupation and on the need to establish constitutional rule respectful of equality and human rights.

As a result of his failure to quell the rebellion General Sarrail was replaced in late 1925 by a new high commissioner, Henry de Jouvenel, a civilian member of the French senate who also represented France at the League of Nations. In his first pronouncements on being charged with the new mission, de Jouvenel was at pains to sound reasonable and receptive to the demands of the Syrian nationalists, emphasising that the essence of his task was, indeed, to bring Syria to independence. He added, somewhat cryptically, that he would like the country no longer to be the subject of front-page headlines but to feature only in the back pages. In furtherance of this 'enlightened' approach de Jouvenel put out feelers towards the nationalist leaders both inside and outside Syria. He held talks with representatives of the executive committee of the Syrian-Palestinian Congress in Cairo, and an unofficial agreement was drafted that included the setting up of a national government and constitutional rule, as a prelude to negotiations over a treaty between a sovereign Syria and France.

The discussions between de Jouvenel and the nationalists lasted nine months. They eventually collapsed amid widely held suspicions that the French were merely buying time to allow their military to consolidate their positions on the ground and re-establish control over those areas where the rebellion still held sway. In effect the overwhelming force that the French were eventually able to muster succeeded in substantially weakening the power of the rebellion. After two years of a struggle that, despite the odds stacked against it, carried the voice of Syrian resistance to colonial rule to the ears of many at home and abroad, the final chapter for the armed uprising came in the spring of 1927 when a team of Druze leaders surrendered to the French. They had run out of ammunition and could no longer hold out. In beating back the rebellion (particularly in the southern Druze Mountain region) the French had benefitted greatly from help and cooperation received from the British stationed across the border in Palestine. Sultan Pasha Al Atrash escaped capture and went into hiding before re-emerging ten years later.

The Great Syrian Revolt of 1925-27 may have been crushed militarily but it nevertheless had the lasting and ultimately victorious effect of galvanising a nationalist sentiment to which the vast majority of Syrians could rally. Henceforth it strengthened the hand of those political leaders carrying the banner of independence and unity against a shrinking minority still trying to ride on the coattails of French rule, while the latter openly or tacitly sought both continued dependency on their colonial masters and sectarian and regional separatism. The rebellion also had the impact of convincing the French, especially those with liberal or left-wing tendencies, that their neo-imperial strategy in Syria was doomed to failure and that a new chapter must be opened – one in which plausible arrangements must be reached with the force of Syrian nationalism. A first step in that direction was the replacement of Henry de Jouvenel as high commissioner at the end of summer 1926. Despite his early hyperbolic expressions of good intentions towards Syrian demands, de Jouvenel was seen to have failed in his mission. As an experienced diplomat it was believed that Henri Ponsot had the wherewithal to achieve progress where his predecessors had failed and that he would find the means to begin a political process satisfactory to Syrian opinion. To that end Ponsot produced a programme of action in July 1927 by which he intended to respond to some of the nationalist demands. He proposed a 'political truce' and the establishment of constitutional rule ensuring national unity, yet reasserted his country's wish to maintain its international responsibilities under the mandate: there would be no climbing down on the issue of granting independence in the foreseeable future. The result was a rejection of the proposals by the nationalists through the voice of the Syrian-Palestinian Congress. Instead they renewed their call for a strong and united opposition to French rule. Nevertheless Ponsot ploughed ahead with his declared policy and invited from the ranks of the nationalists Sheikh Taj al-Din Hasani to form a new government to preside over the formation of a constitutional assembly. The government announced its programme of action in February 1928. It centred on the planned assembly and the promise that power would be handed over to a cabinet duly elected by the new parliamentary body.

Although highly sceptical of the new approach adopted by the mandate authorities, and seeing in the details little that would firmly set the country on the path to true independence, the nationalist camp, on the whole, declared its readiness to respond positively to Ponsot's initiative. Nonetheless, ominous signs of division started to appear within the nationalist ranks between hardliners wanting no truck with any promises falling short of the immediate fulfilment of their demands and those seeing an opportunity for a gradualist political strategy that would deliver those same objectives in the longer term. Activists outside Syria, particularly the Cairo-based Syrian-Palestinian Congress, were more likely to reject the compromise on offer, while within the country the leaders of the newly formed National Bloc decided – albeit with reservations – to go along with the political process that was taking shape.

The position taken by the National Bloc bore fruit when the elections for the constituent assembly delivered a resounding victory to the nationalists. Forming a clear majority, they elected as speaker of the assembly Hashem Al Atassi – a nationalist leader commanding great respect throughout Syria. With momentum behind them the nationalists soon began the work of drafting a constitution, and the process almost immediately set them at odds with the French. Certain major clauses of the draft, voted on by the assembly in August 1928, were rejected as France claimed they ran counter to her commitments as a mandatory power entrusted by the League of Nations. The clauses in question all related to the issues of sovereignty, independence and unity – matters that had lain for so long at the heart of Syrian aspirations. Ponsot insisted on the need to remove all such contentious clauses from the draft constitution, but the assembly members voted almost unanimously in favour of their retention. The resulting standoff soon led the French authorities to declare the suspension of the constituent assembly – a decision that led to mass demonstrations and protests throughout the land.

The struggle over the constitution was to overshadow Syrian political affairs for the next two years. During that time the nationalists who gambled by entering the political fray in the face of the hardline rejectionists demonstrated that the path they had chosen did not signal weakness or softness towards the occupier. The kudos that they gained by standing fast on core principles when drafting the constitution – in defiance of French pressures – reinforced their position, and that of the National Bloc, in their claim to represent, henceforth, the rights and aspirations of liberty-seeking Syrians. In the two years that followed the suspension of the constituent assembly the nationalist members as well as other leaders of Syrian opinion loyal to the National Bloc maintained the pressure on the French through popular rallies and mass activities. They demanded the reconvening of the constituent assembly and the adoption of the constitution it had drafted with all its clauses intact. Finally, at a conference held in Damascus in March 1930, the nationalists agreed to embark on a new initiative in an attempt to break the long political impasse. Hashem Al Atassi met with Henri Ponsot, who promised to revive the political process and reinvigorate the spirit of cooperation and openness with which he had begun his mission. The result was the promulgation on 14 May 1930 of the first Syrian constitution since the establishment of the French mandate. It varied little from the draft adopted by the assembly in 1928 and, crucially, kept those clauses insisted upon by the nationalists that had caused the French to reject it and suspend the assembly. However, an additional clause (number 116), imposed by the French upon the enacted constitution, watered down the impact of this milestone in Syrian political history by tacitly enshrining a right of veto by the mandatory power over those parts of the constitution the French regarded as contravening their rights.

Clause 116 of the Syrian constitution was to become a major bone of contention in future years between the nationalists and the French. Nevertheless, despite the general mood of consternation and resentment that greeted the announcement of the constitution, the nationalist leadership continued to participate in the revived political process and, after much internal deliberation, decided to take part in elections for the new parliament. This time, though, the French rulers pulled out all the stops in support of candidates they saw as friends opposed to the nationalist leadership. The result was an assembly packed with members loyal to the French, or at least much more pliable to their wishes. The nationalists, now in a minority, were faced with the difficult choice of behaving like a loyal opposition or resorting to the popular 'street' where they manifestly held the reins of power. In effect both tracks saw an infusion of nationalist fervour, and the French-leaning majority in the parliament was never allowed to set the political agenda as it might have wished or as their French masters had hoped. At the same time, however, the nationalist ranks were suffering a deep fissure, and a new political force (named the Constitutional Group) emerged in opposition to the National Bloc. Led by Dr. Abdulrahman Shahbandar, a prominent and highly regarded early pioneer of resistance to French rule, the group took the mainstream nationalist leadership to task, accusing it of turning a blind eye to collaborators in its midst.

The permutations in and outside the parliament and the power struggles over the shaping of the country's future and its relationship with France coalesced around the issue of a treaty to replace the mandate and so set Syria along the path to independence. A model loomed in neighbouring Iraq where a treaty was signed with Britain in 1930, giving that country a formal, albeit heavily qualified, independence. The possibility of such a treaty and the debate over what it may or may not contain dominated the political discourse of mid-thirties Syria. Ponsot had already received instructions from his government to begin talks with Syrian leaders over the proposed treaty, and, indeed, he proceeded in late 1932 and early 1933 to engage in such talks. But it soon became apparent to the nationalists that the issue dearest to their hearts – Syrian unity – was not being given the importance it deserved, and at a conference held in Damascus in April 1933 the nationalists declared their intention to boycott future meetings and withdrew their representatives in the cabinet. By the middle of the year Ponsot, who had been in his post for seven years (the longest serving of the high commissioners for Syria and Lebanon), was to leave Syria having largely failed in the goal he had proclaimed for himself – that of guiding Syria to a new era of independent governance in close association with his country, France.

It was left to his successor, Count Damien de Martel, another seasoned diplomat, to try to pick up the pieces left by Ponsot, and especially to revive the stalled treaty negotiations. On his arrival in Syria in October 1933 he unilaterally announced the terms of a Treaty of Friendship and Alliance, which he pretended to have negotiated with the compliant Syrian cabinet – now completely devoid of any nationalist representation. The treaty was duly signed and declared valid in late November. However, it was a move that soon ignited a storm of protest across the spectrum of Syrian public opinion, including large sections of those identified as mandate loyalists. The treaty had surrounded the precious prize of independence with such caveats and restrictions as to render it a hollow promise, and it became difficult to defend even for the most supine of Syrians. In fact it was not long before that treaty became an acknowledged dead letter, with the Syrian parliament, notwithstanding its being loaded with pro-French members, finally rejecting it. This led to the adjournment of parliament, the suspension of the constitution and a return to rule by diktat as the country once again entered a period of major turbulence, strikes and political protest led by the forces of nationalism, still mostly under the banner of the National Bloc. Many of Syria's women were now emerging from centuries of traditionally inconspicuous existence and actively taking part in the struggle for independence. They joined and even helped organise rallies and demonstrations all across the country. At the same time a growing movement for women's emancipation was taking shape, led by activists from the urban and educated elites who started to form into organised pressure groups. The bolder members began storming the barriers of gender discrimination, such as refusing to sit in designated 'women-only' tram enclosures.

The political paralysis lasted until January 1936, when the funeral of the legendary leader of the earliest rebellion against French rule, Ibrahim Hanano, sparked a renewed and escalating wave of nationalist agitation. This was met with harsh measures of repression by the French, including an assault by the security forces on the offices of the National Bloc. The rising tension threatened to unleash a new, countrywide rebellion and prompted the high commissioner to revise his failed hardline approach. The result was a declaration by de Martel that strongly hinted at the opening of a new chapter and a readiness to begin serious negotiations with the National Bloc to reach agreement on the vexed question of the treaty. A meeting was held in Beirut between de Martel and Atassi, where an agreement was signed containing an invitation to an official Syrian delegation to visit Paris with the purpose of negotiating the details of the treaty. This overt French attempt at a rapprochement was accompanied by the release of political prisoners and a general easing of the heavy-handed tactics that had hitherto marked the policies of de Martel.

Most of Syria responded to the developments with a degree of relief, even jubilation, seeing in them a clear triumph for the independence movement and the National Bloc. A sizeable minority within that movement, however, stood against what it deemed a climb-down by the Bloc and rejected the very concept of a treaty that would shackle Syria irreversibly to France. Nonetheless a Syrian team, representing the National Bloc and led by the venerable nationalist Hashem Al Atassi, left for France in March 1936. After months of very hard bargaining a treaty was eventually signed in September of that year which provided for the ending of the mandate and the recognition of Syrian independence, while maintaining for France a privileged position in its former domain. At first the French government had seemed as inflexible as ever in agreeing the terms of the proposed treaty, but when that summer produced for France a radical new administration – the socialist-communist coalition of the *Front populaire* – the mood of the talks changed for the positive, allowing both parties to reach the landmark agreement. Despite falling short of the full aspirations of the independence movement, the treaty was received favourably on the whole and the Syrian delegation was warmly welcomed by large crowds upon its return to the country. A new, post-treaty momentum was created that carried Atassi to the presidency of the country and, importantly, passed to the central government in Damascus full sovereignty over the self-governing regions of the Druze and Alawites.

Looming menacingly over the new climate of national liberation was the perilous status of the province of Alexandretta, which the treaty left hanging in the balance. At all stages in the course of administering the mandate the French had kept the issue of that province's future in doubt as they managed the vicissitudes of their relationship with Ataturk's Turkey. As Syria approached what seemed like certain independence so the voices grew louder in Turkey for the pre-emptive move of laying claim to Alexandretta while the French were still in charge. This would build on earlier agreements with the French that had given the province an autonomous regime and conceded special rights and privileges to the minority Turkish population. The new nationalist government in Syria sensed that a Franco-Turkish deal over the future of Alexandretta was taking shape behind its back.

Indeed it raised the alarm in its first address to the parliament, stating that the issue of Alexandretta was the gravest facing the nascent nationalist administration and stressing the deep historical and geographical links between the province and the rest of Syria. The Turks, meanwhile, having sensed France's weakening resolve, pursued an escalating campaign, both diplomatically – at the level of the League of Nations – and by stirring Turkish nationalist emotions inside and outside Alexandretta. They succeeded first in detaching the province from Syria and creating an independent state of Hatai. This was finally annexed wholesale in 1939 by the signing of an agreement with France in June under which the territory was formally ceded to Turkey. In doing so France – eager at the time to gain the goodwill of Ankara as war clouds gathered over Europe – betrayed the primary responsibility entrusted to it as (still officially) a mandatory power: that of maintaining the territorial integrity of the country under its care.

The loss of Alexandretta, and with it the historical Syrian capital of Antioch, was a devastating blow felt by all Syrians – one which continues to be felt, particularly as families were left either side of the new border. As if this stark example of riding roughshod over Syrian rights were not enough, it was soon to become apparent that the French government was less than honest in advancing the process of independence as envisaged by the treaty of 1936. At every turn in the Syrian nationalist government's attempt to bring into effect the provisions of the treaty the French raised objections and put up impediments, revealing their true intentions. They also resorted to underhand tactics in encouraging dissent by groups opposed to the National Bloc, including stirring up regional and ethno-sectarian resentment. Moreover, the fate of the treaty itself was increasingly in doubt. The French government continued to prevaricate over official ratification by the National Assembly of the treaty it had solemnly signed. The procrastination only served to deepen the chasm between the supporters and opponents of the treaty within the Syrian national movement, especially as de Martel insisted on maintaining his hold on the levers of power, in particular those applied to security and the military. Syrian opponents to the still-unratified treaty argued with some justification that it represented a mere front to the outside world while it remained business as usual for French colonial rule in Syria.

Against a background of distrust and new waves of unrest the National Bloc was hard pressed to keep hold of the loyalty of its supporters. Nonetheless it clung on to the stalled treaty, believing that ultimately it would deliver the promised independence. All efforts were directed at convincing French politicians of the need to ratify it, and delegations were dispatched to France to lobby for that purpose. All that to no avail, however, for the treaty was never ratified, and the Syrian cause was left hanging in the air as France's attention was consumed by the sound of battle drums very close to home. By early 1939 Syria's nationalists had all but given up hope of resurrecting the treaty and were preparing for a return to earlier forms of struggle. The French, on their part, were preparing for what seemed an inevitable conflict with the Axis powers and were ill-disposed to loosening control over territories they anticipated becoming key battlegrounds.

With the outbreak of the Second World War, and using the pretext of the national emergency that arose from it, the French clamped down hard on all challenges to their authority in Syria. All manner of repression was applied, targeting leaders and activists deemed subversive with arbitrary arrest, imprisonment and exile. The Syrians held their breath, expecting the worst, and political life entered a ponderous phase as all minds focused on the great power struggle in Europe and the prospective impact on their own destiny as a nation tied – against its will – to a principal combatant. When France suffered its catastrophic defeat at the hands of the Germans in the spring of 1940 many Syrians could hardly contain their joy at the collapse of their oppressor, believing, for an instant, that the fall of France was the harbinger of the liberation of Syria. However, it soon became clear that while the French Republic may have been brought to its knees, the successor, Axis-leaning state of France, based in Vichy, was determined to hang on to its *Outre-Mer* possessions, including Syria. The high commissioner, Gabriel Puaux, who had succeeded de Martel in early 1939 before the outbreak of war, simply carried on with his duties, answerable now to Vichy instead of Paris. It came as a shock to Syrians to find their country passed on seamlessly from the victorious France of 1918 to the defeated vassal regime of Marshal Pétain, without any question of the legitimacy of the transfer.

Despite the anti-climax of the French defeat, Puaux sensed the potential delicacy of his position and began to tone down the harsh anti-nationalist measures he had hitherto adopted. He re-established dialogue with Syria's political leaders in a bid to forestall any negative repercussions of serving a defeated country. In July 1940, however, an assassination in Damascus would shake the very foundations of the National Bloc and further divide and weaken the nationalist camp. The victim was Dr. Shahbandar, who, as already mentioned, had split from the National Bloc, having been sharply opposed to its policy of pursuing the path of the (now dead) treaty with France. For a period of time the finger of suspicion pointed at the National Bloc, leading a number of high-ranking leaders to flee the country. However, the court hearings before which the captured assassins were arraigned soon established that the perpetrators were acting under the instructions of a religiously motivated group hostile to the secularist ideology purportedly being propagated by Shahbandar. Thus the name of the National Bloc was cleared, and those leaders who had fled returned. Nevertheless the Shahbandar affair would not die entirely and continued to fuel the flames of turmoil within the nationalist ranks.

While the Vichy government continued to maintain the legitimacy of its inherited rule in Syria (and Lebanon) there was growing concern among the Allies, especially the British, that allowing Syria to remain in the hands of a regime accused of being a tacit collaborator with the Axis powers endangered their positions in Palestine and Egypt. Furthermore, the British forces were feeling great pressure from General Rommel's Africa Corps attacking from the west. The suspicions as to Vichy's ultimate loyalties were fed by reports of an increasing presence of German and Italian agents in Syria and Lebanon in the latter half of 1940. A war of words between Vichy France and Britain reached fever pitch as the latter pointed to examples of overt collaboration with Germany (including a protocol signed between France and the Reich in May 1941 that committed the French authorities to providing logistical facilities in Syria for German forces in transit). Meanwhile the high commission, now under General Dentz, made much of Britain's so-called threat to supplant France's imperial interests in the Levant and closed down the British consulate general.

The die was cast for an invasion of Syria. Indeed the Free French, under General de Gaulle, had for some time been actively seeking to convince their reluctant British patron of the need to launch a joint campaign. On 8 June 1941 troops from Britain, Australia and India, together with Free French soldiers, crossed into Syria from the south and engaged the defending forces of Vichy France, heralding a campaign of thirty-four days that ended with Syria and Lebanon firmly in the grasp of the Allies. To the surprise of many Dentz and his military fought stubbornly, defying the hopes of the Gaullists that there would be mass defections to their ranks. General de Gaulle, through the commander of the Free French forces, General Catroux, issued a solemn proclamation, declaring 'in the name of Free France' the end of the mandate and the independence of Syria and Lebanon, to be guaranteed by 'a treaty in which our mutual relations will be defined.' The proclamation ended with the following resounding words: 'A great hour in your history has struck; France declares you independent by the voice of her sons who are fighting for her life and for the liberty of the world.' This pledge to the Syrian people was reinforced by a simultaneous British guarantee, issued by Britain's ambassador in Cairo, which expressed support for the announcement by the Free French.

The Syrians reacted positively to the Allied promises, although some cynicism remained, thanks to their long experience of French duplicity. They were reassured by the fact that the French no longer had the total power that they previously enjoyed, having to bow to Britain as the principal military player in the region. General Catroux assumed the duties of the ousted Dentz (but with the title of general delegate rather than high commissioner as a sign of the post-Proclamation of Independence changes) and was eager, in the first flush of victory, to signal the start of a new era. When General de Gaulle himself visited Syria in June, he and Catroux enjoyed a warm reception from the notables and politicians they met. Cordial messages were exchanged, with de Gaulle keen to secure the cooperation of the former president, Atassi, in the formation of a new government that would gain the blessings of the National Bloc. Contacts and discussions carried on for some time but no understanding was reached and little progress made in putting flesh to the bones of the Proclamation of Independence, aside from some nods towards a sovereignty that remained largely symbolic.

It soon dawned on the Syrian nationalists that the real purpose of the Free French dragging their feet over the interpretation of the Proclamation of Independence was nothing less than a restoration of the canon of the mandate under a new name. At the same time the British and Free French were engaging in a scarcely hidden game of geopolitical chess in the Levant, with Syria seemingly again a prize to be fought over. The British were giving the French repeated assurances that they respected the latter's primary position in Syria and Lebanon. Yet de Gaulle and his followers saw in the Syrian nationalists' every move in opposition to their rule the treacherous hand of their British 'ally,' as testified by the memoirs of many French actors of the day, including those of de Gaulle and Catroux. The former, of course, was to carry forward his bitterness at British behaviour in the Levant in his attitude of *froideur* towards Britain for many years to come. Meanwhile Syria's nationalists saw an opportunity in the British counterweight to French hegemony and were not averse to exploiting to their own advantage the lack of trust between the allies.

The pressure exerted by the nationalists, with quiet but solid backing from the British (and other leading international powers such as the United States and the Soviet Union), finally forced the hand of the French and in early 1943 they announced preparations for the holding of free elections in both Syria and Lebanon. The elections, as expected, returned a parliament dominated by the National Bloc. It was an historic moment for Syria when that new parliament met on 17 April and unanimously elected Shukri Al Quwatly to be president of the Syrian Republic and Faris Al Khouri (a leading Christian politician) speaker of the parliament. A new government was formed under the prime minister, Saad Allah al Jabiri – a prominent nationalist leader from Aleppo. Syria, it seemed, was well on its way to achieving its dream of genuine independence.

De Gaulle and his representatives had other ideas. They were not about to abandon their hold on these eastern Mediterranean outposts so readily. Surprisingly, their harshest response to the unpalatable new political realities came not in Syria but in Lebanon, where French rule historically had faced the least resistance; indeed it was welcomed by large sections of the Christian population who remained grateful for the creation of *Grand Liban* (Greater Lebanon) by a French decree in 1920. Notwithstanding that large reservoir of good will, the French authorities in Lebanon reacted with severity to the emergence of a strong movement for independence in that country following the parliamentary elections held there. Leading politicians from all Lebanese factions were summarily rounded up in November 1943, triggering mass protests and demonstrations that only ended with a complete French climb-down and the release of the arrested leaders. The date, 22 November, is annually celebrated as Lebanese National Day. Syrians of all shades stood solidly behind the Lebanese people as they confronted and ultimately prevailed over coarse attempts by the French to suppress their bid for freedom. Expressions of popular support for their sister country erupted throughout Syria. Henceforth the Syrian and Lebanese struggles to cast off the shackles of French domination were inextricably linked, and both countries sought to present to the outside world an image of a common front.[2]

Those Arab countries that had achieved a degree of internationally recognised independence and sovereignty – Egypt, Iraq and Saudi Arabia – strongly backed Syria and Lebanon in their continued campaign to wrest control from a French government that, despite its official declarations, refused to surrender full sovereign authority to its erstwhile dominions. A firm message of Arab solidarity came in the form of meetings that took place in 1943 and 1944 to prepare the ground for the establishment of the League of Arab States. Syria and Lebanon were solemnly recognised as independent countries and founding members of the incipient regional body. Expressions of formal recognition also came from beyond the Arab world, including the Soviet Union and then the United States of America. Yet the French continued to pursue a rearguard action, demanding that their allies, especially Britain, agree to recognise Syrian and Lebanese independence only on condition that it be accompanied by an affirmation of French pre-eminence in both countries enshrined by binding treaties. Britain, on her part, was caught between the demands of the French – who were already deeply suspicious of her plans for the Levant – and the Syrian nationalist leadership, who refused to concede any privileged position for France in an independent Syria. This tug-of-war between France and Syria was to mark the remaining two years (1945-46) of the former's reign in the Levant. Using all manner of pressure at its disposal Paris continued to insist on a treaty as the price for loosening its hold on Syria. It succeeded, initially, in delaying the issuing of invitations to Syria and Lebanon to attend the inaugural meeting of the United Nations to be held in San Francisco in April 1945. However, after much protest by and on behalf of the two governments, invitations were delivered to Damascus and Beirut. Faris Al Khouri, who had by then become Syria's prime minister, headed his country's delegation to the meeting, where it seemed that Syria's long struggle for independence had reached a triumphal conclusion with recognition on the highest international stage.

Yet still the French clung desperately to the last vestiges of an eastern Mediterranean empire. Emboldened by the illusion of having been restored to its former glory as a victorious power – after the humiliation of its defeat in 1940 – the government in Paris decided on a defiant course of action, even though most of the world had by now recognised Syria and Lebanon as fully independent and sovereign republics. Relying on the effect of its de facto military presence in the two countries, and believing it could do a deal with Britain to conjure up the spirit of Sykes-Picot, France kept delaying on its promise to hand over full political, economic and security powers to the governments in Damascus and Beirut. It was partly sustained in its obduracy by mixed messages from London that referred to the need for the parties, France on the one hand and Syria and Lebanon on the other, to reach agreements that respected the pre-eminence of French interests in the two countries. The British were also careful in almost every declaration on the issue to assure the French that they had no intention of replacing them – a deeply ingrained suspicion held by de Gaulle and his entourage.

The spark that detonated the final explosion of the struggle for Syrian independence came on 7 May 1945 with the landing in Beirut of a French force (comprised almost entirely of Senegalese recruits). This set off alarm bells in Syria, as well as Lebanon, with memories still alive of the landings in 1919-20 which had preceded General Gouraud's invasion of Syria and the dissolution of its first experience of independence. The Syrian government immediately protested this provocative move, which was accompanied by a memorandum citing

French conditions for handing over the command of Syrian and Lebanese military units (the Special Forces, as they were called) to the respective national governments. The demands reiterated that French interests in the strategic, cultural and economic domains be guaranteed by treaty. The Syrian and Lebanese government representatives held a joint emergency meeting and denounced the arrival of the new troops, which they saw as a violation of the sovereignty of both states. They also rejected the demands contained in the memorandum as they ran counter to the principles of independence. This was France's cue for the unleashing of an armed offensive that spread all over Syria and included the heavy shelling of Damascus. The Syrian parliament was attacked and set on fire, and its garrison perished, after a stand that became an object of pride in the history of modern Syria. The Syrians refused to submit to the terror of French arms. Much of the world reacted with shock and indignation at this blatant act of neo-colonial aggression, with the United States, the Soviet Union and Great Britain all expressing their deepest concern at France's actions. The *coup de grâce* to this last desperate French adventure came in the form of a letter (the contents of which were announced by the British foreign secretary in the House of Commons on 31 May 1945) from Prime Minister Winston Churchill to General de Gaulle. He stated that, due to the grave situation created by the fighting in Syria, instructions were given to the British commander-in-chief in the Middle East to intervene to prevent further bloodshed and maintain security and the routes of transport. He added that in order to forestall any clashes between British and French forces immediate orders should be issued to the French military to cease fire and withdraw to their barracks. Indeed, on 1 June the French representative in Damascus was handed a British note, amounting to an ultimatum, requiring immediate compliance with these demands. The humiliated French had little choice other than to comply, but never reconciled themselves graciously to the ending of a quarter of a century of dominance in the Levant. From that date on, the inexorable march towards Syrian independence was assured, and finally accomplished on 15 April 1946. It was an episode in Anglo-French relations that was to stick bitterly in the craw of de Gaulle and many of his compatriots for decades to come. At the same time Britain's standing was never so high in Syria.[3]

Notes

1. The river that flows through Damascus.
2. Indeed, the Lebanese minister Camille Chamoun, who headed his country's legation in London, was the acting representative of both governments for a few months from late 1944. He relinquished his Syrian hat when the Syrian minister Najib Armanazi (this author's father) arrived in London to assume his duties as head of the Syrian legation in March 1945.
3. Indeed, a cousin of this author, born during those turbulent days of late May 1945, was given the middle name Eden after the British foreign secretary of the time and in appreciation of the country's stand against the French onslaught. It was a tag he would regret just over ten years later when Anthony Eden, the architect of the Suez War Crisis, became the *bête noire* of all Arabs.

CHAPTER FOUR

The Early Years of Independence

*Greater Syria [Bilad Al Sham], the fount of Arabism
and the birthplace of its earliest advocates and immortal
martyrs ... Greater Syria, from which radiated the light
of the Arabs and which was the first of the Arab states to
carry its civilising mission to the furthest horizons, up to
the banks of the Loire, the orchards of Andalusia and the
walls of China ... declares today its belief in the widest
meaning of Arabism and its mission towards human
civilisation based on the highest principles of Right and
Just Peace. As for Arab Palestine, the southern part of
the Syrian homeland, its cause, and saving it from the
Zionist threat, is a principal cornerstone of our policy,
and by rescuing it we set on firm ground the policies of
our country and the future of our children.*

- Shukri Al Quwatly, president of the republic, at an
oration delivered on 17 April 1946 during a parade in
Damascus marking the evacuation of foreign troops and
the attainment of Syria's full independence.

The 17th of April 1946 was a day of exultation celebrated by all Syrians. After what had seemed like an eternity of struggle, first against the Turks and more recently against the French, at last the flag of independent Syria was raised, unchallenged, high over the horizon. A small country with a population of barely three million inhabitants had succeeded in defeating a powerful colonial empire to become master of its own fate. It was a moment to seize with joy but also to reflect on all that had been sacrificed in the achievement of that cherished goal. Syrians would pride themselves on having secured unconditional independence beyond anything attained by other Arab states at that period in history. Egypt, Iraq and Transjordan, for example, while all ostensibly independent, remained shackled to their former colonial master (Britain) through treaties that severely restricted that independence for years to come. Alongside Lebanon, which also saw the evacuation of all foreign troops later in 1946, Syria had set the standard of a stubborn nationalism that refused any such restrictions, rejecting even the most minor remnants of privilege for the departing French. The firm stand which Syria took, and its success in completely liberating itself from any postcolonial connections, served as a beacon and exemplar for many of the evolving independence movements in areas such as India, Indochina and North Africa.

It was also a day for looking forward to the challenges ahead. The quote above from the speech by the president of the republic provides an eloquent and prophetic insight into those challenges which would have a profound impact on the course of Syrian history for decades to come. The president singled out for special emphasis the two issues that burned then, and still burn in the hearts of Syrians. The first was that of Arabism or Arab nationalism. Quwatly was at pains to stress his belief that Syrian independence, treasured as it was, did not represent the final prize of the struggle. The ultimate goal was Arab unity, and Syria – or rather Greater Syria – was historically the torchbearer of that mission. In fact, in that same speech he asserted that the only flag 'which we shall raise above that of independent Syria is the flag of Arab unity.' The other overwhelming national duty was 'rescuing Palestine,' which, he stressed, forms an integral part of the Greater Syrian homeland. These dual, almost sacred, objectives have for decades informed the narrative of Syrian political life, and, as we shall see in the pages to follow, they are at the heart of much of the mixture of drama, elation and distress that will colour the twists and turns of Syria's story following that fateful day in April 1946.

Clearly, the great challenges of both Arab unity and Palestine were bearing strongly and immediately on the agenda of the fledgling republic, and would not allow any basking in the victory of independence. From the moment it took charge of an independent Syria the political class, organised around the National Bloc, could no longer assume the role of admired leader of the struggle for independence or command the kudos and allegiances that went with that role. Not long after those heady days of the April celebrations, cracks started to appear in the nationalist front that had largely coalesced in unified strength prior to achieving freedom from colonial rule. Divided loyalties across regional, tribal and communitarian lines started to be felt in a system of government that took the superficial shape of a liberal democracy but contained much that harped back to an age of semi-feudal patronage. The National Bloc soon split into two political parties: the National Party, mainly based on the Damascene political and social elites, and the People's Party, with its base in Aleppo, the industrial and commercial hub of the country. Defeating the French had been a feat that the governing class could no doubt largely attribute to its dedication and shrewdness throughout the mandate years. But the challenges that it now faced were of a different nature altogether, not just in the great trials over Palestine and the ideals of Arab unity that loomed very forcefully ahead, but most importantly in delivering on the raised aspirations of good governance and economic and social advancement that, in the eyes of the new breed of political activists, should follow independence.

However, the generation that transitioned from the phase of leading the struggle against the French to running the newly independent country emanated from a milieu that was not structurally adept at dealing with the changed environment. Largely representative of the land-owning class and the *haute bourgeoisie,* it was ill-suited to responding to the needs of a society and economy that cried out for growth and reform as well as social justice, having endured many years of upheaval and deprivation. Furthermore, the period of struggle against the French had produced among the educated class, especially the student youth, an energetic and insurgent mentality honed on the many riots, strikes and other forms of protest that marked the mandate years. This younger generation started to feel alienated from the political establishment, which, having successfully delivered independence, appeared less sure-footed in dealing with the challenges of its aftermath. Thus it was predominantly the youth that started to gravitate towards emerging new parties with radical and modern ideologies and much sharper discipline and organisation than was the case with the loose confederation of politicians forming the older National Bloc and its offshoots. One such party was the Syrian Nationalist Party—later to become the Syrian Social Nationalist Party, or SSNP, which was established in the early thirties by a dynamic Lebanese thinker, Antun Saadeh. Highly ideological and organised on strict disciplinary lines the SSNP advocated the cause of a united Syrian homeland. It had a vision of the Syrian nation – formed of those living in that stretch of the eastern Mediterranean known as the Levant or Greater Syria – rising up and shedding all that kept it backward, divided and weak and prevented it from assuming its historical destiny among leading nations. Shunning pan-Arabism in favour of pan-Syrianism (albeit insisting that a strong and united Syria would in time take a leading place within an Arab 'front') the SSNP faced an ingrained Arab nationalism that prevailed in its surrounding environment. Its uncompromising secularism also set it against the centres of religious power. Nevertheless it gained substantial inroads among the intellectual elite, first in Lebanon and soon after in Syria, especially within the more marginalised minority communities outside the predominant Sunni and Maronite socio-political establishments in Syria and Lebanon respectively.

In the mid-forties, more than ten years after the formation of the SSNP and partly in response to its sharper focus on Syrian nationalism, radical Arab nationalists found voice in the emergence of the Arab Baath Party (*baath* meaning renaissance or revival). Officially launched in April 1947, it was largely the brainchild of a Damascene Christian, Michel Aflaq, who, ironically hailed from the same Greek Orthodox community as Antun Saadeh. The SSNP and the Baath vied with each other in drawing support from an intellectual class with roots in the minority communities, especially Christian and Alawite, but it was the Baath that had the advantage of being able to appeal to a broader Muslim audience by pairing Arab nationalism with the culture and history of Islam. In a celebrated article, written on the occasion of Muhammad's birthday, Aflaq waxed lyrical about the 'Arab' Prophet as the source of the glories of the Arab spirit and its civilising mission. Even more significant in the eventual spread of the Baath beyond its initial intellectual base was a merger in later years with the Arab Socialist Party. The latter was formed in the late forties by Akram Al Horani, a leading young activist from the town of Hama in central Syria. Early in his political life Horani joined Saadeh's SSNP and was the party's representative for the region of Hama. He soon drifted away from that party, however, and discovered an aptitude for the more localised politics of Hama and its countryside where a harsh system of exploitation had produced a skewed relationship between a small class of landowners and a large population of peasant farmers living a semi-feudal existence. Preaching a socialism that promised emancipation through agrarian reform, Horani's populism gained him a mass following. In later years this was to pay substantial political and electoral dividends to the benefit of the restructured and renamed Arab Baath Socialist Party.

In addition to the SSNP and Baath parties some of the younger generation of Syrians were attracted to the Syrian Communist Party. Although originally formed in the early twenties, the Communist Party only started to establish solid populist roots in the mid-thirties to late forties, having benefitted from a towering charismatic leader, Khaled Bikdash (a Kurd from Damascus), and the growing prestige and international influence of the Soviet Union. In a separate camp from the rising new parties with their secular leanings stood the Muslim Brotherhood – it had originated in Egypt in the late twenties and started to spread steadily in Syria, in particular among the religiously conservative and urban Sunni middle class. In common with its sister organisation in Egypt, the Syrian Muslim Brotherhood advocated a society and polity based on the precepts of religion, and an adherence to the concept that Islam was both a spiritual belief and a guide to practical as well as ethical statecraft.

While the underlying political landscape was in a state of flux, with the growing attraction of new currents and ideologies the established political order seemed oblivious to the creeping threat to its power. No serious effort was made to reform an outdated social and economic structure, while the merging of the interests of the old land-owning class with those of the rising industrial-cum-commercial upper middle class served to widen further the chasm between the haves and have-nots in an increasingly politicised Syrian society. Stirrings of protest over living conditions came in the form of a number of strikes and demonstrations. Students, once in the vanguard of popular rallies against the French, were now turning their attention to their own government, whom they denounced for perceived shortcomings in the deliverance of the fruits of independence.

The government's neglect of the domestic agenda was only partly the result of an inability to fathom the new aspirations of a post-colonial generation. It was also a product of very pressing regional challenges that independent Syria was compelled to confront before it had any time to settle down to the business of good governance. Almost immediately after securing independence, the new republic appeared under threat from competing regional and international powers that sought to bring under their wings the hard-won sovereignty achieved by the Syrians, in the knowledge that control over Syria was the key to regional hegemony. The surrounding Arab dominions, especially Egypt, Iraq and Saudi Arabia, all found in the new Syria an opportunity to play an intricate game of assuring a favourable foothold in the new polity, or at least thwarting the ambitions of rival powers. Also entering the fray were the international 'patrons' of the semi-independent Arab rulers. With varying degrees of enthusiasm, Britain in particular, but also significantly a United States with a growing interest in a strategic oil-rich area, backed the regional ambitions of their local allies. Within Syria itself the political and social diversity allowed these outside powers opportunities to influence the domestic agenda, particularly during the early years of liberal government and the freedom it allowed political parties and a thriving newspaper industry.

The most outspoken of the Arab rulers in putting forward a project to co-opt the destiny of the independent Syrian state turned out to be Emir – later King – Abdullah of Transjordan. Emir Abdullah advocated openly and tirelessly the concept of a Greater Syrian Kingdom (to include Jordan, Palestine and Lebanon) with its capital in Damascus and the implication that he would sit on the throne last abandoned by his brother, Faisal, in 1920. While there was another proposal on the table – that of a united Fertile Crescent, which added Iraq to Greater Syria and was the pet project of the Iraqi strongman Nuri Al Said – it was the threat from Abdullah that was seen from Damascus as more serious and immediate. It was rejected very forcefully by the government and by large sections of the population that saw in it a threat to republicanism and the risk of being shackled to a regime well known for its subservience to its (British) colonial master. Syria's leaders, however, were only too conscious of the appeal of Arab unity that had been endorsed so passionately by President Quwatly in his Independence Day speech. They were careful, therefore, to stress that the rejection of Abdullah's project was not against the principle of union per se and that they were ready to enter an arrangement that had republicanism and full sovereignty as its cornerstones. Concerned that Abdullah had the full backing of Britain (a fear largely misplaced as documents from that period reveal) and playing up the populist anticolonial theme, Syrian politicians, including spokesmen of the rising new radical movements, whipped up opposition to the Greater Syria project. They went further and wholeheartedly endorsed a rival Egyptian and Saudi project founded around the League of Arab States. Partly to offset the version of Arab unity backed by the regimes in Baghdad and Amman, Syria was an enthusiastic cheerleader for the Arab League, pushing hard from the outset for giving the newly founded pan-Arab organisation real teeth, even at the expense of the sovereignties of the member states. This was illustrated in the great fanfare and celebration that the anniversary of the League's foundation inspired in Syria, more than in any other Arab state, and Damascus continued to clamour loudly for the League to embody in practice, not just in theory, the notion of a united Arab superstate.

Navigating the rough waters of Arab unity was not the only international challenge confronting the newly independent Syria. Even more daunting were the darkening clouds over Palestine that showed every sign of erupting into violent storm. Syria had always felt that the fate of Palestine was intimately linked with its own, and that history and geography dictated the strength of that bond. Indeed, in Syrian eyes Palestine formed part of southern Syria. Since the earliest days of Zionist colonisation Syrians were at the forefront of calls to recognise the national threat that was looming and the need to mobilise to avert it. One of the early leaders of Palestinian armed resistance to the British occupation of Palestine (seen in Arab eyes as the umbrella under which Zionist colonisation was proceeding) was Izzedine al Qassam who hailed from the Syrian town of Latakia. And in the years preceding the Arab-Israeli war of 1948, the main Arab-Palestinian irregular fighting force, the Palestine Salvation Army, operated from Syria under the command of Fawzi Al Qawukji, originally from Tripoli in Lebanon. A number of leading names in Syrian politics and in the military had fought in the ranks of the PSA, giving a boost to their public image. Among these were Akram Al Horani and Adib Al Shishakli, later to become president of the country.

Given the passions aroused by what had become known widely as the 'Palestine cause' it became incumbent on the untried government to respond to the public mood and take it up as its major preoccupation. The leadership had little time and meagre resources to prepare for the increasingly likely confrontation as it had gained control of its small army barely months before the day independence was declared. Moreover, having taken the plunge in a spirit of almost naive resolve, and in contrast to the other Arab powers, Syria was the least calculating in the countdown to the imminent conflict. As events and documents would reveal, the leaders of Jordan, Egypt and Iraq all held hidden agendas alongside their lofty proclamations of selfless support for the rights of the Palestinians. King Abdullah, in particular, is known to have had secret talks with the Zionist leadership, through their envoy, Golda Meir, in which an understanding was reached, effectively setting boundaries for the territorial division of Palestine and allowing the Jordanian monarch the opportunity to expand his kingdom westward. Egypt's King Farouk, aware of the ambitions of his Hashemite rivals, was resolved to stake his own claims should the conflict result in a dismembered Palestine. Above all, he and the Saudi King, Abdul Aziz, were

85

anxious to thwart any move by Abdullah to profit politically or territorially from the regional shakeup that loomed. Only Syria, it seemed, was preparing to devote itself to the struggle with minimal consideration for its narrow interests. And Syria's was the loudest Arab voice on the issue at the international level as it was occupying a non-permanent seat at the United Nations Security Council at the height of the debates on Palestine's future. The Syrian representative was no other than Faris Al Khouri, the prominent nationalist and Protestant Christian who, while officially speaker of the Syrian parliament, had been charged with leading the Syrian delegation to the UN. During his chairing of the Security Council, Al Khouri's interventions were some of the most eloquent and vehement made in support of the Palestinian cause at this highest international forum. On returning to Syria at the beginning of 1949 he was greeted at the airport as a hero by a huge welcoming crowd, at the head of which was President Quwatly, the prime minister and members of the cabinet.

In the meantime the war, which started on 15 May 1948 with Arab armies entering Palestine, had ended in humiliating defeat. The Syrian front suffered the least as the truce declared at the end of the fighting left Syrian forces in possession of a sliver of territory beyond the old frontier (later to be defined as no man's land in the permanent armistice agreement reached under United Nations auspices). The impact of the 'disaster' (*al nakba*, as it became known in Arab historical folklore) was immense. In Syria huge throngs descended into the streets expressing their anger and frustration. The press was especially critical of governments that had accepted a temporary truce, as demanded by the Security Council, a few weeks into the war while Arab arms appeared to be in the ascendancy. This had allowed the nascent Israeli state to regroup and consolidate, and by the time a second permanent truce came into effect the Israelis had taken the initiative and conquered significant territory beyond that allocated to the Jews by the UN Partition Plan of 1947. By early 1949 Arab ranks were drastically split when first Egypt, then Lebanon followed by Jordan, agreed armistice agreements bilaterally with Israel, leaving Syria high and dry as the last country still to sign up to what was seen across the Arab world as an acceptance of defeat.

The political situation within Syria was reaching boiling point as the humiliating end to the Palestine war played into the hands of the emerging radical and populist parties which were keen to blame the debacle on the 'reactionary and corrupt' political class. That class had already tarnished its own image and that of the fragile democratic system when, in 1947, it forced through parliament a constitutional amendment allowing President Quwatly to stand for a second term as president. A sweeping majority of deputies voted for him amid much fanfare and celebration. But the re-elected president and the new cabinet were unable to quell the rising tide of restlessness and protest that had been given strong impetus by the anger over the loss of Palestine. In response, political leaders – including Quwatly, his entourage and a number of deputies in parliament – began blaming the command of the army. They accused certain high-ranking officers of involvement in a scandal of supplying soldiers with contaminated provisions and of general incompetence in carrying out their duties. The chief of staff of the army, Brigadier Husni Al Zaim, took these criticisms personally, with results that would shake the foundations of the state and open the door to a new era in Syrian politics.

CHAPTER FIVE

1949-58: The 'Revolving Door' of Coups and Counter-Coups

Motivated by our patriotic values and painfully aware of the dire state of the country as a result of the malice and injustices inflicted by those who claimed to be our faithful rulers, we have felt it necessary to take temporary governance of the country ... we shall endeavour to carry out to the full our duty to our beloved patrimony, while harbouring no ambition to keep hold of power as we prepare the ground for sound democratic rule that will replace the current false one.

An excerpt from a communiqué announcing the first of a series of coups that would punctuate Syrian political life for several years.

On 30 March 1949 Syrians awoke to a communiqué broadcast on national radio declaring that an army council had seized power in order to prepare the country for a true democracy and in response to the unjustified attacks on the armed forces who had 'borne great sacrifices in defending the homeland.' It soon emerged that the leader of the coup was the army chief of staff, Brigadier Husni Al Zaim, and that he had ordered the incarceration of the president and prime minister as well as a number of leading politicians. This turn of events shook not only the country but the whole region as those powers that held a stake in the future of Syria sought to comprehend the implications of this shock to the established order.

Zaim insisted that the coup was intended as a temporary intrusion by the army; constitutional government would follow as soon as political life was cleansed of its alleged villainous and corrupt elements and the military would return to its barracks. Quwatly soon offered his resignation to the Syrian people, as did Prime Minister Khaled Al Azm, and Zaim went through the process of consulting parliamentary leaders in a show of good faith. Yet it was not long before his true objectives became apparent as he introduced broad measures of censorship and repression. One of many victims was the founder of Al Baath, Michel Aflaq, who endured very harsh and humiliating treatment in prison, which ended only when he wrote a letter of supplication to Zaim – a document that would haunt Aflaq for the rest of his life. Zaim also hurried through the finalisation of two important issues: the first was the signing by Syria of an armistice agreement with Israel, becoming the last of the frontline Arab states to do so, and the second an accord relating to the 'Tapline project' – the extension of a pipeline through Syrian territory to carry American-extracted crude oil from Saudi Arabia to the Mediterranean. Debate over the accord had been causing political controversy for several months. Many argued that agreement to the pipeline should be accompanied by clear geopolitical and economic benefits for the country. The fact that Zaim waved through such an accord, together with the signing of the armistice, gave credence to suspicions that he had sold out to foreign powers, in particular the United States. Indeed, years later a CIA operative, Miles Copeland, was to claim that the coup of 30 March was planned with American support. Much later the Israeli academic and diplomat Itamar Rabinovich revealed that Zaim offered Israel a full peace treaty – even an alliance – that would secure the two countries' regional pre-eminence. The Israeli government of the day rejected Zaim's overtures, believing that they lacked seriousness. The new Syrian leader was soon also deeply immersed in the game of Arab regional rivalries, tilting towards the Egyptian-Saudi axis and thus inviting the wrath of the Hashemites in Baghdad and Amman. And he was quick to paint himself as an enemy of communism in an attempt to cosy up to the West, in particular the United States, at a time when the region was becoming a Cold War battleground.

Meanwhile Zaim's tendency for megalomania asserted itself on many levels. He declared himself 'field marshal' and carried a baton and wore a monocle in true 'Prussian' tradition. He also abandoned all promise of a return to constitutionalism by ensuring he was elected president by an ad hoc plebiscite. Spin doctors were encouraged to portray him as a new Ataturk who would carry Syria into the modern age. Indeed some of his measures were daring in the Arab and Syrian contexts, including the granting of full voting rights to women, but they could not hide the deep flaws of megalomania, fantasy and even pathos that were to result in his bloody demise only four and a half months after his dramatic power-grab. A notorious act of both folly and betrayal helped to bring about that end. The story began in Lebanon in early summer 1949 where militants from the Christian Phalangist Party provoked a clash with members of the Syrian Social Nationalist Party in Beirut by burning down their printing press. The Lebanese government used the incident as a pretext to order a massive roundup of SSNP supporters and the arrest of its leader, Antun Saadeh. Fleeing to Damascus, Saadeh was received by Zaim, who pledged his full support should Saadeh declare an uprising in Lebanon in retaliation for what was regarded by the SSNP as a plan to crush the party. As a token of his good faith Zaim even offered his personal handgun to his prospective ally.

Partly believing in the word of Zaim but also driven by the pressure to respond to the clear incitements by the Lebanese government and its Phalangist accomplices, Saadeh proclaimed a rebellion. In effect it was easily suppressed, not least because Zaim's support never materialised. Nevertheless, Saadeh continued to maintain contact with Zaim, who arranged to see him on 6 July at the presidential palace. When Saadeh arrived, however, he was delivered into the hands of an armed security contingent from Lebanon's government. He was then taken at speed past the frontier, arraigned before a hastily convened military tribunal, tried, convicted and shot outside Beirut within a matter of hours. The manner of his arrest and execution outraged not just his followers but many of his adversaries as well. In Syria the repercussions centred on the betrayal by Zaim of his solemn oath to Saadeh and the violation of the honoured tradition of protection and refuge. Later revelations point to the fact that pressure by Egypt's King Farouk, acting on strong appeals from the Lebanese premier,

Riyad Al Solh, was instrumental in persuading Zaim to hand over the man seen as a danger to the established order in Lebanon and beyond.

His act of apparent treachery sealed Zaim's fate. On 15 August 1949 a second military coup quickly gained control of Damascus. A group of officers loyal to the SSNP led an armoured column to Zaim's residence in the early hours and, after overwhelming his guards, seized hold of him. He was taken in an armed convoy to a site just outside Damascus, where the arrested prime minister, Mohsen Al Barazi, joined him. Their captors shouted abuse at Zaim for his betrayal of Saadeh and wasted no time in carrying out his execution and that of Barazi by firing squad.[1] Meanwhile the overall leader of the coup, Brigadier Sami Al Hinnawi, was addressing the nation by radio and heralding the end of the period of tyranny and corruption. In a repeat of the assurances first heard when Zaim announced his takeover, Hinnawi swore that the army had no intention of retaining power and would return in due course to its regular duty of safeguarding the homeland, keeping 'far away from politics.' It soon became evident, however, that the coup against Zaim had more to it than avenging the death of Saadeh. In fact it represented a geopolitical shift that was to mark Syrian politics for the next decade. In this instance Hinnawi redressed the earlier shift by Zaim towards the Egypt-Saudi Arabia axis and was clearly intent on promoting a Syrian-Iraqi union instead – a cherished dream of the Hashemites ruling Baghdad. This gave rise to the received wisdom of the day that Hinnawi's takeover was a direct result of an operation planned in association not just with the Iraqis but also with their British masters – a favourite target of the rising tide of Arab nationalism. In his attempt to pivot towards Baghdad Hinnawi was able to draw on the support of a substantial constituency built around the merchant and industrial class in Aleppo, and their political arm, the People's Party. At elections for a new constituent assembly held in November that year the People's Party and its allies gained a clear majority. The stage was then set, it seemed, for decisive steps leading to union with Iraq, and a resolution in favour of such a union was soon adopted by the new assembly.

The Egyptian-Saudi axis was alarmed by these developments, as were the defenders of Syrian republicanism fronted by Akram Al Horani, who had gained a reputation for political shrewdness and opportunism and for having unique access to ambitious power-seeking army officers. One such officer, Colonel Adib Al Shishakli, took decisive action, striking the night of 18 December and so leading the third military coup d'état in a span of just seven months. Hinnawi and his closest colleagues were arrested and deposed from their positions in the supreme army council, and a new military command was set up. Hinnawi was later to meet a grim fate when assassinated in Beirut by a member of the Barazi family avenging the execution of Mohsen Barazi the day Hinnawi had seized power in Damascus. The communiqué that announced the latest coup justified the move by claiming that it was done in order to preserve the republican system (a reference to the risks to that system posed by an association with the Iraqi monarchy). Repeating almost verbatim the words that Syrian ears had become accustomed to, the communiqué solemnly declared that the military had no intention of meddling in politics and would soon hand the country over to civilian rule.

Despite his role behind the latest coup, Shishakli did not at first take centre stage. He was satisfied with assuming command of the army while paying lip service to the constitutional institutions that had recently reemerged, including the constituent assembly and the office of head of state occupied by the veteran leader Hashem Al Atassi since the overthrow of Zaim. A facade of civilian rule was maintained and cabinets with theoretical authority were formed and reformed. Yet behind the scenes the invisible hand of the clique of officers headed by Shishakli carried the real clout. The tide was now turning decisively against those political forces, such as the People's Party, who had almost succeeded in pushing Damascus into the embrace of Baghdad. Shishakly was eager to steer the country into the opposite Arab camp – Cairo and Riyadh – and carefully calibrated his powers of persuasion to make sure that the civilian political class, nominally in charge of the country, knew the limits of their freedom of action. Meanwhile, after some heated deliberations, the constituent assembly finally agreed the wording of the new constitution. Particularly at issue was the question of the status of religion. A strong group formed of the Muslim Brotherhood and various Islamic figures insisted Islam be enshrined in the draft constitution as the religion of the state. However, the progressive and more secular-minded members succeeded in watering down that provision while accepting a wording to the effect that the religion of the head of state be Islam. The 1950 constitution stands out even today as an enlightened document well ahead of its time, especially in comparison with other constitutions in neighbouring lands.

By autumn 1951 the cosy relationship between the de facto military government and a more or less compliant political class was starting to fray. Parliamentary voices started to be heard that were critical of the army's interference in the affairs of the state. Cue the fourth in the series of coups that had punctuated Syria's political landscape in the space of two and a half years. On the morning of 29 November 1951 yet another burst of martial music on Damascus Radio prefaced the solemn announcement that the armed forces had once again felt compelled to take over the reins of the country in order to flout the ambitions of politicians bent on 'destroying the independence of the country.' A communiqué, issued by Shishakly, launched a vitriolic attack on the People's Party, accusing it of conspiring (with Iraq) to undermine the republic and install monarchical rule.

It was the second coup to be led by Shishakly and this time he used it to dispense with the institutions of constitutional government that he and his fellow officers had maintained at least in form during the previous two years. The president, Hashem Al Atassi, resigned and parliament was dissolved, as were all political parties save one created by Shishakly named the Arab Liberation Movement. Many politicians were arrested, with the People's Party feeling the brunt of the new regime's hostility. For a long spell though Shishakly, while recognised as the strongman of the regime, shied away from claiming for himself the title of head of state, leaving that post in the hands of Brigadier Fawzi Selo, who everyone knew was the front man for, if not the puppet of, Shishakly. By 1953, however, his personal egotism got the better of him: a referendum in July of that year finally anointed Shishakly as president with near dictatorial powers. By that time he was busy forging relations with Egypt where a coup in July 1952 had put an end to King Farouk's reign, and a new leader, Colonel Gamal Abdel Nasser, was emerging. Shishakly saw in Nasser's military background and his approach to politics a special kinship and potential for a partnership that could have strong bearing on Arab and regional affairs. On other issues, such as the economy, Shishakly was receiving some kudos. A new industrial and commercial class was benefitting from his protectionist measures, which included breaking away from the customs union and other 'joint interests' shared previously with a laissez-faire lebanon. Shishakly also took credit for strengthening the capabilities of the military and standing up to Israel in a number of armed confrontations following attempts by Israeli forces to lay claim to the territory on the border designated no man's land by the UN and in connection with a festering dispute over Israeli water and irrigation projects in the Galilee area.

Internationally Shishakly was mostly accepted as a stabilising factor after the years of turbulence and quick-fire changes at the top of Syrian politics. He even became the object of courtship by competing Western capitals, with Paris doing much of the running but Washington also showing clear interest in warming up to him as a potential recruit for the putative Middle Eastern Defence Pact being forged in the face of the threat from communist expansion in the region. Aid was promised, especially through the American 'Point Four' programme, which offered assistance to those countries in the Middle East that joined the Western-backed alliance. It was hoped that Syria – considered a linchpin state in the region – would sign up to the new and heavily promoted geopolitical strategy. Shishakly, however, declined the offer despite heavy pressure and attempts by the West to lure him into the proposed anti-Soviet camp. Regardless of whatever private thoughts he may have held regarding Washington's overtures, Shishakly was certainly restricted in his policy choice by a wave of popular opposition to the Point Four programme which was seen by the bulk of public opinion as a vehicle for neo-colonial domination. America's reputation was already at its nadir due to its support for Israel. Despite the setback Washington continued to work for closer ties with Shishakly and his government, especially as the Syrian leader maintained his opposition to communism as a creed foreign to Syrian society. Thus American arms were sold to Syria during that period although it was France that had the lion's share in Shishakly's drive to modernise and strengthen the Syrian army. As for Britain, despite substantial improvement in its trade relations with Syria (including a small number of military shipments), relations between Damascus and London were uneasy. Shishakly remained wary, even paranoid, about British involvement in the continuing campaign by Iraq to undermine his rule and promote the hated Fertile Crescent project.

Shishakly's rule was becoming increasingly despotic. One by one he alienated the forces that formed the political landscape, whether of the left or right. Meanwhile the Iraqis, as suspected, were as active as ever in sowing dissent through their influence within the ranks of the People's Party and their approaches towards sympathetic officers. And those other political groupings who could have rallied around Shishakly at his time of need were instead snubbed as he pursued an increasingly idiosyncratic policy, which banned all parties except his own – the tailor-made Arab Liberation Movement. It was not long after he took on the presidency that rioting and strikes had started to spread, especially among the student population which was increasingly drawn to the rising radical parties: the Baath, the SSNP and the communists. These were countered with increased repression and arrests, which only served to feed further the forces arraigned against him. Yet as 1954 dawned there seemed to be little sign that Shishakly's rule was in real danger, and Western diplomatic despatches from that period mostly pointed to the regime's resilience.

However, in January a badly judged response to disturbances in the area of the Druze Mountain south of Damascus started a chain of events that quickly got out of control. The army resorted to brute force, including heavy bombardment, to pacify the region, causing many casualties as well as a tide of anger that swept through the entire country. Shishakly blamed the Iraqis (and even the British) for the uprising by the Druze, but his political enemies, supported by some disgruntled army officers principally owing allegiance to the Baath, decided that the time had come to strike. The spark was lit in the north of the country and centred on Aleppo where Shishakly's rule was least popular. The rebels took over the local radio on 24 February 1954 and called for the overthrow of the 'tyrant' and the restitution of political freedoms. A number of commanders of army units in the north and central sectors, along with the coast, soon pledged their loyalty to the rebellion. In the south, however, and around the capital where the bulk of the Syrian army's strike force was stationed, the president remained in command and the prospect of a full-scale civil war loomed. The next morning Shishakly made an attempt to restore the dignity and reputation that his final weeks as president had seen melt away. In a message to the Syrian people he acknowledged that certain army officers, 'acting under the influence of their party affiliations,' had risen against the 'constitutional government' of the country. He continued that it 'would not have been difficult' for him to quell the rebellion but that in order to avoid infighting within the army and the spilling of blood of the people and the army to 'whom [he] is devoted' he announced his resignation.[2]

The nature of Shishakly's departure was met with sighs of relief across the country. Yet it took a number of days for the spectre of civil war to lift as elements in the army still loyal to the departed president threatened to hold fast against the rebellious units. The crisis was finally overcome when a 'national convention,' including almost the entire spectrum of political and army leaders, met in the city of Homs and decided on the restoration of constitutional life as had existed before Shishakly's coup in late 1949. So it was that the president at that time, Hashem Al Atassi, was restored to his position. The event was marked with his triumphal entrance through the streets of Damascus amid a torch-lit parade, which this author witnessed as a child. The national assembly of 1949 reconvened and made a point of announcing the formal end of its 'adjournment' that had lasted over four years, as well as the restoration of the constitution of 1950. All political prisoners were released and political parties given licence to operate openly. The freedom of the press and the rights to street assembly and trade union organisation were ensured. Indeed Syria now seemed at the apex of democratic transformation – well ahead of virtually any country in the Middle East.

The summer of 1954 also saw the return to the country of the former president Shukri Al Quwatly who had been living in exile in Alexandria. His return felt like one more nail in the coffin of the turbulent era of successive military dictatorships that had begun when Quwatly was removed by Zaim five years previously. The country was set, it was hoped, for a bright and stable future, even though the old guard, represented by Quwatly, had lost much of their shine due to past failures that were not easily forgotten. While welcoming the end of the series of dictatorships, the fact that the country was not prepared to submit readily to the old political class was evident in the parliamentary elections held that autumn. They resulted in a sharp increase in the representation of left-leaning radicals, especially the Baath party, which, with its allies, formed a substantial bloc to rival that of the traditionalist and conservative elements that had dominated previous assemblies.

The triumph of the Baathists was due almost entirely to the success of Akram Al Horani in mobilising the votes of the bulk of peasants and the deprived communities in and around the central region of Hama and other areas in opposition to the established land-owning families that had held sway in past elections. Furthermore, for the first time in Syrian history a communist was elected to the new assembly – a precedent in post-war Arab politics. This was the secretary general of the Syrian Communist Party, Khaled Bikdash – a towering figure in the regional and international pro-Soviet community. Another power centre in the ascendant was a bloc of independents headed by the famously shrewd Khaled Azm. A scion of one of the wealthiest and most aristocratic dynasties, he positioned himself on the side of those left-wing forces newly on the rise, earning for himself the sobriquet the 'red millionaire.' The realignment of forces in parliament was mirrored in the armed services, where Horani continued to be as active as ever in drawing into his orbit prospective adherents to the Baathist cause. In that he was not alone as other ideological adversaries, particularly the SSNP and the communists, busied themselves in carving out fiefdoms within the military establishment.

The fluidity of the new political landscape and its lack of a strongman at the top imposing a firm hand on domestic affairs, or restricting the opportunities for foreign intervention, provided easy pickings for the international powers in their geostrategic competition for Syria's favours. So it was that over the next few years the country became a prime battleground in the grand struggle to determine the destiny of the Middle East. An important milestone in those power alignments was marked in February 1955 when a defence treaty was signed between Iraq and Turkey, soon to be joined by Pakistan and the United Kingdom. Dubbed the Baghdad Pact, it was the result of months of pressure by Western governments, especially Britain, aimed at bringing the Arab countries into their fold within the context of an anti-Soviet strategic alliance. Syria was seen by Western chancelleries as the key prize in the push to expand the Baghdad Pact beyond its founding signatories and into the heart of the Arab world. In Egypt, Nasser announced from the outset his country's vehement opposition to the Western-inspired pact, seeing in it a means to buttress the arch regional rival, Iraq. He also felt its threat to the concept of 'non-alignment' that he was busy promoting in partnership with other stars of the international stage such as Prime Minister Nehru of India and President Tito of Yugoslavia.

Cairo and Baghdad were locked in an aggravated recurrence of the bitter struggle over Syria's future, which in earlier years had fuelled the cycle of military coups. This time, though, the stakes were higher than ever as Baghdad had behind it an aggressive Western strategy of containment aimed at the communist bloc. On the other side Nasser was counting on, and receiving, the support of Moscow and the growing tide of anti-imperial and nationalist Arab opinion in standing fast against the West's latest attempt to subjugate the region. For a number of months in late 1954 and well into 1955 Syria wobbled as domestic political forces, with their shadow extensions into the military, jockeyed for influence and ranged themselves overtly or tacitly on either side of the great debate over the Baghdad Pact. Despite the growing appeal of Nasser's anticolonial message, his reputation in Syria was suffering due to his perceived close association with the hated Shishakly regime. This was compounded when, in the autumn of 1954, he blamed the assassination on his life on Egypt's Muslim Brotherhood and subsequently executed a number of its adherents. This brought large anti-Nasser demonstrations onto the streets of Syria. Yet it was a single act of violence that eventually tipped the balance decisively in favour of the anti-Baghdad Pact camp.

On the afternoon of 22 April 1955 a football match was being played at the main stadium in Damascus between the Syrian and Egyptian national teams. In attendance were various officials from the two countries including the Syrian deputy chief of staff, Colonel Adnan Malki, known to be a Baath sympathiser and the leader of a powerful bloc in the military. Suddenly a corporal on guard duty protecting the VIP enclosure drew his revolver and fired two shots at Malki, killing him almost immediately. In the ensuing melee the assassin himself was shot in an act that remained shrouded in some mystery, although it is generally believed that he committed suicide. Not long afterwards Damascus Radio announced the news of the assassination and, crucially, identified the assassin as a member of the SSNP. As if on cue a mass roundup began of known party members in Damascus and across the country, while a mob attacked the SSNP's offices and the printing presses of its daily newspaper. In a single blow the main rival to the Baathist-communist presence in the military, and a force considered a strong counterweight to the ideological lurch to the left in the land as a whole, was virtually eliminated from Syrian political life. But the events surrounding the assassination of Malki resonated beyond the fate that befell the SSNP. They signalled the first stage in the triumphal march of the camp that opposed the Baghdad Pact and strove for a radicalised Syria – a country transformed not only by its external alignments but also the shifts in its internal socio-political and economic order.

One of the first to benefit from the changing environment was a major in the army, Abdul Hamid Al Sarraj, the head of the *Deuxième Bureau*, a name borrowed from the French military and given to the army's intelligence department. Sarraj unleashed the new security powers in his possession not only against followers of the SSNP – many of whom had harrowing experiences in jails that would become notorious for the brutal treatment of their inmates[3] – but gradually against those he saw as a threat to the emerging radical order. Under his tutelage members of the *Deuxième Bureau* – later commonly known as the *mukhabarat* – would grow into a fearsome breed that would terrorise Syrians in the decades to come. Sarraj was an early admirer of Egypt's Nasser, and relying on the support of Horani's Baath and other fervent Arab nationalist forces (such as the Arab Nationalist Movement which was attracting many intellectuals of the middle class) he hoped to inherit Malki's mantle as a main driving force in forging a new leftist-nationalist direction for the country.[4] The trial that was soon to take place of SSNP leaders provided the opportunity to submit dubious evidence of a strong relationship between the accused and US government agents. The latter, it was claimed, used the SSNP as a bulwark against the communist threat and a vehicle for tying Syria to the Baghdad Pact. The proceedings of the court, which, on occasion, took the shape of a political show trial, fanned the flames of anti-Western emotion. This was reflected in much of the press and in Syria's political 'street.' It was also clear that Sarraj, Horani and their communist allies were exploiting the SSNP affair to the full, and damning through guilt by association all those right-wing and conservative forces in the country who still owed allegiance to Baghdad and believed in an alliance with the West.

The old political class, meanwhile, despite losing out on the 'street,' was not yet done. The return of former president Quwatly gave a new lease of life to conservative forces within the state and parliamentary establishment. A victory of sorts was achieved for these forces when Quwatly was re-elected to the post of president by a vote in parliament in September 1955. His opponent was Khaled Azm, who had the support of the Baathists and his own group of independents allied to the broad nationalist-leftist front. In the months to follow, however, Quwatly's triumph was to prove increasingly illusory. The initiative was dramatically shifting in the direction of the pro-Cairo, pro-Moscow and anti-Baghdad camp, with ultimate power being exercised not by the president and the cabinet but by the group of radical and nationalist officers closely tied to the Sarraj-Horani axis.

From the start of his tenure Quwatly would face the reality that his writ was severely curtailed by the growing power of the ideologically driven officer clique that wanted to tie Syria firmly to the anti-imperial, Arab nationalist front that was becoming the zeitgeist. The leader whose charismatic personality most personified that growing mood was Gamal Abdul Nasser. He succeeded as no one before in stirring the passions of an Arab public hungry for the glories he was promising. His oratory was exceptionally effective, as was the message relentlessly broadcast from the Cairo-based propaganda arm, the Voice of the Arabs, denouncing Western colonialism, the Zionist enemy and the rulers in Baghdad who were betraying the Arab nation by signing up to security deals devised in Washington and London. Quwatly and his followers, as well as the broader swathe of non-radical and conservative politicians, were hamstrung and dared not defy the surging popular sentiment. Thus having prevaricated for as long as it could Syria now tied its colours firmly to the mast of the anti-Western camp. A sign of the times was the sealing of a bilateral mutual defence pact between Egypt and Syria in October 1955, with Saudi Arabia joining them almost immediately.

Apparently in response to the defence pact that Syria had just signed, in December 1955 Israel mounted a large-scale raid across the armistice line, causing significant casualties among the Syrian forces. It was a strike that further fired up emotions within the country and, very importantly, steered Syria into overtly cosying up to the Soviet Union from where it sought, as Egypt had, to obtain shipments of arms, including MiG aircraft. Damascus claimed that it needed these arms to deter future Israeli aggression, especially as Western powers were refusing to supply the necessary military equipment. In April 1956, on Independence Day, the streets of Damascus shook with the weight of freshly supplied Eastern-bloc (mainly Czechoslovak) hardware as the roar of MiG 15s echoed from the skies. Syria was now firmly set on a path that was already giving rise to much concern among Western politicians and diplomats worried about losing Syria to their Cold War adversaries. The summer of 1956 soon provoked the greatest Western angst for at least a decade when, in a shock move, Nasser announced the nationalisation of the Suez Canal. Paroxysms of protest from Western capitals immediately followed, but in Syria, and across the Arab world, Nasser was hailed as a hero, having dismantled the last vestiges of a bygone colonial era. The political balance within Syria, already heavily weighted in favour of the nationalist-leftist front, was now almost completely tilted against the old conservative political class as Nasser garnered the adulation of the crowds and became the talisman of the Baathists and their fellow riders on the broader Arab nationalist wave. When a tripartite (Israeli-British-French) attack on Egypt was launched later in the autumn Syria was at the forefront of countries offering direct help to Nasser. A team of army engineers (acting on the instructions of Sarraj and without the authority of the civilian regime) blew up the pipelines that traversed Syria carrying crude oil to the Mediterranean. Syria immediately broke off diplomatic relations with Britain and France and urged other Arab countries to do the same. President Quwatly also embarked on a visit to the Soviet Union on 31 October, an occasion that was used to maximum effect in underpinning the new relationship with Moscow and in ramping up the rhetoric by both sides against the 'imperialist' attack on Egypt. (It also provided a useful distraction for the Kremlin from the impact of its widely condemned simultaneous invasion of Hungary and the crushing of the rebellion there.) Quwatly's visit saw the signing of a far-reaching trade and economic agreement. It also secured Soviet assurances of an increase in arm shipments to Syria to bolster its defences as it squared up to deeper involvement in Egypt's resistance to the tripartite aggression.

On the regional front Syria played a crucial role in the convening of an emergency Arab summit in Beirut in mid-November, which voiced strong support for Egypt. Albeit with varying degrees of enthusiasm, it further consented to the breaking off or at least the downgrading of relations with London and Paris. In a show of solidarity with Jordan, which was anxious about the possibility of having to face Israel on its own, a Syrian force was stationed alongside the Jordanian army. By that time Jordan had allied itself very closely with the Syrian-Egyptian axis, a process that had been given dramatic resonance earlier that year when King Hussein summarily dismissed the British Brigadier Glubb Pasha from his post as commander-in-chief of Jordan's armed forces. By the time Nasser emerged seemingly victorious (politically if not militarily) from the ill-fated campaign launched by his nemesis, the British prime minster, Anthony Eden, he had risen in Arab eyes to a level unprecedented in modern history. Syrians in particular hero-worshipped him as a saviour of the Arab pride that had long been trampled under the feet of the colonial master. Almost all the political forces in the country started on a stampede to prove their loyalty to the new champion. The Baathists, along with the communists, went as far as to clamour for a union with Egypt. Those who could have opposed this sweeping current were reluctant to voice any dissenting view, especially as Damascus had solemnly announced, in the midst of the Suez battle, the uncovering of a plot to mount a pro-Iraqi coup.

The abortive coup revealed by the Syrian government had indeed been in a state of preparation for several months. The Iraqis had played a major role in bringing together opponents of the Sarraj-Baath-communist alliance that was threatening to take over the country and its institutions, especially the army. These opponents included right-wing conservative politicians, the SSNP, the ex-president Shishakly, retired officers and tribal forces neighbouring Iraq. A detailed plan for the overthrow of the regime, much of it put together during meetings in Lebanon involving the Iraqi military attaché in Beirut, was ready for execution but at the last minute put on hold at the outbreak of the Suez Crisis. The reason given was that a coup at such a time would be seen as highly damaging and deeply unpopular when Egypt was bravely defending itself and requiring the closing of Arab ranks behind it. The postponement of its zero hour proved fatal to the planners of the operation. The secrecy they had hoped to maintain was soon exposed and they were to face the full wrath of those now wielding power in Damascus. The latter would exploit the opportunity to the full, relishing the chance to defame the plotters as agents of imperialism. The accused included many prominent names from the political establishment and the involvement of such noted figures cast suspicion well beyond those individuals and into the heart of the traditional ruling class. This prompted President Quwatly and his allies to distance themselves as much as possible from their erstwhile brethren and even to try to outdo the Baathists and communists in their denunciation of the 'treacherous plotters.' A further purge of those who could still act as a barrier to the ambitions of the Sarraj-Horani-communist juggernaut followed, and by early 1957 Syria was almost completely in the grips of a radicalised and fiercely nationalist military-political consortium. Consisting of a strong Baathist and communist presence at the higher military echelons and controlled by Sarraj's iron hold as the head of military intelligence, the seemingly all-powerful grouping was firmly allied to a growing parliamentary bloc headed by Horani and Khaled Azm. It also had at its disposal a well-drilled network of street activists ready to whip up anti-Western nationalist feelings on every occasion. The facade of moderate civilian rule still maintained by Quwatly and the bulk of cabinet ministers had by now ceased to convince anybody with a realistic appreciation of the rapidly changing dynamics of Syrian politics. Indeed, early that year, when President Quwatly tried to exercise his constitutional authority by ordering transfers at the top of the military command that would shift the balance in favour of the old guard he was met with the threat of an army takeover, and swiftly backed down.

By the spring of 1957 Syria was attracting global attention. The West was becoming increasingly alarmed as diplomatic despatches and frequent press reports pointed to a country 'going red' and to the prospect of the Soviet camp gaining a satellite and hence a foothold in one of the most geo-strategically sensitive regions of the world. The spotlight was directed at the ultra-nationalist Sarraj and the newly appointed pro-communist head of the army, Brigadier Afif Bizri, as the real rulers of the country, setting it on a path seen as dangerous to the security and stability of the whole Middle East. Syrian officials responded by declaring the discovery of yet another pro-Western plot, this time planned with the direct complicity of American diplomatic agents stationed in Damascus. On 13 August three US diplomats were given twenty-four hours to leave the country. A storm of protest and denials erupted from Washington, and American-Syrian relations descended to a new low. Almost on cue, sabre-rattling was soon to be loudly heard from across the frontier as the Baghdad Pact camp moved into action. Tens of thousands of Turkish troops amassed on the northern border, ostensibly to ward off the communist threat from Turkey's neighbour to the south. The crisis soon escalated when Nasser, in a show of solidarity with his embattled Syrian ally, sent a force of Egyptian troops to 'stand alongside their Syrian brothers-in-arms.' For an instant the world feared the worst as the Cold War threatened to heat up in a regional tinderbox. But cool heads prevailed, and, through some Arab diplomatic brokerage, particularly that undertaken by the Saudi Arabian king, the Turkish military deployment stood down.

The crisis of autumn 1957 succeeded in its desired effect of alerting many Syrians to the looming threat of communism. A shift was suddenly in evidence in the Baathist attitude and narrative towards their erstwhile allies. Communism was now spoken of as contrary to Arab nationalism. At the same time, and as a means to rescue Syria from the clutches of the newly acknowledged 'evil,' the same Baathists joined ranks with others from traditional mainstream politics to call for union with Egypt. The attraction of such a union was felt and even tacitly encouraged by Western officials who saw in it the chance to prevent Syria falling into the lap of the

Soviets.[5] The resulting rush to unity with Cairo was feverish. Syria's parliament, by now dominated by Baathists and their allies, with Akram Al Horani recently elected speaker, held a joint session in October with forty visiting members from the Egyptian parliament (a session presided over by Anwar Sadat). The merged assembly passed a resolution calling on the two governments to take steps to achieve a federal union between their countries. There followed a period of intense debate over the terms of the union between the political factions that formed the nationalist-leftist coalition. The communists and their major ally, the group led by Khaled Azm, were holding out for a loose federation that would maintain their growing powerbase and ensure the survival of Syria's vibrant political life and the freedoms associated with it. At the same time the Baathists, by now obsessed with the communist threat, saw a strong and integrated union as providing security and a means to propel them to the role of main partners in the formation of the new state.

Nasser, meanwhile, had ideas of his own. Although initially paying lip service to the idea of a federal union, he was aware that through such a loose structure he could be inheriting a troubled and troublesome Syria. While nominally united under his rule the danger was that the volatile neighbour would effectively remain outside his control. Hence he worked behind the scenes, through trusted associates, to establish solid contacts within the Syrian military, encouraging members of its high command to push for a union that went well beyond the objectives of most of Syria's established political class. The lack of cohesion within that class was now accompanied by a developing rift in the nationalist-leftist alliance, which was starting to be mirrored in the military. The instability played into Nasser's hands as Syrians seeking shelter from the gathering domestic political storms went running to him. In a humiliating slap in the face for the political leadership, a group of Syrian army officers led by the chief of staff, Afif Bizri, and with the blessings of Sarraj, left for Cairo in January 1958. With a total disregard for constitutional proprieties, these men agreed the terms of the union. Nasser was able to impose all of his conditions: a completely integrated union to be headed by him as president with almost unlimited powers and with Cairo as its capital, and the dissolution of all Syrian political parties – in effect a takeover of Syria by Egypt.

Upon its return to Damascus the military delegation brazenly informed the civilian leadership of the agreement with Nasser. Swept along by the tide of public opinion few in that leadership dared oppose the sudden and fundamental transformation that had been agreed over their heads. Only the communists overtly signalled their opposition, with their leader, Khaled Bikdash, deciding to leave the country on an extensive international tour. Their ally Khaled Azm also voiced criticism, if somewhat muted, seeing in the impending union the stifling of Syria's political life. The Baathists, on the other hand, while suspicious of Nasser in his insistence on the abolition of political parties, approached the dawn of the union with unbounded enthusiasm. They went so far as to claim for themselves almost all the credit for this momentous victory of Arab nationalism and the realisation of the age-old dream of Arab unity. The Baathists calculated that despite the theoretical dissolution of their party they would remain an organised force that Nasser would require as a partner in the rule of Syria. Nothing now stood in the way of that fateful moment when Syria would become the Northern Region of the United Arab Republic.

Notes

1. It is said that the officer commanding the force that executed Zaim took his blood-stained tunic to Saadeh's widow as a token of the exacted revenge.
2. Ten years later, seeking revenge for his bloody assault on their mountain stronghold, a Druze man tracked Shishakly down to a remote farm in Brazil and murdered him.
3. The most infamous of these was the Mezze jail overlooking a Damascus suburb. Its name became synonymous throughout the Arab world with the legendary Bastille because of the dark horrors faced by the prisoners inside.
4. The fact that Sarraj rose so suddenly and to such a position of power following the death of Malki gave rise to suspicions that he was implicated in the assassination. These were given credence by a number of authoritative sources.
5. Writing his end-of-year report, Britain's ambassador to Syria sounded positive on the impending union and called for support for the Baathists in their bid to confront communism.

CHAPTER SIX

The Rise and Fall of the United Arab Republic

The tide that has swept though Syria will engulf all Arab states and the winds of change that sprang from Damascus will blow their way across the whole of the Arab World.

- Gamal Abdul Nasser addressing a mass rally in Damascus on 27 February 1958 after the plebiscite that confirmed the merger between Syria and Egypt and his election as president of thenascent United Arab Republic.

It is not imperative that Syria remain part of the United Arab Republic but it is imperative that Syria remains.

- Nasser speaking on Cairo Radio on 5 October 1961, conceding Syria's secession from the UAR.

On 5 February 1958 the parliaments of Syria and Egypt, meeting separately in Damascus and Cairo, approved the historic document that laid the foundations of the United Arab Republic. Syria's president, Shukri Al Quwatly, addressed his assembled deputies in florid terms, speaking of the merger with Egypt as a moment of destiny crowning the hard struggle of the Arab nation against colonialism. Echoing that message, President Nasser declared to the Egyptian parliament that the union about to be achieved sprang from the hopes of the forefathers and met the aspirations of the new generation. In the national plebiscite held on 21 February an overwhelming majority of Syrians and Egyptians voted in favour of the union and agreed to the appointment of Nasser as the president of the new state. Even allowing for the inflated figures of ninety-nine per cent turnouts and 'yes' votes common in the practices of heavily state-controlled referenda there is no doubting that in Syria at least (less so in Egypt where the public was more subdued) the union was greeted with unbridled enthusiasm, almost to the point of delirium. When Gamal Abdul Nasser paid his first visit to Syria following the vote he was mobbed by adoring crowds everywhere he went. Pointedly he insisted on paying a visit to the tomb of Saladin in Damascus in a scarcely veiled bid to claim the mantle of the warrior-hero of ancient glory who united Egypt and Syria.

Yet the seeds of trouble were already being sown even in those heady days of unprecedented exultation. Behind the scenes the various actors playing a part in the rush to union were examining the opportunities – and pitfalls – ahead. The first to feel a negative impact on their position within Syria were the communists and their ally Khaled Azm. As had been clear in the months leading up to Syria's being thrown into the lap of Nasser the main motive driving the Baathists and the conservative political forces to such a drastic act of state self-sacrifice was the dangerously combustible internal divisions within Syrian army ranks and the political class as a whole. The Baathists, who had hitherto engaged in a partnership with the communists in pushing the country on a leftist, anti-imperial tangent, awoke belatedly to the threat of communism's hostility to Arab nationalism. This, ironically, led them to make common cause with those voices in the West that spoke with alarm of Syria 'going red.' The Baathists and their supporters in the army, as well as the strongman Abdul Hamid Al Sarraj, saw in the merger with Nasser's Egypt the means to outflank and ultimately destroy that enemy within. The communists and Azm, meanwhile, were aware of the trap being set for them but could do little to challenge the emotional wave that was sweeping the country and opted to go into a state of political sulk. They held on to a threadbare hope in the shape of the army's chief of staff, the pro-communist General Afif Bizri, who maintained his position in the initial post-merger distribution of leading government appointments. But that was not to last; on 23 March Bizri was given his marching orders as he and a host of officers with known communist sympathies were spontaneously cashiered in the first major political shakeup in the life of the union.

Getting rid of political rivals was only the start of the ambitions that the Baathist command entertained while rushing headlong into the union. They felt confident that Nasser would have little choice but to rely on them to maintain his hold on a famously unruly and heavily politicised Syrian population.[1] In the agreement that set up the union they had had to swallow Nasser's condition that all political parties be disbanded in favour of a 'national union' as the only recognised political force in both regions of the UAR. (The concession had irked many cadres and party faithful in Syria and the other Arab countries where party chapters were active.) However, the party's secretary general, Michel Aflaq, and its shrewd strategist, Akram Al Horani, argued that Baathism, even if officially subsumed into a larger political body, would continue to be the lifeblood of the union and exercise power where it mattered most within and outside the all-embracing new state. The first period of the union era did indeed bear the Baathist leaders out as Horani was appointed to key posts, including that of vice-president of the republic. Other Baathists and their sympathisers were generously rewarded with the distribution of governmental and bureaucratic largesse ensuing from the new bloated administration. In the governance of the Northern (Syrian) Region the influence of Horani and his cohorts was palpable, at least during the first year of the union. The other great beneficiary of Nasser's favours was Sarraj, who was given charge of the interior ministry, consolidating the iron grip he already exercised in Syria as head of security before the union. If there was one man upon whom Nasser depended to maintain his hold on Syria it was Sarraj. Aware of how indispensable he was to Nasser, at least in the early stages of the merger with Egypt, he behaved with that authority in mind. This meant a severe clampdown on all potential opposition. Inevitably it was the communists who felt most keenly the brutal force of Sarraj's secret police, the infamous *mukhabarat*. A notorious example of the lengths to which Sarraj's henchmen would go was the capture, torture and the melting in acid of the body of the Lebanese communist leader, Farajallah Helou, in Syria in 1959. It became a cause célèbre that echoed through much of the region. It also gave rise to a degree of tension between the Soviets and their ally in the broad anti-imperial camp: Nasser.

As far as Western governments were concerned, the birth of the UAR was greeted with mixed reactions. There was a sense of relief that Syria had been rescued from the maelstrom that was gripping it and that stability had been achieved – as well, of course, as the allaying of the communist menace. But the same governments were not comfortable with Nasser. London still harboured bitter memories from the Suez fiasco, as did Paris with, in its case, the added injury of Nasser's support for the nationalist rebellion in Algeria. While less hostile than the other two capitals, Washington considered Nasser's high profile in the non-alignment camp and the inspiration he provided to radical movements of national liberation as inimical to its strategy of containing the spread of communism. Also weighing heavily in the thoughts of Western policy-makers was the continuing stability – even the viability – of the conservative, pro-Western Arab states bordering the UAR: Iraq, Jordan, Lebanon and especially Saudi Arabia. There was no doubting the power that had been unleashed by the realisation of the dream of Arab unity encapsulated by the merger of Egypt and Syria, and by the charismatic leader now basking in the glow of that triumph. Arab public opinion, from North Africa and eastwards through to the Gulf, experienced a wave of emotional outpourings that alarmed the ruling elites and carried with it the inescapable necessity of at least seeming to join in the feast of Arab unity. Yemen was quick off the mark, announcing a federation with the UAR (a move that largely remained on paper). The conservative Arab camp, however, had a different plan: rather than join the UAR – an act of political suicide – it decided to set up, with obvious Western backing, a rival project of Arab unity. Almost immediately after the establishment of the

Egyptian-Syrian union, the Arab Federation was declared, linking the Hashemite monarchies of Iraq and Jordan.

The two Arab unionist projects – one centred on Cairo, the other on Baghdad – soon entered into a fierce war of words. Syrian and Egyptian proponents of the UAR claimed they best represented the progressive ideal of the union: a republic that gave voice to the masses and promised a future of national liberation and social justice, at the expense of the forces of Arab reaction. The advocates of the Hashemite version of Arab unity evoked the glorious history of the Hashemite dynasty – the mainstay of the original Arab revolt against Turkish rule – and laid into the Nasserist 'dictatorship' and its 'usurpation' of the proud Syrian homeland. Yet there was no doubting that Nasser held the trump card. By far the most potent instrument of partisan propaganda, the Cairo-based Voice of the Arabs (fronted by the iconic firebrand of the era, the irrepressible Ahmad Said) dominated the airwaves and stoked the fires of rebellion in the streets of Iraq and Jordan. The ideological sparring was almost immediately accompanied by a more violent exchange, for which the arena was Lebanon. The spring and summer of 1958 saw an insurgency against the pro-Western sitting president, Camille Chamoun (who had provoked anger by actively seeking re-election, requiring an amendment of the constitution), that turned into a proxy conflict between the supporters of the UAR – mostly Muslim and Arab nationalist – and its opponents – predominantly Christian and anti-Nasserist. Both rival Arab union camps weighed in heavily on each side, with Sarraj masterminding a sustained system of support for the rebels from across the frontier in Syria, while Baghdad did its best to shore up the beleaguered Chamoun presidency.

Before the Lebanese conflict could run its course, however, a momentous cataclysm was to strike at the very heart of the anti-Nasser regional coalition. On 14 July 1958 Baghdad Radio announced in fiery terms the overthrow of the monarchy and the birth of the Iraqi Republic. As the day unfolded the true extent of the ensuing carnage was revealed: the almost total obliteration of the royal family and the hunting down and lynching on the streets of stalwarts of the old regime, including the veteran strongman Nuri Al Said. This was a geopolitical earthquake of the first order and it set off resounding alarms in regional and Western capitals. Panic-stricken, London and Washington immediately responded – the first by sending a force of paratroopers to Jordan and the second by dispatching a formation of marines that landed on the shores of Lebanon. In the wake of the Iraqi coup many observers foretold the collapse of most of what remained of the old conservative and pro-Western Arab order, with the Hashemite king of Jordan facing his most perilous hour. Of course, Nasser and the Baathists, with their ally Sarraj, were celebrating reaching the apex of their triumphal journey. The strategic nemesis had been eradicated, and what Nasser had forecast as the relentless march from the Egyptian-Syrian union towards a union of all Arabs seemed to have become reality.

The new rulers in Baghdad had other ideas. While initially paying lip service to Nasser and the idea of Arab unity, and borrowing heavily from the lexicon of Arab nationalism, they were not ready to commit to following in Syria's tracks. A deep split had developed between the two main factions that carried out the anti-Hashemite coup. While a pro-Nasser-pro-Baath faction led by colonel Abdul Salam Aref was positively disposed to an immediate tying of the knot with the UAR, the more powerful faction led by the senior commander of the coup, Brigadier Abdul Karim Qassem, was much less eager to do so. Qassem, who soon became the unchallenged leader of Iraq, wasted little time in sidelining Aref and removing him from power as his second-in-command. It soon became clear that Qassem was riding high on a powerbase provided mainly by a resurgent Communist Party, which was taking over the streets of the capital and other parts of the country, and he entered into a phase of bitter and often bloody struggle against the Baathists and Nasserists. The turn of events in Iraq proved to be a body blow to Nasser's dream of building on the momentum created at the beginning of the year by the establishment of the UAR. It was not long before the old rivalry with Baghdad was revived, this time with added venom as Nasser's propaganda machine hammered away at Qassem's 'godless' communist regime and its insidious creed standing in the way of the glorious unity so cherished by Arabs. The newly republican Iraq attacked Nasser for his hegemonic greed and for faking his pretentions to be a truly progressive leader. It also appealed to Syrian *amour-propre* by posing as the champion of Syria's liberation from the yoke of Nasser's Egypt. As he was wont to do previously in Lebanon, Sarraj embarked on a campaign of sedition inside Iraq. It culminated in a violent uprising in the spring of 1959 when a group of Nasserist Iraqi officers took over the northern city of Mosul and raised the flag of the UAR. Qassem and his communist allies quickly overcame the rebels, killing their leaders and inaugurating a period of state-sponsored street terror that consumed many Baathist and Nasserist lives. The prize that was Iraq, having seemed so tantalisingly within reach on the morning of 14 July 1958, had turned into a monstrous blight.

It was not only in Iraq that Nasser's ambition was hitting the rocks. In Lebanon those aligned against Chamoun, who were promising to put in place a regime to draw the country into the unionist fold, were held in check by the arrival of the

American marines. A counter-revolution by allies of Chamoun (mainly Maronite Phalangists) threatened to split the country further and render it ungovernable. A settlement was eventually achieved, however, with the help of an American go-between, Robert Murphy. He was aided by the tacit support of President Nasser who took steps to restrain Sarraj's hot-headed approach having acknowledged the futility of continuing to engage with the Lebanese crisis. The new president, General Fouad Shehab, met Nasser on the Lebanese-Syrian border and an understanding was reached that ensured Lebanon's good neighbourliness, while laying to rest any prospect of its being integrated into the UAR. Jordan, meanwhile, had regained its balance after the shock of the overthrow of its Hashemite kin in Baghdad. At one point it had seemed likely to succumb to a wave of almost fanatical support for Nasser and the UAR, especially within the areas of Palestine annexed by Amman, but a new confidence had emerged as a consequence of Britain's swift rendering of military support. As a result Jordan's King Hussein, vigorously supported by that other pillar of Arab conservatism, King Saud of Saudi Arabia, took to spearheading the drive to undermine Nasser's hold on Syria.

By the time the UAR was celebrating its first anniversary much of the shine of that historic Arab enterprise had started to fade. The tide of unionism had been stemmed if not reversed, and the UAR remained stuck within ossified borders having to face its own internal challenges. While the dream of an ever-expanding union may have served as an emotional rallying-point, serving to distract attention from the mundane exercise of everyday politics and economics, the moment had now arrived when no such distraction was forthcoming. This was indeed the end of the honeymoon between Nasser and Syria. The Syrian public had been prepared for a great degree of self-sacrifice and the downgrading of narrow national ego if that was the price to be paid for the holy grail of Arab unity. But as that vision disappeared over the horizon, attention began to be directed at the inner workings of the Egyptian-Syrian merger, which left a lot to be desired, at least in Syrian eyes. It was not long before the Syrians began to feel that what was spoken of as a union disguised the reality of an Egyptian takeover of their country. All major government appointments were given to Egyptians while Damascus, the proud and ancient capital of the first Arab empire, was turned into little more than a provincial centre. While Egypt's population dwarfed that of Syria (around thirty-five million to Syria's just over four million), and its dominance of senior posts, especially those based in Cairo, could be justified to some extent, what seemed to trouble many Syrians was the disproportionate flow of Egyptian manpower into almost every vestige of Syrian military and civil life. Cast as 'advisers' and 'experts' they behaved as a semi-colonial class with little appreciation of or sensitivity to local culture and custom. Although each region of the UAR had its own executive council to manage its affairs, in Syria the authority of that body was significantly curtailed as appointees from Egypt, answering directly to Nasser, often had the final say. The discontent that was brewing in Syria may have been contained had the two political and security pillars that brought Syria to the union, namely Sarraj and the Baath, remained loyal. But tensions were about to rise between them and Nasser's mighty leadership. Deciding that the Baathists were a barrier rather than an asset in building bridges with the Syrian public and were therefore standing in the way of a satisfactory merger of Egypt and Syria, Nasser thought the time had come to clip their wings. In the summer of 1959 elections were held for the National Union – the body that was to replace the multiparty system that had been abolished when the UAR was formed. The campaign was especially energetic in Syria, where forces opposed to the Baathists were given open encouragement by agents answering to Nasser. In the event the Baathists gained no more than 250 out of a total of 9,445 members allocated for the Syrian branch of the new organisation. The meagre two per cent share stood in sharp contrast with the fifteen per cent they had managed at the parliamentary elections of 1954. The leaders of the Baath could see the writing on the wall. At the end of 1959, following a series of resignations, Cairo announced the departure from office of all five Baathist ministers, including the leading stars of Baathism, Akram Al Horani and Salah Eldin Bitar. By that time Nasser had appointed his second-in-command, Marshal Abdul Hakim Amer, in executive charge of the affairs of the Northern Region. In his first few months acting as Nasser's personal representative, and a virtual viceroy, Amer busied himself in a mass purge of Baathist officers. Many were replaced by hand-picked Egyptian officers, fuelling still further a resentment that had been building up inside and outside the Syrian military establishment.

The breach between Nasser and the Baath echoed throughout the region. It split the party's ranks within and beyond Syria as members found themselves having to choose between the union and the party. The schism would continue to blight the course of Baathism for years to come. As for Sarraj, he was not at first too troubled by the fate of his Baathist colleagues in government; on the contrary he foresaw his role as being strengthened in Nasser's eyes as the remaining 'native' enforcer of Syria's allegiance. Yet Sarraj could not but be anxious in seeing his authority jeopardised by Marshal Amer's new title. Hence the year that followed witnessed an intensifying tug-of-war between Amer and Sarraj who had assumed the position of secretary general of the national union, in addition to his other powers. The struggle seemed to have been resolved in September 1960 when Nasser ordered Amer's withdrawal from Syria and placed in Sarraj's hands the power to rule Syria with an iron fist. Indeed, Sarraj lost little time in imposing an even harsher police state than that which had existed previously. He reversed most of the measures that Amer had taken in an effort to relax tensions with a restless Syrian public and to restore a modicum of trust between government and governed. Arrests were widespread and the suppression and torture of 'seditious' elements were ratcheted up as the country entered a dark and ominous epoch. Nasser, it seemed, had lost any faith in a consensual approach to his rule, deciding instead to entrust the fate of the union to the whip hand that Sarraj was deploying with gusto.

While the union had started with élan and fanfare, all pointed now to its having lost its soul. Syrians watched as it collapsed into the kind of closed dictatorship they had hoped to escape when they rid themselves of past army juntas. Yet Nasser's popularity remained high among Syrians, despite the Egyptian political and military hegemony that followed his appointment as their ruler. They even seemed prepared to endure the excesses of Sarraj in the belief that his boss would not long tolerate them. Ultimately it was his economic policy that spelled the end for Nasser in Syria. It began in 1959 when the central government in Cairo enacted land reform laws across Syria replicating those previously implemented in Egypt. Where the reform may have been necessary and desirable in Egypt with its vast amounts of land in the hands of a relatively small number of landowners (and the peasantry locked in semi-perpetual serfdom) it was ill-judged to apply it blindly to a different socioeconomic landscape. The negative consequences on the Syrian agricultural sector were immediate (a matter not helped by a coincidental season of drought). Although Syria had a problem of feudalism that affected many agricultural tenants and farm labourers – a fact that had been crucial in helping the spread of Horani's appeal in the central regions of the country – its scale was much smaller than in the case of Egypt. The mid- to late fifties had also seen a successful drive by entrepreneurs with access to capital to bring into marketable production a very sparsely populated but potentially rich region of the northeast (known as *Al Jazeera* or 'the island,' bordered as it is by the Euphrates and Tigris valleys). Expensive agricultural machinery was put to good effect on the newly exploited soil and the results in the expansion of Syrian agriculture had been spectacular. None of this could continue with the land divided into small tracts as determined by laws that seemed to pay little attention to the specificities of Syria's circumstances. Syrian interests were again shown to be subservient to half-baked Egyptian policies lacking judgement and foresight.[2]

Nasser's ignorance of the Syrian context shown in the case of land reform was to become evident again with grave consequences in the summer of 1961. A series of laws nationalising a number of leading industrial corporations was proclaimed as part of the socialist transformation of the economy. Although the laws applied to both Egypt and Syria, the impact on the latter was far more severe in undercutting the interests of the middle class. It was a matter of historical record that the course of commercial and industrial growth in Egypt had owed a lot to capital seen as foreign-sourced and had been identified with a class that was either expatriate or at least rigidly separated from the indigenous population. In Syria, by contrast, the economic growth witnessed by the country in the forties and especially the fifties was credited to an entrepreneurial bourgeoisie, which, despite its class credentials, was considered much more integral to the welfare of the broader society. The nationalisation laws of 1961 added one more block to the growing coalition of forces that was becoming hostile to the whole experiment in unionism – at least as practised by Nasser and his henchman, Sarraj. The Baathists had long been ostracised, the army purged and penetrated by domineering Egyptians; landowners had lost out to the land reform laws, and now – the last straw – the middle class had been alienated. The stage was surely set for a moment of reckoning.

The inevitable backlash was hastened by two decisions taken by Nasser in 1961. The first was the announcement in August of a major reorganisation of the internal administration of the republic. The executive councils pertaining separately to the Northern (Syrian) Region and the Southern (Egyptian) Region were abolished and their authorities amalgamated within a central cabinet based in Cairo. Thus the last vestige of Syrian autonomy was lost within the wider union. The second step was the kicking upstairs of Sarraj, who was appointed minister and one of several vice-presidents based in Cairo, thereby removing him from the position of *Gauleiter* in Damascus. Marshal Amer was once more dispatched to Syria to take up his previous role as viceroy. Nasser had believed the move certain to prove popular with a Syrian public deeply antagonised by the brutal hand of Sarraj's police state, but he gave little weight to the downside of shunting aside the last pillar of control over a country on the verge of rebellion. And Sarraj did not relinquish his position without a struggle. His agents in Syria made life difficult for Amer who had his eyes focused (wrongly as it turned out) on an incipient pro-Sarraj insurgency, ignoring the behind-the-scenes workings of real conspirators. Two days before the latter would strike, on 26 September 1961, Cairo announced the acceptance of Sarraj's resignation. On 28 September Syrians would awake to a familiar clarion call from Damascus Radio.

Notes

1. According to a popular anecdote the Syrian president is reported to have said to Nasser, 'I leave in your care a Syrian population half of whom believe they are entitled to run the country while the other half think they already do run the country.'
2. Rumours had begun to circulate that the lands seized in the Al Jazeera region would be given over to large numbers of Egyptian peasants – a poisonous anti-Egyptian story among many others.

CHAPTER SEVEN

1961-63: The Last Hurrah of the Old Political Class

This revolutionary movement is a popular movement, which aims at protecting the dignity of the people and the army, and is not capitalist, imperialist or reactionary. It reflects the people's demand for the protection of Arab Nationalism and its sacred principles and will endeavour to establish a union between willing Arab states. It will implement a socialism that is sound and not arbitrary and a true democracy that is far removed from chaos, despotism and dictatorship.

From a statement issued by the Syrian army command following the coup that put an end to the union with Egypt.

Ali Armanazi, author's uncle. A prominent publisher executed in 1915, along with other leading Syrian and Lebanese nationalists who advocated independence from Ottoman rule.

Prince (later King) Faisal in Damascus in 1918 with T.E. Lawrence.

King Faisal 1st, 1920.

Yusef Al Azmeh, Syrian War Minister, killed in 1920 in the battle of Maysaloun while leading the fight against the invading French army.

General Gouraud, commander of the French forces that invaded and occupied Damascus in July 1920.

Sultan Pasha al Atrash, leader of the 1925 Syrian Revolution against French rule.

First Conference for the advancement of Arab women, held in Damascus 1930.

Abdul Rahman
Shahbandar, Syrian
nationalist leader.

Duke of Edinburgh, visiting Damascus in
1950.

Street protest against French rule, circa 1934.

Rally in Damascus addressed by leaders of the National Bloc, circa 1936.

Syrian parliament, early 1930s.

Antun Saadeh, founder and leader of the Syrian Social Nationalist Party.

First President of Independent Syria, Shukri al Kuwatly.

Ceremony in 1945 held in honour of Britain's representative to Syria. To the left of President Kuwatly is the Prime Minister Jamil Mardam Bey, and to the right of the British envoy is the author's father, Dr. Najib Armanazi.

Brigadier, later Field Marshal, Hosni Zaim. Led in March 1949 the first of Syria's coups d'état. Was overthrown and summarily executed in August the same year.

Akram Horani, leader of the Arab Socialist Party which merged with the Baath in the 1950s. Played a crucial role in the transformation towards radicalism of Syrian politics.

Syrian Delegation at the meeting in Cairo in 1944 to form the Arab League. In the white suit is Foreign Minister Jamil Mardam Bey, at the other end of the sofa is Saadallah al Jabiri, Prime Minister and to his right is the author's father.

Colonel Adib Shishakly, Coup leader and later President who ruled Syria from 1949 till 1954.

Khaled Bikdash, longtime leader of Syrian Communist Party.

Veteran President Hashem Atassi (centre of photograph in dark suit), at a palace reception after the restoration of civilian rule in 1954.

Egyptian leader Gamal Abdul Nasser and to his left Syrian
Ambassador to Cairo, the author's father (1954).

Gamal Abdul Nasser, greeting Syria's Prime Minister
Fares al Khouri, wearing a fez, at Cairo' s airport in 1954.
To Khouri's right is the author's father and on the left
of the photograph, also wearing a fez, is Abdul Khalek
Hassouna, Secretary-General of the Arab League.

Nadhem al Kudsi, Speaker of Parliament and later, in 1962, President of Syria after the breakup of the Egyptian-Syrian Union.

Khaled Al Azm, a very influential 50s politician, and last premier before the Baathist coup of March 1963.

Syrian women demonstrating (late 1950s).

نساء سوريات يمارسن حق الانتخاب في عام 1955. يُذكر
أن سوريا أول دولة عربية منحت النساء هذا الحق في عام
1949 ...

Syrian women exercising their right to vote in 1955.

Colonel Abdul Hamid Sarraj, Syrian Head of Intelligence in the late 50s. Sarraj was Nasser's right-hand man during the short-lived Union with Egypt.

Brigadier Amine al Hafez, Baathist Head of State, 1964-66.

Brigadier Salah Jadid, leader of the radical leftwing faction of the Baath Party, overthrown by Hafez Assad in the 1970 coup.

Michel Aflaq, founder of the Baath Party, 1947.

The Egyptian president, Gamal Abul Nasser, and the Syrian president Shukri Al Quwatly, signing the Treaty of Union establishing the United Arab Republic, in 1958.

Nur Al Din Al Atassi, Head of State 1966-70, overthrown November 1970 by Hafez Assad.

Poster Depicting President Hafez Assad and his two sons
Bassel and Bashar.

President Assad Receiving President Sadat in Damascus
1977.

Presidents Hafez Assad and Bill Clinton at their last meeting in
Geneva in March 2000.

Syrian 'cafe society', 1965. In the forefront is a young Sami al Khiyami, due to become many years later Syrian Ambassador to the United Kingdom.

The communiqué broadcast on the morning of 28 September 1961 took Syrians back to an era they thought they had left behind. In the early fifties they would habitually wake up to a solemn announcement by the army of the latest coup made necessary by the appalling state of the nation that cried out for salvation by the valiant guardians of the homeland. That would be followed by the strongest condemnation of the nefarious legacy of the overthrown regime and a pledge to return to barracks and deliver power to civilian hands at the 'earliest opportunity.' However, for the current rebels, calling themselves the Arab Revolutionary Command of the Armed Forces, the task of taking over the country was complicated by the fact that the regime they were confronting was in charge not just of Syria but of the United Arab Republic within which Syria was a (junior) partner. Moreover, the UAR spoke for tens of millions of Arabs who saw in it the embodiment of the dreams of generations, and at its head stood a leader of exceptional charisma who was hero-worshipped as no other in modern Arab history. Comprehending the challenge, the rebels trod carefully in their first communiqués and chose their words with acumen. The message was that the ruling 'clique' was making mistakes that were injurious to the principle of Arab unity, hence the need to set the derailed union back on the right track. Their actions were the last resort, 'after all efforts at reform had been thwarted,' and ostensibly had the interests of the entire UAR at heart. The personage of Nasser was deftly sidestepped, notwithstanding subtle references to grievances and 'high-handed' measures, meaning the recently enacted nationalisation laws, as well as the arbitrary reorganisation of the armed forces to the detriment of the Syrian officer class.

It was clear that the insurrection was intended to be more a reformist strike than a full-blown bid for power. That impression was strengthened when, a few hours after the first radio announcement, a surprise communiqué (number nine) declared that an understanding had been reached with Marshal Amer, who had promised that the concerns of the rebels would be addressed 'in the interests of safeguarding the unity of the UAR.' The communiqué signalled a possible defusing of the situation and was interpreted momentarily as reflecting the failure – or at least the standing down – of the rebellion. However, it seemed that Amer had made promises his boss, Nasser, could not sensibly endorse without a loss of face and authority that would prove fatal to his rule both in Syria and in Egypt.[1] The tenth communiqué soon followed and rescinded the previous proclamation, claiming that Amer had reneged on his word. This triggered the pursuit of the aims of the revolution. The die had now been cast and the fate of the UAR was hanging by a thread. Nasser, in the meantime, denounced the rebels and refused to acknowledge their demands, accusing them of being agents of reactionaries and foreign imperialists. Believing he could still win the day, and relying on evidence of resistance to the coup in Aleppo and other parts of northern Syria, including, crucially, the coast, he prepared to send an expeditionary force by sea to quell the rebellion. An advance force of commandos landed by parachute near the port of Latakia. By then, however, the local garrison had already switched to backing the rebels and the newly dispatched Egyptian troops were easily surrounded and captured. Any attempt to regain Syria by force seemed forlorn as almost all Syrian-based military commands soon pledged their loyalty to the group of officers who had seized Damascus. Marshal Amer was promptly and unceremoniously bundled off to Cairo, as, subsequently, were all Egyptians – military and civilian – who had served (to much local resentment) in the governing of the Northern Region.

Nasser soon bowed to the inevitable. On 5 October 1961 he publicly acknowledged Syria's secession, adding that the United Arab Republic would retain its name and continue in its role as the embodiment and standard-bearer of Arab unity. Yet while bidding a sad farewell to Syria there was no sign that Nasser was willing to reconcile with the new regime in Damascus. On the contrary, the powerful propaganda machine that had proved so deadly in undermining previous foes of Nasserism was immediately deployed with full venom against the 'reactionary' rulers – agents of the West, the Hashemites and the Saudis – who were about to take Syria back into the 'dark times' of feudalism and greedy and exploitative capitalism. Meanwhile, in Damascus, the military council that had taken charge was desperate to gather the support of civilian politicians. It succeeded in convening a meeting of figures from Syria's pre-union past as well as, in a particular tour de force, the two leading Baathists, Akram Al Horani, and Salah Bitar. A common declaration was signed in support of the army and its stated objectives of ending tyranny, restoring those rights and freedoms that had fallen prey to despotic rule and advancing the true and pure ideals of Arab unity.[2] A cabinet was soon announced and was headed by Mamoun Kuzbari, a noted lawyer and former speaker of the parliament elected under Shishakly in 1953. The cabinet was composed largely of non-political professionals but had a distinctly liberal and right-wing flavour. However, it became clear that the military council that had planned the coup was the real centre of power, and this soon began to show cracks as rival officers jockeyed for position and influence. With the military breathing down its neck, and Nasser's propaganda machine in full, hostile throttle, Kuzbari's government had little time or space to be anything more than a fragile caretaker. But there was an attempt by the newly formed authority to play up the Syrian riposte to the shrill Egyptian campaign. Thus the old Syrian flag was officially reinstated, as was the national anthem of the antecedent state. At the same time, in a sign of nervousness regarding the blow that had been struck against the sanctity of Arab unity, and to demonstrate the rebellion's attachment to that unity, the restored republic was rebranded the Syrian Arab Republic (having previously been known simply as the Syrian Republic). Nonetheless the new rulers spent that first period of secession desperately fending off the accusation that they had betrayed Arab nationalism. They took every opportunity to swear that as a matter of urgency they would seek to enter a union with one or more Arab countries on a basis that would safeguard it against the 'errors' that had doomed the UAR. It was a very hollow message that found few takers. For the vast majority no amount of window-dressing could hide the fact that Syria's split from Egypt to regain its independence represented a severe setback to the cause of Arab unity.

As it struggled to prove its Arab nationalist credentials the putative government hesitated to affirm its Syrian credentials and so was reluctant to rescind the social and economic measures that Nasser had enacted in setting up the foundations of a socialist state. There was little doubt that those reforms had contributed to the climate that led to the coup of 28 September, yet there was real anxiety over the impact of appearing to rob the masses of the gains attributed to them, especially when Cairo Radio and the Voice of the Arabs were screaming vitriol at the 'feudalists and reactionaries from a bygone era' who had usurped power in Damascus. The officers in charge of the military council – the shadow government still lurking in the background – were also applying the brakes to any abrupt rollback of the socialist agenda. Finally, a return to political pluralism and civil rights, the stifling of which had been declared as a major justification for the rising against Nasser, was also put on hold and the ban on political parties remained in effect – at least officially. One move that marked a sharp break with the structure of political life under the UAR was the official disbanding of that Nasserist monolith, the National Union.

With little to show by way of real achievements the Kuzbari cabinet soon gave way, on 1 December, to another cabinet of largely neutral administrators. It was charged with overseeing elections to a parliamentary assembly, leading the way to the formation of a representative government. The elections held that month were based on lists of individual candidates ostensibly independent of party affiliations. Nevertheless it was known to all and sundry that the old political parties were pulling the strings of many of those candidates. The result of the vote, which witnessed a significantly high turnout of electors, was an assembly heavily weighted in favour of the traditional right-wing parties – the People's Party and the National Party – while the Baathists suffered considerably, with their leader, Salah Bitar, being one of the losers.[3] Among the winners were the veteran politician Khaled Azm and that stalwart of the Syrian political scene, Akram Al Horani, whose list in his stronghold of rural Hama swept the board. Horani had already signalled his split with the Baath Party following his enthusiastic backing for the coup. (This had been seen as treasonable by many Baathists, including Aflaq, because while critical of Nasser and the UAR they could not bring themselves to endorse the breakup of the sacred token of Arab nationalism.) Horani instead restored life to the Arab Socialist Party, which he had headed in the early fifties before it merged with the Baath. The Muslim Brotherhood also gained a respectable number of seats.

Following the elections a new government was formed from a coalition of the traditional and right-wing forces represented in the new parliament. At its head stood Maarouf Dawalibi, a prominent politician with conservative leanings. His close connections to the Saudi Kingdom hardly endeared him to Nasser who lost little time in directing his wrath at the latest manifestation of Syria's lurch to the right. The elected assembly also voted to appoint as president of the republic Nazem Al Qudsi, a softly spoken and well-respected politician from Aleppo who was a leading figure in the People's Party. It seemed, for a fleeting moment, that Syria was set on the path to democratic civilian rule. But powerful enemies were standing in the way, both inside and outside the country. Not least of these was Nasser himself, whose hunger for the restoration of his power and pride was as intense as ever, and he used every means available to stir trouble for the 'apostatic' regime in Damascus. To that end he relied on the substantial support he still enjoyed within Syria. This included students honed on the romantic appeal of Arab nationalism and bitterly resenting the fact that the union had been so treacherously aborted, as well as large sections of the working and farming communities who feared the impending loss of the rights granted to them by the socialist and anti-feudal laws enacted by the UAR. So it was that almost from the day the Syrian Arab Republic came into existence its rulers had to deal with recurrent riots and strikes that threatened their ability to govern with ease and security. Even more menacing was the fact that the military council itself was beginning to show signs of unease at the drift to the right, with a number of officers still labouring under the stigma of having blown asunder the cherished union. In fact it was not long before one of the leaders of the coup, Colonel Haydar Kuzbari, a relative of Mamoun, lost out in a mini-purge when he was accused by his comrades of having close links with, and even of receiving funding from, the Jordanians. It seemed that the more progressive elements within the army hierarchy were getting impatient with what they regarded as an attempt by conservative forces to steer Syria in a reactionary direction that went beyond the original reformist agenda of the 'intifada' of 28 September.[4] They saw the greedy pursuit of class privilege in the government's move to rescind the nationalisation laws and to modify the land reform laws in a manner favourable to the land-owning class.

Crucially the officers began to operate behind the scenes to test the possibility of a reconciliation with Nasser in order to re-establish the union on new and equitable lines. Emissaries established secret contacts with Nasser during which the Syrian army officers were led to believe that a move to overthrow the secessionist regime would get the support of Cairo, which would also engage in good faith with plans for a new and reformed union between Egypt and Syria. The Syrian officers and their Egyptian interlocutors also shared a growing concern over a sudden rapprochement between the political leadership in Damascus and the Iraqi regime. This culminated in an alliance signed in mid-March 1962 at the border between Iraq and Syria by President Qudsi and General Qassem. The two parties at the summit meeting pledged to work together to achieve an Arab federation that was inclusive and comprehensive in nature, and agreed to closer economic and military ties. For the Egyptians this smacked of a return to the dreaded spectre of Baghdad trying to usurp Cairo's regional role. Meanwhile the Syrian officers were worried that if Iraq (and its relatively strong army) were to consolidate its presence inside Syria in partnership with the political establishment, then the power of the Syrian military to continue pulling the strings from behind the edifice of civilian rule would be hampered.

The hour for action struck exactly six months after September's coup. On 28 March 1962 the customary refrain of the army coming to the rescue was heard once again over the airwaves. The Arab Revolutionary Command of the Armed Forces announced it was again taking the reins of power. It did so through communiqué number twenty-six – a clear linkage with the last communiqué (number twenty-five) that had been broadcast at the time of the original September takeover. Almost the same collegium of officers – minus Haydar Kuzbari and led by Major Abdul Karim Nahlawi – was behind the new coup. It said it had been staged 'in response to the wishes of the people and to protect the gains, security and stability that were achieved as a result of the revolution of 28 September.' They attacked the corruption and ineptitude of the overthrown government and promised to restore the union as well as the land reform laws and nationalisations. Further pronouncements went on to dissolve the constituent assembly, dismiss the president and the council of ministers and place full legislative and executive power in the hands of the military command. But almost immediately Syria found itself face to face with the spectre of civil war. The Nasserists in the army and on the streets took the announcements as a cue to launch their own takeover bid and call for an immediate return of the union with Egypt. In Aleppo and other parts of Syria crowds raised the flag of the UAR as they took over military and government installations. It seemed that Nasser – or at least his followers in Syria – had little intention of living up to the unofficial arrangement Nahlawi and his putschist colleagues thought they had reached with Cairo in the countdown to their takeover. Indeed there was no sign of what they had believed would be a negotiated return to the union that would constitute neither a surrender nor a dismissal of the valid grievances that had led to the September coup. A showdown seemed inevitable and the army was starting to split. Many in the military, especially those hailing from the provinces, were showing resentment towards Nahlawi and his clique of Damascene officers seen to be claiming too much authority. A hastily arranged conference held in Homs at the beginning of April reorganised the army command and resulted in Nahlawi and many of his allies being shunted aside. The new command had at its head the minister of defence, Brigadier Abdul Karim Zahreddin – a Druze. They issued a proclamation that appeared to be a scarcely concealed attempt to ward off the Nasserists' demands for an immediate restoration of the union with Egypt. It called for union with the 'liberated' Arab states, at the head of which was Egypt, subject to the 'necessary conditions so as to avert the mistakes of the past and secure Syria's entity and dignity.'

Inevitably the Nasserists rejected the decisions of the Homs gathering and continued their defiance. They were now in control of Aleppo, and broadcast through its radio station appeals for a national uprising that would return Syria to the fold of the United Arab Republic. Their appeal resonated strongly with the students roaming the streets of Damascus and other cities, brandishing the flag of the UAR and banners bearing Nasser's image. The new army command decided to act swiftly to quell the rebellion and Syria hovered on the edge of a precipice. Broadcasts from Aleppo and other rebel-controlled areas called for the organisation of popular resistance and pleaded loudly for the intervention of Egyptian troops. Nasser, however, calculated that any such intervention would be fraught with risk. Instead he equivocated and called for restraint, expressing his readiness to 'exert every effort' and 'participate positively in sparing Syria from all danger.' The rebels were on their own and, in the face of overwhelming military power heading towards Aleppo, especially with the air force remaining loyal to Damascus, the Nasserist uprising fizzled out and its leaders fled or went underground. Meanwhile, the army command, having become conscious of its own vulnerability, sought an accommodation with the politicians: Nazem Al Qudsi was restored to his position as president and political leaders were released from detention. The assembly was to remain dissolved with Qudsi and a new cabinet charged with legislative and executive powers pending elections. A new and very uneasy relationship between the military and the civilian authorities was to start, keeping Syria, as ever, on the path to further grave unpredictability.

An interim government was soon sworn in. Headed by a known progressive, Bashir Azmeh, it included representatives of the Horani as well as the Aflaq branches of the old Baath, which had by now split into a number of factions. One called for an immediate return to the union with Egypt – an idea opposed vehemently by Horani and his supporters, now organised into the Arab Socialists. Aflaq and Bitar remained head of what could be termed the historic Baath. This was ideologically opposed to the secessionist regime but was in practice making use of the downfall of Nasser's version of Arab unity to revive its own distinct Arab nationalist brand and preparing the ground for gaining power in the country. In that process an underground Baathist military committee had been playing a vital role. The committee had been formed during the union from a hardcore nucleus of Syrian officers who had been relocated to Egypt – to tedious desk jobs – as part of Nasser's attempts to get rid of potentially troublesome Syrian army cadres with political affiliations. The founders were five: Lieutenant Colonel Mohammad Omran, Major Salah Jadid, Captain Hafez Assad, Major Ahmad Al Mir and Captain Abd

Al Karim Al Jundi. They all came from rural, and relatively deprived, backgrounds with the first three being Alawites and the remaining two belonging to the small Ismaili community. While ideologically Baathist the five were far removed from the urbane and intellectual Damascene leadership represented by Aflaq and Bitar. That socioeconomic (and implicitly sectarian) divide would have huge implications for the political destiny awaiting the country.

Meanwhile, blissfully unaware of the spreading underground threat from the activities of the military committee, the government of Bashir Azmeh tried to present a progressive face that was pro-Arab unity, hoping that a new approach would calm the waters and lead to an understanding with Cairo. It started by abandoning the plans set out by the previous government to rescind the socialist-inspired nationalisation laws and revise the land reform programme. On 6 June it announced a readiness to achieve a new union with Egypt that would 'form the backbone of a comprehensive Arab union.' But Nasser's Egypt was not impressed and continued its propaganda assault against the regime in Damascus, even raising its invective to new levels. It was able to use its allies and mouthpieces in neighbouring Lebanon to maximum effect, as the country had become a powerbase for Egypt over the previous months. Lebanon's President Shehab was using his *Deuxième Bureau* in the exercise of increasingly authoritarian control of the anti-Nasserist and right-wing forces in the country that were broadly sympathetic to the government in Syria. The marked increase in Egyptian influence in Lebanon had resulted from a failed coup attempt at the beginning of 1962 by the fervently anti-Nasser Syrian Social Nationalist Party. The defeat of the attempt and the ensuing widespread arrests not only of SSNP sympathisers but even of suspected co-plotters opposing Shehab and his perceived patron, Nasser, had cleared the way for the growing dominance of an Egyptian lobby in Beirut.

Matters came to a head in the summer of 1962. Increasingly frustrated in its attempts to chart a conciliatory course, the Syrian government accused Egypt of being behind a plot to overthrow it. Indeed a rebellion was hatched by the Egyptian embassy in Beirut and involved a number of Nasserists and Baathists in the country and in exile, foremost among whom was Jassim Alwan, the leader of the uprising in Aleppo back in early April. Syria upped the ante by lodging a formal complaint against Egypt at the Arab League and calling for an extraordinary session of the council of the League to deal with the Egyptian aggression. The council met in August 1962 in the Lebanese border town of Chtaura and the Syrians and Egyptians exchanged verbal blows almost unprecedented in their rancour. The Syrians, in particular, cast aside all the restraint they had tried to show following the March coup and accused Nasser and his regime of the worst crimes of treachery, not just towards Syria but against the very principle of Arab unity and the cause of Palestine. The Egyptians responded in kind and decided to withdraw from the meeting in protest at the insults to which they had been subjected. The Arab League meeting ended indecisively, with Damascus finding few allies apart from Jordan. It did, however, signal the end of any chance of a deal between Nasser and the regime that was establishing a shaky footing in Damascus. From this point on no holds were barred as the adversaries went for the jugular in an intensified propaganda war.

The pressure was now particularly focused on Syria's rulers as they struggled to navigate a minefield of challenges. Encouraged into agitation as never before by intrigues and harangues from Cairo, students and workers joined in riots and strikes countrywide. The Nasserists, particularly those belonging to the expanding network of the Arab Nationalist Movement, were organised into well-functioning cells, and made common cause with those Baathists loyal to Aflaq in clamouring for the overthrow of the regime and the return of the UAR. At the same time the progressive and left-leaning character of the Azmeh cabinet and its message of social and economic reform was not going down well with the traditional political and merchant class that had enthusiastically embraced the intifada of 28 September only to be at least partially elbowed aside by the ambivalent putsch of 28 March. Their insistent call was for the reinstatement of the legitimacy that was overthrown in March and the return of the constituent assembly that had been dissolved. But this was resisted by the army, leading to months of uncertainty as negotiations were held to resolve the political and constitutional impasse. Finally, a face-saving formula was reached, whereby the assembly would meet once outside the parliament building and dissolve itself after the appointment of a new government. In accordance with the agreement so reached a majority of the members of the assembly convened in September in the house of Khaled Azm. The result was a new government with full powers, headed by Azm, until the election of a new assembly. It was agreed that the constitution of 1950 would be considered valid until that election. This patched-up compromise was the last attempt to breathe life into a faltering and increasingly frail regime.

As it limped on the Azm government increasingly took on the appearance of a beleaguered and doomed enterprise trying to ward off a host of enemies from within the country and abroad. The looming coup de grâce was foretold very alarmingly when, on 8 February 1963, Baghdad announced the bloody end of the Iraqi regime accompanied by gruesome images of the slain leader, Abdul Karim Qassem. A triumphant new revolutionary regime formed of a coalition of Nasserists and Baathists seized power under the leadership of the known pro-Nasser officer, Abdul Salam Aref. The stage was set for mass violent assaults against Iraqi communists, as Baathists and Arab nationalists sought retribution for years of oppression suffered under Qassem. Damascus shuddered as it saw its close ally against Nasser so brutally destroyed. The new rulers of Iraq lost little time in driving home the message that they regarded Syria's position outside the UAR as an aberration to be rolled back. A high-level delegation from Baghdad was soon on its way to Cairo to take part in the celebrations marking the fifth anniversary of the birth of the Egyptian-Syrian union. Meanwhile a team from Damascus attempted to head to Baghdad to congratulate the new masters of Iraq – somewhat lamely and obviously hypocritically – but was humiliatingly prevented from entering the country.

The events in Iraq came at a propitious time for those in Syria who had been engaged for months in planning their own strike against the ailing regime. The nerve centre of that planning was the military committee and its hardcore of former Baathist officers, Omran, Jadid and Assad. Theoretically they owed loyalty to the civilian command of the party led by Aflaq and they kept it informed of the broad outlines of the coup. However, the serious task facing the military committee was putting together, and keeping secret, a coalition of army commanders with real clout in the field that could guarantee success. That meant reaching beyond the limited ranks of Baathists and Nasserists still on active duty within the military to seek allies with loose or no political affiliations who could be lured by personal ambition to participate in the plan. Their choice fell on Major Ziad Hariri, among others, who had held the position of commander of the front with Israel. When the hour struck on 8 March – precisely one month after the coup in Iraq – it was Hariri and the force under his command that constituted the main strike force of the rebellion putting an end to the tottering secessionist regime. In a repeat of the tried and tested formula of the series of largely bloodless Syrian military coups the takeover was completed in a few hours. Leading politicians of the overthrown order were arrested. (Azm managed to escape that fate, however, by finding refuge in the Turkish embassy – housed in a building that he owned and lived in.) The broadcasting services and the main military and civilian installations were all occupied in the face of minimal resistance. Syria's final experiment with a desultory and vaguely democratic and pluralistic system of government lay in tatters.

Notes

1. It remains an open question whether Amer was sincere in trying to placate the rebels but was overruled by Nasser or whether he was merely playing for time in pretending to respond to their demands.
2. Michel Aflaq, the founder of the Baath Party, refused to sign the declaration, and his founding colleague, Salah Bitar, later renounced his adherence to it.
3. It is believed that Nasserists played a decisive role in depriving Bitar of victory as retribution for having appended his signature to the manifesto that welcomed September's coup.
4. The term 'intifada,' later to gain much global currency when applied to the uprisings in Palestine, was the favourite official label attached to the coup of September 1961.

CHAPTER EIGHT

A Fractured Baath Turns on Itself

*One Arab Nation with an Eternal Mission: Unity,
Liberty, Socialism.*

- The enshrined motto of the Arab Baath Socialist Party

The coup of 8 March had much in common with previous
army takeovers in terms of the functional aspects of
seizing power: the physical control of the nerve centres of
government, the broadcasting of revolutionary communiqués
and the arrest of the leaders of the deposed regime. Where it
differed substantially from its long line of predecessors was the
immediate tag of ideological party commitment. On television
screens there suddenly appeared as a constant byline the words
'Unity, Liberty, Socialism' – the familiar, three-pronged mantra
of the Baath Party. Representing a sharp break with the past, a
new and highly distinctive political and social era had dawned.
Yet, in those early days and weeks the Baathists in control of

the airwaves were still faced with the predicament of unruly allies with differing agendas even when agreeing to join forces with the Baath in order to overthrow the secessionist regime. The easiest of those allies to handle was Major Ziad Hariri, the leader of the strike force behind the coup's success. Having served his purpose naively well, and after a brief period as chief of staff, Hariri was easily disposed of by his erstwhile allies. Sent abroad as a military attaché he eventually disappeared into obscurity. The real challenge to the Baathists' authority came from the Nasserists both in the army and more broadly within the country. They had taken part in the overthrow of the secessionists for the sole purpose of returning to the fold of the United Arab Republic and had no interest in a new Baathist-led order in Syria.

A return to the union appeared feasible for a while. Following the 8 March coup talks were held in Cairo between delegations representing Egypt, Syria and Iraq to consider the establishment of a union between all three. Indeed it was agreed, and proclaimed in principle on 17 April 1963. However, even as the agreement was being hailed it was obvious that Nasser was becoming increasingly irritated by the attitude of the Baathist Syrian-Iraqi axis that he found haughty and patronising. He particularly took exception to the tone adopted by the Baathist leader, Michel Aflaq, whom the Egyptian propaganda machine was to brand a supercilious upstart trying to lecture everyone else on the true meaning of Arabism. In fact events on the ground in Syria were already moving inexorably towards a showdown as the revolutionary command council, which had assumed power in the wake of the coup (and in which Baathist officers, including the triumvirate of Omran, Jadid and Assad, held sway), moved to expel from the army dozens of key Nasserists. In the streets mass demonstrations were organised by pro-Egyptian factions. These included the Arab Nationalist Movement (ANM), considered the main rival to the Baathists in claiming the mantle of pan-Arabism. There was little doubt that Egyptian intelligence, supported by the powerful broadcasting arm of Cairo, was active in fomenting the growing wave of protest that demanded immediate union with Egypt and challenged the still-shaky Baathist-led regime. In turn the Baathists used the security forces at their disposal with increasing ferocity to suppress the street demonstrations. Additionally, in a clear replication of what their Iraqi comrades had set up, Syria's leaders inaugurated a national guard of armed party militants who acted as street vigilantes. Eventually, on 18 July 1963, a group of Nasserist officers, led by the emblematic hero of past Nasserist insurgencies, Colonel Jasim Alwan, and supported by ANM militants, attempted an assault on army headquarters and the capital's radio station. The attempt failed and resulted instead in the deaths of hundreds and the capture of dozens of Nasserist officers who were brought before military courts and summarily executed. This was a first in the history of Syrian coups and countercoups, which had traditionally been carried out with little bloodshed.

The Baathists were by now in full and uncontested control. Yet they bore the brunt of accusations from many directions of having established their rule by brute force and the physical elimination not just of reactionary enemies but of ideologically aligned former partners who had played a big part in the triumph achieved on 8 March. The loudest condemnation of their tactics came, as expected, from Cairo. In a thunderous speech delivered that same month Nasser attacked with unprecedented venom the 'fascist Baath Party' and announced the formal burial of the Egypt-Iraq-Syria union accord signed on 17 April. While comfortable for the time being with a secure grip on power the Baathists were aware of the long-term vulnerability of their political message, as they now bore the stigma of scuttling yet another pan-Arab union scheme. Thus they continued to maintain a commitment to an Arab union and sought to deflect Nasser's accusations of perfidy by moving in the direction of Baghdad. It was a natural choice since both countries were now under the undisputed rule of the one Baath Party. Steps were immediately taken to bring the two governments and armies into close liaison. The Syrians even dispatched units of their army to northern Iraq in support of their comrades fighting Kurdish separatists. But this strategic realignment was soon dealt a critical blow. After a period of fratricidal feuding that jolted the very essence of Baathist rule in Iraq (and even led to the Syrian founder and leader of the party, Michel Aflaq, theatrically declaring himself in charge of Iraqi affairs) Baghdad Radio announced a change of regime. The new ruler, Brigadier Adbdul Salam Aref, a leading figure in the 1958 antimonarchist coup, was quick to proclaim his fealty to Nasser and the UAR. Iraq's Baathists were in disarray while their Syrian counterparts sought refuge within 'fortress Syria.'

The Baathists were left with little to show for their lofty pronouncements on Arab unity. Instead they turned their attention to the one component of the trinity of Baathist doctrine – Unity, Liberty, Socialism – that they could realistically implement within the boundaries of the polity they now controlled, namely socialism (liberty supposedly having already been achieved with the revolt of 8 March). Before that, however, there still was much tidying up to be done to consolidate their hold on power. Importantly, the military committee that had been so successful in the planning and execution of the Baathist-led coup, and was now openly forming the core of the revolutionary command council (RCC), was quick to realise that it needed a swift infusion of Sunni blood to counter any accusations of minority rule. Brigadier Luay Al Atassi, who hailed from a well-known dynasty in Homs, was chosen as the first head of the RCC. However, after the bloodletting of the summer Atassi found the going too challenging and resigned. He was replaced by the much tougher Brigadier Amine Hafiz, who had recently been co-opted into the military committee. A much-needed Sunni frontman, Hafiz had earned his spurs among fellow Baathists by personally taking charge – machinegun in hand – of the attacks that had foiled the Nasserist putsch in July. He took over not only from Atassi but also from the civilian prime minister, Salah Bitar, who had formed the first cabinet after 8 March. With his abrasiveness and no-nonsense approach he soon acquired the form and the essence of power that went beyond the military committee's plans in first raising him to those positions. His status as protector of the new revolutionary regime was further enhanced when he stood up to mass stirrings of revolt in Hama, Aleppo and Damascus by opponents of the Baath, many of which were summoned by fervent Islamic slogans attacking the Baathist 'unbelievers.' In a particularly controversial encounter security forces sent by Hafiz shelled and heavily damaged the Sultan mosque in Hama, killing dozens of insurgents – mainly Muslim Brothers. Echoes from that shelling reverberated throughout the country and sowed the seeds of far bloodier confrontations to come. In the immediate aftermath steps were taken to reduce tensions, including the reappointment of Salah Bitar as prime minister in the hope that his would be the more acceptable, if false, face of civilian authority. The fundamental consequence of the action, however, was the establishment of coercion as the main instrument of Baathist rule.

By early 1965 the regime felt secure enough in its authority to embark on a radical socioeconomic transformation of the country in accordance with Baathist socialist dogma. A list of decrees was announced that nationalised the major industrial enterprises and the banking system, turning Syria into a quasi-socialist economy purportedly being run in the interests of the masses. In effect what emerged was a hybrid system where statism coexisted with traditional bazaar culture, leaving room for much activity in the black market and other greyer areas of commercial life. The flight of Syrian capitalists, and capital, already having started at the time of the Nasserist nationalisation programme, now reached its peak (to the benefit of neighbouring countries, such as Lebanon and Jordan). This in turn triggered further restrictive and intrusive measures affecting trade, travel and currency exchange. The legendary entrepreneurial spirit of the Syrian merchant class was steadily smothered and surrounded by a bloated bureaucracy of party apparatchiks given charge of state-owned enterprises. Employment by the state also saw an influx to the major cities of large numbers of rural migrants. A significant social transformation was taking shape, with the old order giving way to newly empowered, formerly marginalised communities. On the international front the war of words with Nasser's Egypt continued unabated and reached new heights of calumny with Baghdad now weighing in on Cairo's side. Syria's rulers tried to up the ante by acting as the authentic voice of true Arabism. To that end they resorted to a loud championing of the Palestinian cause. Thus began the continuous haranguing and provoking of Nasser as being soft on Israel – a sneering campaign that would lead to catastrophic results two years later.

By stirring up feelings on Palestine the Baathist leaders were not out of step with the sentiments of the population at large. For a number of deep-seated reasons of history, geography and identity Syrians held the cause of Palestine close to their hearts. Moreover, for many years, particularly since the ending of the Palestine war, the Syrian-Israeli armistice lines witnessed recurrent armed skirmishes and sometimes larger engagements. UN observers stationed there confirmed that the vast majority of clashes were caused by Israel's repeated encroachments into territory designated as no man's land by the armistice agreements of 1949. By the mid-sixties the prevalent issue was Israel's determination to divert the waters of the Jordan river in order to irrigate its northern farmlands. For Syrians this was a *casus belli*, as it posed a threat to its own water resources as well as those of Jordan and Lebanon. The Baathists also saw a rallying cause in the issue that could not only lift their isolation but also put Nasser on the spot and finally expose his timidity when it came to a serious confrontation with Israel. Aware of the Syrians' motives and wary of being lured into the trap of fighting a war for which Egypt was not prepared (especially as its forces were embroiled in Yemen's vicious civil war at the time), Nasser came up with the idea of an Arab Summit. The first of its kind since the forties, its aim would be to address the issues raised by, and formulate a response to, Israel's diversion plans for the river. In this manner he hoped to take the wind out of the Baathists' sails and avoid plunging into an open war as they were loudly exhorting him to do.

The summit took place in Cairo in January 1965 but stopped short of making preparations for war against Israel, despite much beating of the drum by the Syrian delegation, whose head, Amine Hafiz, advocated an immediate assault on Israel. This was seen as bombastic and fanciful by the other delegations. Nevertheless two decisions taken at the summit would soon prove to have far-reaching consequences. The first was the approval of an 'Arab' water diversion project, with installations mainly on Syrian territory, which would forestall and ultimately render useless Israel's own irrigation programme further downstream. The second was the establishment of the Palestine Liberation Organisation, or PLO: the framework within which the Palestinian people would be gathered, represented and able to claim their rights and aspirations, independent of Arab governments. Both decisions directly challenged Israel and were fraught with complications that would immediately arise. The Syrians would find themselves in Israel's crosshairs as soon as they committed to starting the water diversion works, with only vague assurances of support and solidarity from other Arabs. The creation of the PLO also represented a significant shift in the intra-Arab power struggle. It threatened to undermine King Hussein's hold on his Palestinian territories (the West Bank and East Jerusalem) and the loyalty of his subjects of Palestinian origin. Meanwhile, Nasser, to Syria's annoyance, stood to profit from having under his wing the newly created PLO, whose chairman was a known protégé of Cairo, the barnstorming but largely ineffectual Ahmad Shuqairi.

Syria, however, had a card to play even before the birth of the PLO. It had been encouraging the rise of a clandestine, armed Palestinian organisation later to be known through the reverse acronym of its Arabic title: Fatah. Formed around a group of Palestinian expatriates gathered in Kuwait it adopted the doctrine of armed struggle by Palestinians themselves as the means by which to liberate their land, thereby shunning many years of mistaken dependence on Arab states and armies to restore the country to its rightful owners. The message was clear: Palestinians had to take matters into their own hands rather than allowing their destiny to be subject to the whims and ultimately self-serving policies of Arab leaders. The world soon became aware of the presence of this new political-military reality when, on 1 January 1965, a communiqué by Al Assifa (The Storm), the armed wing of Fatah, announced an attack on an installation inside Israel. That attack and those that followed were mere pinpricks and often resulted in sham claims, but they did introduce a new and unsettling factor in a Middle East that seemed to be on the verge of a very ominous test of nerves. In the immediate circumstance of the start of Fatah's guerrilla campaign the Baathist government in Syria saw a golden opportunity to upstage their Arab rivals, particularly Nasser, Hussein, and Aref in Iraq, by positioning themselves as the patrons of the new 'people's liberation war' – the star attraction of the revolutionary era to which they had nailed their colours.

The reshaping of Middle Eastern geopolitics was in full flow. Bubbling beneath the surface in Syria, meanwhile, was a different power struggle with equally crucial ramifications for the region. It began at the very core of the military committee. The trio of Omran, Jadid and Assad had succeeded beyond even their dreams in plotting their way to the ultimate triumph of taking over the Syrian state, and were now engaged in a fratricidal struggle for supremacy. The result was that the senior member of the trio, Omran, was ganged up on and sent into exile by a Jadid-Assad internal putsch. Omran had taken exception to the brutal approach adopted in relation to the protests in Hama and elsewhere and was known to be unhappy with the harsh policies associated with the regime's frontman, Amine Hafiz. The more important settling of scores was to follow. It ranged the Jadid-Assad faction, which had dominated the so-called regional command of the Baath Party (the organisation responsible for the Syrian branch of the broader, pan-Arab movement) against the national command, which theoretically had ultimate authority over each country's branch. The latter was headed by the veteran, civilian figures of Aflaq and Bitar while the former had a near stranglehold on the military, which was steadily becoming an ideologically indoctrinated arm of the Baath after deep and widespread purges of all opposing political tendencies. Jadid had become deputy chief of staff while Assad was put in charge of the air force. For most of the rest of the year 1965 the Syrian political scene was consumed by the visible manoeuvrings for ascendancy of the two Baathist factions, who were now locked in a fight for the soul of the party. The supporters of the regional command, drawn mainly from the lesser-privileged and rural communities, veered sharply towards a radical leftist agenda, while the national command represented the more mainstream origins of the Baath, prioritising pan-Arabism writ large over the domestic socioeconomic issues cherished by the 'regionalists.' Amine Hafiz, the man who had been chosen by the military committee to head the RCC and thus the organs of state, had by now acquired an independent and empowered status. By the end of the year he had distanced himself from the committee and the regionalists to become a loyal ally of the civilian national command. The power struggle within the Baath troubled a good number of party stalwarts who continued to search for a means to bridge the rift that was threatening the very existence of the party. In a move to appease the regionalists their *bête noire*, Michel Aflaq, was gently detached from his position of secretary general in favour of a largely unknown Jordanian, Munif Razzaz.

All attempts to reach an accommodation between the opposing wings of the Baath Party were to no avail. On 23 February 1966 the regionalists struck, and after some violent clashes, especially around Amine Hafiz's residence in central Damascus, they overwhelmed the forces of Baathist orthodoxy and installed the most radically left-wing regime ever to have governed Syria – or any other Arab country for that matter. The new strongman was Salah Jadid, who, with other likeminded ideologues, such as the newly appointed head of state, Nur Al Din Al Atassi, Prime Minister Yusef Zuaiyin and Foreign Minister Ibrahim Makhos, formed a ruling establishment whose revolutionary rhetoric would have done the most earnest of Marxist theoreticians proud. Hafez Assad, who had joined with Jadid in seeing off the rival presence within the military committee of Mohammad Omran, played his part in the coup by securing for the plotters the loyalty of the air force under his command. He was now firmly in the spotlight as minister of defence in the newly formed cabinet. The new left-wing Baathists disowned the old guard of Aflaq, Bitar and their associates in the national command, many of whom either fled the country or suffered arrest. From that point on the Baath Arab Socialist Party was irredeemably split into two major factions fiercely competing for the loyalty of grassroots Baathists in Syria and elsewhere in the Arab world where the party had established its branches.

The new rulers in Damascus lost little time in asserting the revolutionary radicalism that motivated their souls. Domestically, inspired by the hubris of their swift victory, they raised aloft the banner of class war. On a number of occasions they allowed militant throngs led by trade-union activists to roam the streets intimidating and sometimes violently assaulting merchants and heads of businesses accused of greed and exploitation. The Syrian middle class, already battered by the nationalisation laws of previous years, was further squeezed and subjected to 'street' retribution. The neo-Baathists now in charge went to great – even absurd – lengths to underline their lurch to the left.[1] Not for them the soft socialism of others.

Even the Soviet Union was deemed not far enough to the left, with the Chinese brand of Marxism, energised by the Cultural Revolution, proving a magnet to some of the firebrands of the new order.

The new rulers' real passion was aroused by the developing regional tensions. They expounded even more forcefully than their predecessors on notions of a 'people's war' that would not only sweep Israel away but also its imperialist backers and their henchmen among the Arab 'reactionaries.' By that time Israel was fully engaged in making sure that the water diversion project conceived at the Arab summit never got off the ground. To that end from time to time Israeli aircraft would attack engineering installations on Syrian territory related to the project, leading to intermittent clashes of varying degrees of intensity. These punctuated much of the remainder of 1966 and continued into early 1967. Indeed, the Syrian-Israeli armistice lines threatened to become a major flashpoint as the weeks and months progressed and alarm bells started to sound in the region and around the world. The increasingly frequent attacks by the *fedayeen* militants of Fatah and other Palestinian guerrilla groups, loudly hailed by Damascus, added to the general raising of the temperature. The Israelis were quick to hold the Arab governments responsible for these attacks, in particular that of Syria, and talk was heard in Tel Aviv of the need to teach Syria a lesson, even hinting that the overthrow of the Baathist government was under serious consideration.

It became abundantly clear that Israel had in its sights a final settling of scores with Damascus. Evidence suggested that the Israeli provocations had been intended as a precursor to a battle long in the preparation by which Israel would break the mould of the territorial boundaries set by the 1949 armistice, particularly as they applied to the West Bank and East Jerusalem. Such a strategy would explain why the bloodiest of Israel's forays into Arab territory during the period of rising tension with its arch-enemy was directed not at Syria but, bizarrely, against the most placid of its enemies, Jordan. That occasion was in November 1966 when a large Israeli force launched an attack on a wide front well into Jordanian territory, targeting the undefended village of Samu and exacting a heavy price in blood and destruction. The Israelis claimed that the raid was in retaliation for guerrilla attacks, although their own propaganda had been laying most of the blame for those attacks on Damascus. The result was widespread rioting inside the Hashemite kingdom and a surge in anti-Hussein propaganda emanating from Damascus. Syria took the opportunity to mount accusations of cowardice and feebleness against the regime in Amman for failing to stand up to Israeli aggression. It did not escape the attention of contemporary observers that Israel's action came only a few days after the signing of an Egyptian-Syrian defence pact that partly repaired the acrimonious relationship that had existed until then between Nasserist Egypt and Baathist Syria. By attacking Jordan in such a manner Israel was in all probability hastening the process by which King Hussein would feel compelled to tie his fortunes to the newly emerging Egyptian-Syrian axis. This would lay the ground for the strategic battle that Israel anticipated by creating the opportunity for the land it was coveting to fall into its lap.

The build-up to the showdown gathered pace with great intensity and the first months of 1967 witnessed a series of flare-ups. The most significant of these was a major aerial dogfight over Syrian territory on 7 April, in which the Syrians lost six fighter aircraft and endured the humiliation of a subsequent victory roll over Damascus by the triumphant Israel pilots. Syria was furious and pressed Egypt hard for a military response in accordance with the defence pact between the two countries. Nasser also received messages from Moscow implying that the Syrian regime was in existential danger from an Israel bent on carrying out its threat of completely overhauling the Baathist leadership. Nasser was faced with the most acute of conundrums: either tie his fortunes to a maverick regime, which he secretly loathed but had to appear convincingly to back in its confrontation with the common Zionist enemy, or allow it to suffer ignominious defeat. The latter would mean looking the Arab people in the eyes having betrayed an ally with whom he had recently signed, amid much fanfare, a solemn military pact. He felt that he had little option but to choose the first course of action; otherwise his reputation as leader and champion of Arab national pride would be in shreds. Nasser's decision to act so as to deter Israel from raising the military ante may have been taken on the mistaken assumption that pressure would be brought to bear by the Soviet Union and United States to avert the prospect of all-out war. This is what he appeared to have in mind when ordering his troops into the Sinai Peninsula in mid-May. In so doing he was in violation of the status quo that had existed since 1957 limiting the presence of the Egyptian military in the peninsula in exchange for Israel's withdrawal from that territory after its invasion of 1956 (carried out in connivance with Britain and France). It was a clear challenge to Israel but fell short of an outright *casus belli*. Nasser probably would have let his small victory suffice in the hope that international pressure would restrain Israel's hand. However, he did not count on the UN Secretary General U Thant's response of pre-emptively ordering a withdrawal of the peacekeeping force that had been stationed in the Sinai for more than a decade. The order from U Thant also seemed to apply to the contingent guarding the southern entrance to the Gulf of Akaba – the Strait of Tiran at Sharm El-Sheikh. The UN's presence there had been allowing Israeli shipping to navigate the waters freely to reach Eilat at Israel's southern tip since 1957. It also served as a convenient argument for Egypt to offset complaints from its Arab enemies that it was showing weakness by not closing the Strait of Tiran to Israel. With the UN no longer there Nasser was pushed into a potentially explosive situation: Syrians and other Arab-nationalist voices, now in a state of near hysteria, urged him to announce the closure of the straits to Israeli shipping, while Israel had made it abundantly clear that such a move would constitute an unequivocal *casus belli*. Again Nasser was forced to make a choice he probably wished he had not been cornered into. But the rising clamour of Arab-nationalist emotion had by now reached a crescendo. Abandoning the restraint he would arguably have shown in less heady times, Nasser went for broke.

It was a crossing of the Rubicon when Nasser announced that his forces would take control of the entrance to the Strait of Tiran from the forces of the United Nations and impose a blockade against Israeli shipping, restoring the status quo ante. It caused wild cheer in the Arab street, and Nasser's reputation as a national hero rose to levels not known since his stand on Suez eleven years earlier. Lifted to new heights by this burst of popular adulation the Egyptian leader seemed consumed by his hubris. He openly challenged Israel to start a war that would, in the florid language used by some leading Egyptian commentators, result in a decisive defeat for the Hebrew state. Even King Hussein of Jordan, the most reluctant of Arab leaders when it came to military confrontation, seemed caught up in the combative mood. He flew to Cairo to make up with Nasser and signed a joint treaty of defence that reverberated across the Arab world. It even took the fiercely anti-Hashemite Syrians by surprise and left them with some bitter pills to swallow. In the meantime Israel played the role of a country facing an existential threat.[2] It undertook an intensive and frantic diplomatic campaign that included a highly publicised visit to Washington by its foreign minister, Abba Eban. Having thereby ensured its case would be presented in the best possible light Israel took the decision to go to war. Tel Aviv was convinced that Washington, and particularly President Johnson, would not translate the American administration's public calls for restraint into real action that would prevent it calling Nasser's bluff. It also appreciated the fact that the situation presented Israel with a golden opportunity, not only to settle scores with Egypt and Syria, but also to seize the prized lands of 'Judea and Samaria' – the West Bank – and, of course, East Jerusalem, which the Jordanians controlled. In the meantime Nasser had been persuaded not to fire the first shot (by his advisers and by the success of the Israelis in presenting to the outside world the picture of an aggrieved victim). His most trusted confidant, the editor of the nation's *Al Ahram* newspaper, wrote that Egypt should be prepared to absorb the first strike as the only choice available to it, but that it could then respond in a massive counter-offensive that would result in a fatal blow to Israel.

The mood back in Syria was as bellicose as ever. The Baathist rulers seemed to be at the apex of their triumphalism, taking credit for having drawn Nasser, and even their reluctant ideological adversaries, into confronting the pernicious national enemy. The glorious hour of reckoning with the Zionists and their imperial masters had arrived and the hyperbolic language went into overdrive.[3] No effort was spared in the ostentatious building up of the country's defences, including the much-publicised digging of trenches and exhortations to the populace to prepare for a 'people's war.' Indeed, on the morning of 5

June Syrians at home and abroad were consumed by a rallying national spirit that overcame any historical antagonism towards the regime in Damascus. They believed (or wanted to believe) that Nasser's much-vaunted strike force, which was claimed to comprise an arsenal of devastating ballistic missiles, combined with the aggressive punch that Syria promised to land, would decisively rout the Israelis who were now cornered and in the grip of an Arab world bent on avenging the shame of 1948. In the early hours of that fateful morning Arab broadcasts trumpeted victories on all fronts. Scores of Israeli aircraft had allegedly and very fancifully been shot down, and Arab forces were on the move across the armistice lines. Jordan had joined the fray and, in the eyes of an aroused Arab opinion, was threatening the very heart of the malignant entity that had blighted the Arab nation for so long.

The rest of the world and its media, of course, knew better. That very evening the BBC correspondent covering the conflict announced with absolute certainty that Israel had won the war. The mass of Arab opinion at first dismissed such 'biased' reports and continued to trust the propaganda spouted by Cairo that maintained the myth of a battle being won. The reality soon dawned, however, as there was no denying the footage showing the destruction of the Egyptian and other Arab air forces in the first hours of the Israeli attack. Harrowing images of Israel's advances into Sinai (accompanied by columns of bedraggled Egyptian prisoners) and the triumphal entry into Jerusalem of its troops, led by the minister of defence – the very recognisably eye-patched Moshe Dayan – rammed home the message of an ignominious defeat. To justify the now undeniable humiliation and finally seal any hope of an Arab counterattack, Cairo suddenly announced that Israel was being actively supported by forces belonging to the United States and Britain, and that it was breaking diplomatic ties with both countries. By day three of the war almost all of Sinai and the whole of the West Bank were firmly in Israel's hands.

Syria was left on its own as both Cairo and Amman announced their readiness to abide by a ceasefire resolution adopted by the UN Security Council. In sharp contrast with its hyperbolic pre-war rhetoric the Syrian military's role after the breakout of war was very subdued. Its air force having been crippled within the first hours of Israel's air assault did not seem to explain the relative sheepishness that the Syrian armed forces demonstrated by only engaging in small and tentative skirmishing in the northern area of operation. Their reticence was even more perplexing given that the Israeli forces were very heavily committed fighting the Egyptians and Jordanians during the first three days of the war. This meant the northern front was left relatively exposed and could have been open to severe testing had there been a determined and coordinated offensive by an army supposedly ready to wage all-out war. Once the Egyptians and Jordanians had agreed the ceasefire the Syrians understandably feared the worst. Naturally it was expected that from their well dug-in and heavily protected defences in the Golan Heights, overlooking the Israeli enemy below, they would strongly resist an attempt to storm their positions. In fact, the Israeli leadership was not at one in mounting such an operation, with some ministers fearing the costly losses that could ensue. It took some heavy lobbying from the Israeli settlers in the north of the country, who endured occasional shelling (in response to Israeli military provocation) from the Syrian heights, to produce the decision to attack. It was indeed a costly operation, with the Israelis describing dogged resistance by the Syrian soldiers. But what took place in the midst of battle has remained a mystery: Syrian radio suddenly and precipitately announced the fall of Quneitra, the regional capital of the Golan, at a time when it was yet to be seized by the invading Israelis. Syrian troops still fighting in territory well in advance of Quneitra were confronted with the likelihood of being cut off from their rear and a panicky retreat was the result. A chaotic exodus of soldiers and civilians headed in the direction of Damascus. The inglorious performance of Syrian commanders, civilian and military, including the calamitous pre-emption of the fall of Quneitra,[4] marked the darkest moment to have faced the neo-Baathist rulers. The UN Security Council issued a resolution demanding a ceasefire, which Syria promptly accepted. Israel procrastinated (with tacit American approval it was later alleged) until it had achieved its objective of gaining full control of Syria's Golan Heights. This was soon accomplished and the guns finally fell silent on 11 June – just six days after the start of Israel's campaign and much to the relief of a Syrian government whose appeals for the ending of its tribulations grew more frenzied by the hour.

The most urgent task now facing the Syrian regime was making sure that the catastrophic defeat did not translate into a threat to its very existence. In Egypt Nasser had resigned after taking full responsibility, only to retract the resignation in response to large demonstrations in his favour. Having decided to stay in power himself he encouraged Syria's leaders to insist on no change at the top. They also borrowed from Nasser the terminology to be disingenuously used in reference to the disastrous outcome of the war: it was not a defeat, they claimed, simply a setback that could be overcome by remaining committed to the high principles of Baathist ideology. The Syrian leadership went further and started churning the line that a victory had in fact been achieved, since Israel's declared purpose in waging war, the overthrow of the regime in Damascus, had clearly failed. Notwithstanding the general contempt felt by most Syrians for this twisting of the tragic reality visible to all, the regime survived thanks to a psychology of deep malaise that served to subdue a population almost frozen in a state of shock combined with increased oppression of any dissent. At the same time eyes were starting to turn to a fledging movement that promised Arab public opinion a salvation of sorts from the humiliation of the war. This was an invigorated Palestinian resistance in the shape of Fatah and other organisations which were beginning to gain prominence. They embodied armed struggle as the spirit of the age in contrast to the conventional wars of the past fought by regular Arab armies that utterly failed to deliver a liberated Palestine. Although the actual hurt inflicted on the Israeli forces of occupation by the intensified guerrilla campaign was relatively modest, Fatah was now recognised as a serious challenge not just to Israel but also to the geopolitical status quo that underpinned the Arab state system and which had been severely shaken by the fallout from the June war.

An indication of the power Fatah was now gaining came in 1968 when the organisation effectively launched a takeover of the PLO. Yasser Arafat, who had emerged as the first among equals in the Fatah hierarchy, became chairman of the PLO, replacing the hapless Ahmad Shuqairi. The organisation formed three years earlier as a convenient appendage to the Arab political establishment became the tool of a movement that spoke copiously of revolution as the way ahead. This was music to the ears of Palestinian and other Arab political activists thoroughly disillusioned with Arab regimes, whether of the left or right. The new Fatah-run PLO, however, officially distanced itself from the domestic politics of the Arab countries; non-interference in their internal affairs was a cornerstone of Fatah strategy. Meanwhile, more radical and Marxist-oriented groups, such as the Popular Front for the Liberation of Palestine (PFLP) and its offshoot, the Democratic Front for the Liberation of Palestine, were already starting to outflank the organisation. These groups had few qualms about their links with Arab revolutionaries beyond their natural core support among the Palestinian population in the occupied territories and the refugee camps scattered around the neighbouring countries. Indeed the PFLP, led by the charismatic George Habash, was a creation of the Arab Nationalist Movement, also founded by Habash, which, by the early sixties, had adopted Marxism as its creed.

For a time many politically minded Arabs, including Syrians, turned to the Palestinian resistance as a new dawn. It represented a much-needed psychological boost to overturn the malaise of the June 1967 defeat, and large numbers joined its ranks or became advocates of its cause in the Arab world and beyond. The contrast was striking between the refreshing clarion call of the new breed of freedom fighters, who now bore the brunt of the fight against Zionism, and the discredited message of the Arab regimes whose armies had collapsed so ignominiously when called to account. Yet that generation of Arabs seeking radical change ironically let the disgraced regimes off the hook. They now channelled their energies into support for the Palestinian resistance, and gave their hearts and souls to the promise of a sweeping pan-Arab revolution that would spring from the barrels of the *fedayeen* guns. By neglecting any confrontation with their own despotic rulers they were inadvertently taking the heat off the regimes they detested. They comforted themselves with the thought that the regimes would simply wither on the vine and be replaced by governance that met the high aspirations of the emerging

Arab vanguard without the need to engage directly in the hard slog of politically challenging the discredited regimes. It was a naive reading of history and the dynamics of political and social transformation. The despised regimes proved much more resilient than the expectations of those who were star-struck by the image of the guerrilla fighters. Indeed, as these very regimes feigned support for the Palestinian resistance, verbally anointing them as champions of a struggle they wholeheartedly endorsed, they busied themselves in shoring up their own shaken power structures. Some went further and started a process of infiltrating the PLO and setting up, under its loose umbrella, 'resistance' factions answerable directly to specific Arab state sponsors.

In Syria the infiltration approach spawned Al Saiqa, a Palestinian armed formation affiliated to the ruling Baath Party. Having initially owed its emergence to Syrian logistical and media support, Fatah was sidelined while Al Saiqa was acclaimed as the mainstay of the armed struggle against the Israeli occupier. Yet cynicism and opportunism were not the only driving forces behind the espousal by Damascus of the Palestinian cause. Among the ranks of Baathist cadres, with the party's declared ideology of a 'people's war of liberation' still resonating from pre-war days, there was genuine enthusiasm for the new Palestinian-led guerrilla campaign that would blunt the surge of Israeli triumphalism and serve as a motor for the kind of socio-political transformation that resonated with core Baathist belief. This outlook was strongest in the mind of the arch-leftist Salah Jadid and the coterie of hardcore ideologues who were in charge of the high offices of state. However, for the remaining member of the original military committee, Hafez Assad, minister of defence, the road ahead was treacherous and in need of a more careful and pragmatic approach. For a time Assad went along with his comrade Jadid and the latter's powerbase in government and the party hierarchy, since all had to stand together in the immediate aftermath of the cataclysm of the lost war. In this they were successful and they were able to clamp down hard on any hint of sedition that might emerge from the wreckage of war. With hardly any sign of having been humbled by the experience of defeat on the battlefield the Syrian leaders continued with the rhetoric and the dogmatic inflexibility that had been their trademark in the lead up to war. The attacks against the Arab reactionaries, such as the king of Jordan, were resumed with renewed vigour, as were the denunciations of 'plots' to convert the military 'setback' into a strategy of defeatism and compromise. It was no surprise, therefore, when Syria refused to attend the Arab Summit in Khartoum, held in July, even though the meeting resolved to adhere to the famous trinity: 'no negotiation, no recognition, no reconciliation' with Israel. Later that year, when the UN Security Council adopted Resolution 242, sponsored by the United Kingdom, as the framework for settling the Arab-Israeli conflict, Damascus rejected it with vehemence, in contrast to Cairo and Amman who announced their readiness to abide by it.

Again it seemed Syria was on its own in asserting an unadulterated and principled commitment to the cause that was being sacrificed at the altar of the 'Zionist-Imperialist' agenda. Undeterred by the fact that its superpower patron, the Soviet Union, colluded in the passing of Resolution 242 and that the towering figure of Nasser had accepted it, Syria insisted that the provisions of the resolution – which called for an Israeli withdrawal from occupied territories in exchange for the ending of Arab belligerence – amounted to the surrendering of Arab and Palestinian rights. Behind the facade of a united regime in Damascus, however, the first signs of a new power struggle were beginning to emerge. The protagonists at the head of the smouldering confrontation were the erstwhile brothers-in-arms, Salah Jadid and Hafez Assad. The former was the intellectual and motivating force of the neo-Baathist ideology. He was also well in charge of the Baath Party machine and enjoyed substantial support among the military, many of whose higher echelons he had hand-picked at the cost of summary purges, and even the physical liquidation, of those whose loyalties were suspect. Assad, on the other hand, while downplaying any differences with Jadid in public, was avidly building up his own powerbase, concentrating primarily on the armed services, the ultimate arbiter of political supremacy in Syria.

The fault lines between the incipient adversaries became clearer as the months passed. Jadid and his followers had learned little from the lessons of the June defeat. If anything they raised the volume of their revolutionary rhetoric of class war, driving down the already critically depleted performance of the Syrian economy while driving up the acrimony with potential Arab and international allies. Assad, on the other hand, while firm in his essential Baathist orientation, was aware of the need for Syria to align itself more closely with other Arab states, Egypt in particular, as well as with the international community if it was to repair the huge damage inflicted by the 1967 war. He was also conscious of the deep unpopularity of the neo-Baathist rulers among the bulk of Syria's population. He realised that the continuous stoking up of divisive and class-based passions was inopportune and potentially destructive at a time when society needed to be galvanised under a unifying formula. Both Baathist camps were prepared for an apparently inevitable showdown.

The trigger arrived in the early autumn of 1970 when the simmering hostility between the Jordanian state and an increasingly powerful and overbearing Palestinian resistance, led by Fatah's Yasser Arafat, erupted into a full-scale battle. Conflict was assured by multiple plane hijackings organised by the Popular Front for the Liberation of Palestine that culminated in the spectacular blowing up of aircraft on the ground in Jordan. The stage was further set by the PFLP and other radical Palestinian groups declaring that the time had come for a people's revolution and the setting up of peasant and workers' 'soviets' in the style of Russia's October Revolution. Showing an unwillingness – or inability – to rein in the wilder factions within the PLO, Arafat was dragged into a confrontation that played into the hands of King Hussein and his army. Jordan's monarchy had long been suffering the humiliation of unruly Palestinian guerrillas riding roughshod over its sovereign authority. It now saw the possibility of striking a fatal blow not just against the troublesome renegades but also, and more importantly, against the entire Arafat-PLO franchise that was threatening the legitimacy of Hashemite rule.

For Salah Jadid and his far-left colleagues the choice in Jordan was clear-cut. Syria had to offer support to the revolutionary Palestinians locked in combat with the 'vile and reactionary regime' of King Hussein. The decision was made to intervene militarily on the side of Arafat and his allies, and Syrian troops backed by tanks spilled over the border to occupy parts of northern Jordan. An all-out regional war beckoned as Hussein appealed to the United States and (clandestinely) to Israel to intervene against the Syrians. Amid mounting international tension the Jordanian army launched a counterattack, with air support, against the Syrian tanks. A moment of severe crisis was at hand as Jadid pushed for the Syrian air force to become involved, only for Defence Minister Assad to countermand any such decision. The result was the defeat of the Syrian forces and a humiliating withdrawal back across the border. No single previous point of difference between Assad and Jadid had equalled the enormity of the contest over policy in regard to those fateful events in Jordan later to become known as Black September. The outcome was the signing of a ceasefire accord on 27 September at an emergency Arab summit convened by Nasser. It spelled defeat for Arafat and his forces, and a shifting of the political sands. This was further underlined by the sudden death of Nasser on 28 September – just one day after the summit in which he had been so frantically involved. Earlier that summer Nasser had provoked much controversy, and especially the ire of Damascus, by having accepted the so-called Rogers Plan, named after the then US secretary of state. It had aimed to curtail the intensified fighting on the Suez Canal frontline, dubbed by the Egyptians the 'war of attrition,' and to resume the stalled efforts for a regional peace solution. Nevertheless, the death of such a colossus, with his long legacy of championing the Arab nationalist cause, stirred the deepest emotions of loss all across the Arab world, even among his adversaries.

In Syria, meanwhile, the focus was on the impending clash between the two pillars of Syrian politics, Assad and Jadid. The former had had the final say in the country's approach to the Jordanian crisis and had thereby established his credentials as a pragmatist who understood the limitations and pitfalls of entering an explosive regional confrontation. Jadid and his supporters, on the other hand, were livid at the abandonment of an ally in his hour of need and the betrayal of the revolutionary doctrine seen in Assad's actions. The feud between the two factions reached its apex when an extraordinary congress of the Baath Party convened in Damascus in November 1970. The delegates, most of them solid Jadid supporters, endorsed the left-wing line of the party, with many voicing damning criticism of Assad and his 'pragmatic' approach. Assad himself hardly made an appearance. He was too busy planning the move for which he had been preparing all his adult life. The long Assad era was about to begin.

Notes

1. The minister of information wrote at the time that Baathists should learn to swear by referring to their left rather than right arm in the traditional spoken oath; they should also keep to the left when walking on the street.
2. Western intelligence, particularly that of America, anticipated an overwhelming victory for Israel in any conflict with Egypt, or even an alliance of Arab countries.
3. The Syrian chief of staff promised that his forces would reduce the Mediterranean-based US sixth fleet to 'small morsels that would feed the fish.'
4. What unnerved the commanders acutely was the idea that Israel would penetrate deeper into Syrian territory, even reaching Damascus itself. The panicked announcement regarding Quneitra seemed to be aimed at alerting the UN to this possibility.

CHAPTER NINE

Hafez Assad: The 'Eternal Commander' With the Iron Grip

I was beginning to come to the conclusion that Syria was the key to significant progress. Assad's engagement would signal, in the most dramatic fashion, that our efforts were legitimate in Arab eyes. His participation, in effect, would insulate the process.

- Former US secretary of state James Baker acknowledging the centrality of Syria, and of Hafez Assad, in the build up to the Madrid Peace Conference of 1991.

Hafez Assad met with very little resistance when carrying out his putsch on 16 November 1970. In well-prepared and smoothly executed moves his supporters easily dispersed the party which had congregated in order to rally the faithful against him. Leading neo-Baathists, including Jadid himself and the head of state, Atassi, were easily rounded up while others fled in disarray. It was a completely bloodless affair, with very little sign of meaningful resistance from those who had claimed to have the power of the masses behind them. In strict coup terms this was the most understated in the long line of seizures of power that had convulsed Syria for over twenty years. The official statement labelled it, rather timidly, a 'correctionist movement' that simply aimed to adjust the wayward course that the overthrown Baathist leaders had followed. In fact this takeover was to mark a watershed of unrivalled significance in the history of modern Syria. It laid the foundations of a regime that was to exceed – by far – the endurance, stability and resilience of any before it.

There was little love lost between the Syrian population at large and the ousted far-left neo-Baathists. Assad realised this and was keen to exploit that sentiment in the establishment of a broad base of support. He toured the country and addressed mass rallies, all the time driving home the message that a new era of national unity was at hand and that Syrians could look forward to a future of governance that was inclusive and free of the extreme dogma that had blighted the country's progress and its Arab and international relations. The message was received with relief and genuine approval across all strata of society, not least the merchant community and the middle class in general, which had borne the brunt of the era of Jadid and his followers. Also pleased were those among the side-lined and suppressed political groups and those aspiring to greater freedoms who sensed that Assad might relax the absolutist stranglehold on political life imposed by his predecessors. And there was a feeling that Syria, long ostracised and isolated regionally, would at last mend its fences with fellow Arabs and the wider world.

In what would later prove to be his trademark approach to issues of policy-making, Assad moved with caution even as he was raising the nation's hopes. He initially declined to assume the top office of state, leaving that position to a nondescript acolyte, while appointing himself prime minister. Soon enough, however, he oversaw the drafting of a new constitution that, very importantly, concentrated legislative and executive authority in the hands of an all-powerful president. The constitution, along with his unique candidacy for the job of president, were presented to the public for approval through a referendum in the spring of 1971. The result was overwhelming, with the percentage of votes in favour reaching well into the high nineties. Although a predictable result, most observers of the time conceded that it reflected the bulk of public opinion. Having secured an unchallenged hold on power as newly anointed 'president of the republic' (the first such titleholder since the overthrow of Nazem Qudsi in 1963) Assad started on the path to slow reform that he had signalled in his early pronouncements. Thus, for example, a National Progressive Front (NPF) was established as the nominal highest political authority in the country, ostensibly replacing the one-party rule that had reigned since the coup of March 1963. For the first time several political parties – essentially the Communist Party (under two separate leaderships) and various Nasserist factions, as well as the 'Arab socialists' of the by now largely powerless Akram Al Horani – were implicitly recognised by being made members of the NPF alongside the Baath Party. However, the Baath maintained for itself a position of seniority by having its own secretary general – none other than Assad himself – also installed as the secretary general of the NPF. Moreover, the newly adopted constitution enshrined the Baath, in article 8, as the 'leader of the state and society' – an ordination that even the overthrown neo-Baathists had not attempted to articulate so solemnly or boldly. To leave no doubt of the dominance of the Baath within the NPF the constitution gave the party the sole right to recruit adherents within the armed services and universities. There was no illusion that this was anything but the narrowest of political openings. The creation of the NPF was nevertheless taken as a positive indicator of what could follow, and, suspending disbelief, most Syrians at that point were ready to give Assad the benefit of the doubt.

The business sector was encouraged by Assad's reaching out to leaders of the merchant communities, in particular those of Damascus and Aleppo, promising to take their interests into account and to do away with the exhortations to class war that had informed the policies of the previous rulers. There was no renouncing the socialist doctrine that formed an integral component of Baathist ideology (Unity, Liberty, Socialism), but the mood music had changed. It encouraged the beginnings of an entrepreneurial economic revival, albeit within strictly limited parameters. The new hope invested in Assad's approach to foreign policy, which promised a new era of Arab solidarity, brought with it the anticipation of flows of funds and capital from the oil-rich Arab Gulf states. It also offered the potential for a more hospitable environment for Syrian expatriates working in those countries and therefore an increase in repatriated remittances to bolster the Syrian economy.

Assad basked in the honeymoon of heightened expectations and responded by appointing to government those noted for their qualifications rather than their ideological purity (including the well-regarded prime minster, Abdul Rahman Khleifawi). Yet he was only too aware of the deep wound left by the heavy defeat of the 1967 war. As minister of defence at the time he could not escape responsibility for that debacle, and his *amour-propre* played a big part in his growing desire for a battle to reverse the shame of that devastating episode. By now Assad had mended Damascus's fences with the Arab neighbourhood. (He had even embarked on the creation of an Arab federation to combine Syria, Egypt, Sudan and the new Libyan revolutionary regime under the young and impulsive Colonel Gaddafi – a union, like many of its predecessors, that failed to materialise.) This gave Assad the confidence to turn his attentions to the planning of an unlikely offensive against what all observers believed to be Israel's impregnable strategic dominance following its resounding victory in 1967. Any chance of success, however, would depend on a solid Arab front – and that meant a coordinated plan of action with Egypt.

Egypt was now under the rule of Anwar Sadat. By the time he took office the guns had fallen silent on the Suez front, ending the two-year 'war of attrition' through which Nasser, thanks to strong Soviet backing, had enjoyed some success in redeeming the shame of the 1967 war. Nasser had agreed to a ceasefire, however, as well as the Rogers Plan – the American initiative involving a phased settlement – and Sadat continued along the same path. He was also determined to push for stronger ties with Washington. Sadat firmly believed, and was not shy to state, that the United States held 'ninety-nine per cent of the cards' in determining the fate of the Middle East. He restored diplomatic relations with the Nixon Administration and entered into public, as well as behind-the-scenes, dialogue with the new Secretary of State, the arch-proponent of realpolitik, Henry Kissinger, who saw the advantages of prying Egypt loose from its long and close alliance with Moscow. In a surprising move, Sadat even went so far as to order the expulsion of Soviet military advisers from Egypt in July 1972, hoping that the apparent, and rather sudden, volte-face would prove his good faith and reliability to Washington as a potential strategic ally to rival Tel Aviv. The bombshell was received with astonishment across the Arab world, not least in Damascus, where such a precipitate move clashed sharply with the very cautious attitude to policy changes that was Assad's hallmark. Nevertheless, the latter held his fire knowing that a feud with Sadat's Egypt was to be avoided at all costs as the geopolitical scene had yet to settle following Nasser's death and the convulsions of Black September. Also, the business of building an Arab front to recapture the occupied territories remained uppermost in his mind. Allowing Sadat to pursue to the limit his strategy of cosying up to the United States, and waiting to witness the results, may have served Assad in appraising the possibility of an alternative to war without tarnishing Syria's nationalist reputation by bending its own knee to Washington. As it happened even Sadat had to admit by early 1973 that all his attempts to coax a change of policy out of Washington had fallen flat: America simply would not deliver a compliant Israel as he had so naively hoped.

In 1971 Sadat and Assad began secretly planning a joint military campaign aimed at regaining the territories lost in 1967. These plans remained in abeyance while Sadat entertained hopes of a Kissinger-inspired strategy to push Israel towards an acceptable deal of 'land for peace.' Eventually, however, the lack of such an initiative led to frustration. Kissinger seemed content to play for time, convinced as he was, as the Israelis were, that the Arabs were too weak and divided to consider a military strategy. So Sadat and Assad embarked on a series of secret meetings with their respective military commanders that culminated in an agreement to launch a coordinated military offensive across the fronts separating the two countries from Israeli-occupied territory. In building this new partnership both sides had to overcome lingering points of unease. For

Sadat, as indeed for the Egyptian high command, memories of Syrian backstabbing from the time of the anti-Egyptian coup of 1961 were still alive, while Assad was jittery about Sadat's propensity to rely on shock tactics as an instrument of policy, and his readiness to offer unilateral concessions to the common enemy. This concern arose particularly from a plan by Sadat, soon after taking office, to propose a partial Israeli withdrawal from the eastern bank of the Suez Canal in exchange for the reopening of the waterway to international, and by implication Israeli, shipping – a clear undermining of the Arab demand for a just and comprehensive peace.

Notwithstanding their various concerns the two leaders worked together with resolve and achieved a degree of secrecy in their planning that managed to elude both the Americans and the Israelis. The commitment to the clandestine scheme was demonstrated most compellingly on 13 September 1973 when Israeli fighter planes engaged formations from the Syrian air force over Syrian territory, shooting down twelve aircraft. Assad could have deployed newly acquired antiaircraft SAM missiles against the Israeli jets but refrained from doing so in order to conceal their presence in the build-up to the major offensive under preparation. Ensuring their readiness for battle involved close consultation with the Soviet leaders, who had by then recovered from the dismissal of their advisers from Egypt and proved to be quite forthcoming in meeting the Arabs' requests for shipments of up-to-date military hardware. They also needed assurances of support from other states in the region that could play a vital role: Jordan and Saudi Arabia. King Hussein, who had been largely shunned since the events of Black September three years earlier, was brought back into the fold in the context of a summit meeting held in Cairo on 10 September. Informed of the plans to wage war the

Jordanian monarch pledged support of a limited nature. This was to translate into the sending of an armoured brigade to bolster the Syrian army without – vitally – activating his own, long, frontier with Israel.

In the case of Saudi Arabia Assad knew from the outset that getting the backing of that country would be essential in the building of a solid Arab front capable of striking a blow both militarily and economically. The oil-producing states of the Gulf were able to bring considerable weight to bear on the international geopolitical landscape, including in the capitals of the Israeli-supporting West. Hence one of Assad's priorities upon assuming the leadership in Syria was the restoration of links with Riyadh. These had been dogged by bitter memories of the long campaign waged by the Jadid-led neo-Baathists against Arab 'reactionaries,' including, in particular, the Saudi monarchy. Assad found a responsive King Faisal. The Saudis had become increasingly frustrated by an American administration that seemed blind to Arab concerns and unable or unwilling to exert the required pressure on Tel Aviv to restore the Arab territory seized in 1967. Dear to Faisal's heart was the fate of East Jerusalem and its sacred Al Aqsa Mosque, given the religious importance of the domain over which he ruled as the home of the holiest Islamic sites of Mecca and Medina. For Muslims Jerusalem is the third holiest site, and it had been the earliest *Qibla* (the direction towards which the faithful pray) before the consecration of Mecca in that role. As recently as 1972 Saudi spokesmen had dismissed the use of the 'oil weapon' as running counter to the interests of both oil producers and consumers; yet by the summer of 1973 a hitherto reluctant Faisal was considering it a useful bargaining asset. Both Assad and Sadat had started to believe that a high level of Arab solidarity was available as they authorised the countdown to the great shock they were about to deliver to a stunned world.

On 6 October 1973, at precisely 2.05 p.m.,[1] the Egyptian and Syrian armies launched a coordinated offensive across their respective ceasefire lines with Israel. It was the beginning of what the Arabs would call the Ramadan war as it coincided with the Muslim holy month. The decision to launch the attacks during Ramadan was part of the deception that punctuated all stages of the preparation. It was believed that the Israelis would least expect such a massive offensive at a time when Muslims' energies were restrained by the rituals of fasting. The Israelis, on the other hand, would call it the Yom Kippur war because that very date is the holiest in the Jewish calendar. It was chosen by the Arab leaders as the day to attack in order to catch the Israelis off guard. If the news of the joint offensive was a jolt to the Israelis, it was no less of a rude awakening to most Arabs. Just as the Israelis were caught by surprise, having for years belittled the Arabs' capabilities both in the planning and execution of a serious military campaign, so the Arab street was at first incredulous on hearing of a battle to liberate Arab lands. Early on, however, there were signs that this was not going to be a repeat of the disaster of 1967. For a start there was little of the hyperbole of Arab military communiqués that had proved to be so mendacious during that war. Indeed, if there was a hint of hysterical bombast, it came from the Israeli side, with its leaders and generals threatening to sweep aside with ease the foe that had so audaciously and foolhardily dared to challenge Israel's mighty army.

By the time the Israelis awoke to the reality on the ground major gains had been achieved by the Arabs on both fronts. The Egyptian crossing of the Suez Canal and the successful storming of the vaunted Bar Lev Line were achievements that garnered respect among global military experts. Less newsworthy were the substantial advances made by the Syrian army in the north. Large swathes of the Golan were re-conquered and some units even reached the heights overlooking and threatening the Galilee region itself. Assad was able to address his nation proclaiming that this was a battle conceived not in a spirit of warmongering but of regaining rights. He enjoined his fighters to remember that they carried on their shoulders the 'honour of the Arab soldier.'

Almost immediately the entire Arab world stood in solidarity with the Syrians and Egyptians. Even Iraq, now ruled by a restored and vengeful Baathist government representing the traditional leadership overthrown in Syria in 1966, sent an armoured force to bolster the Syrian army, regardless of the venomous divide between the two factions claiming the soul of Baathism. Morocco also dispatched an expeditionary force to the Syrian front despite being at deep political and ideological odds with Syria. The armoured brigade sent by Jordan joined the battle in the Golan. Most important of all, the Arab oil producers, led by Saudi Arabia, announced the unsheathing of the oil weapon in support of the Arab combatants. In a series of decisions adopted at OAPEC (the Organisation of Arab Petroleum Exporting Countries) graduated reductions in production were introduced and the amount supplied to specific Western countries was made dependent on their policies towards Israel and the Arabs. This was an unprecedented show of Arab economic force. For several months the 'oil shock' and its repercussions were to be felt across the world's markets. The Arabs were regarded, and demonised, as a rising global power, holding the world to ransom. Kissinger now saw it as his urgent mission to roll back the emerging bloc that was threatening the strategic mastery of the First World and empowering not only the Arabs but also kindling the hopes of the entire Third World.

On the military front, meanwhile, Israel was regaining its balance after those first heady days of swift Arab advances. Israel's mobilisation had in fact begun two days before the launch of the offensive when their intelligence reported a massing of Arab forces. Nonetheless the coordinated, surprise attack came as a shock and the Israelis immediately decided on a counter-strategy concentrating on the northern (Syrian) front. The Syrians were getting very close to Israel's populated areas and threatening the very heart of Galilee. The Egyptians were proving less menacing as it appeared that their forces were content to consolidate their positions just east of the canal, with most of Sinai still protecting Israel's territory. Hence the full fury of the Israeli war machine was flung at Syria during the critical third and fourth days of the war. Many of Syria's territorial gains in the Golan were reversed, albeit at a very heavy price for the Israelis whose air force, despite achieving air supremacy, fell prey in mounting numbers to the newly supplied, Soviet-made SAM missiles. Israel's ability to counterattack had much to do with the fact that the United States, from the first day of the war onwards, established an aerial bridge that supplied vast amounts of weapons, ammunition and supplies to the hard-pressed Israelis. That transfusion of war material played a decisive role and the effort by the Soviets to resupply their Arab allies fell well short of that undertaken by Washington.

At this stage fissures started to appear among the Arab allies, bringing into question the presumed strategic understanding between the Egyptian and Syrian leaderships. It soon emerged that each had a different interpretation of the objectives behind the launch of the Ramadan war. While Assad and his commanders were led to believe that the central aim of the war was the liberation of the occupied territories, or at least such a proportion thereof as to strengthen their overall bargaining position at the cessation of hostilities, Sadat seemed intent purely on a military *coup de théâtre* that would spark a renewal of the stalled diplomatic process on which he had banked from the start of his presidency. The divergence in the two men's war aims was made very clear to the Syrians when, hardly forty-eight hours after the start of hostilities, the southern front remained largely static. Having established its presence on the eastern bank of the Suez Canal the Egyptian army did not develop its offensive any deeper into Sinai. This allowed the Israelis to feel relatively secure in the following days and to focus their efforts against the Syrians in the north. With his forces in partial retreat and the Israelis on the verge of breaking through in the northern sector of the front, threatening Damascus itself, Assad was alarmed by his ally's apparent retreat from what he had understood to be the commonly agreed war plan. This had envisaged no such halt on the part of the Egyptian forces – rather a seamless drive towards the strategic Sinai passes (Mitla, Giddi and Khatima), following the storming of the canal.

There was much agonising among the Egyptian commanders as to the steps to be taken following that initial assault. The prevailing view accepted by Sadat and his high command was that to continue the offensive eastward into Sinai, without the defensive antiaircraft missile wall that covered only a limited area on the flank of the canal, would be fraught with risk. A period of consolidation and logistical preparation was required if there was to be any dramatic movement eastward by the Egyptian army. Time was not a luxury available to the Syrians, however, and their appeals for assistance became increasingly desperate. The calls were finally answered in mid-October when an Egyptian armoured offensive was launched towards the interior of Sinai.

But the move amounted to too little too late. The Israelis were far more assured than they had been in the aftermath of the initial strike, as well as being significantly fortified by the massive resupply of ordinance from the Americans. They dealt a crushing blow to the advancing Egyptian formations, with many tanks being destroyed and the surviving units beating a hasty retreat. At that moment the tide turned decisively in Israel's favour. Sadat seemed increasingly intent on achieving an early ceasefire and the revived diplomatic solution that had always been his goal. In a speech delivered on 16 October he announced his readiness for a ceasefire to be followed by a peace conference. The proposal had not been cleared with Assad and caused further strain in the relationship between the two leaders. Meanwhile, under General Ariel Sharon, Israel's forces conducted a sweeping manoeuvre and succeeded in crossing the canal westward, encircling Egypt's Third Army while also laying siege to the town of Suez. After panic-stricken appeals from Cairo the UN Security Council adopted a ceasefire resolution on 22 October. Numbered 338 the resolution fell far short of requiring an Israeli withdrawal. Instead it called for renewed negotiations based on Resolution 242 of 1967. Despite Egypt's hasty acceptance of the resolution, Israel remained intent, it seemed, on pressing home its military advantage, with implicit American support. International alarm was triggered when the Soviet Union threatened to intervene on behalf of the Egyptians, resulting in a well-publicised state of alert declared by the Americans. For a brief moment the world held its breath. The dramatic tension proved short lived, however, as both parties backed down from what eventually amounted to a hollow standoff. The Israelis, solidly backed by Washington, held the whip hand. As the ceasefire finally took hold they were left in possession of acres of new territory on the western side of the canal and beyond the Golan.

While the world's attention had been focused on the critical events on and around the Suez Canal, the fighting had continued on the northern front. Having suffered a substantial loss of territory and with an Israeli-controlled salient protruding ominously towards Damascus, the Syrians had eventually been able to contain the Israeli counterattack, thanks to a strong showing by the Iraqi expeditionary force. They had even managed to push the most advanced Israeli units into a retreat. Stability of some sort was then restored to the Syrian front, and the talk in Damascus was of a long war of attrition and of refusing to end hostilities until the Arabs' basic demands were met. However, this tack had promptly been rendered futile, as Sadat, acting unilaterally, had rushed towards the ceasefire. Reluctantly, and after weighing the alternatives, all of which appeared daunting, the Syrians announced their acceptance of the Security Council's resolution. Despite all the gloss that the Arab leaders were to apply to the war subsequently (both Egypt and Syria mark the anniversary of 6 October as the Day of Victory), there was a strong sense of unfulfilled expectations at the way it ended. Yet, the war's impact, regionally and internationally, was considerable and could have bestowed lasting global influence to the Arab political community as a whole. Firstly, although pushed back eventually by the US-backed Israeli army, the Arab units had shown a degree of prowess and organisation in their advances that belied their catastrophic performance six years earlier. The events had also demonstrated a rare and genuine alliance across the whole of the Arab world. For once Arab unity ceased to be an empty slogan. Significantly, the deployment by Saudi Arabia of their trump card – oil – shook the very foundations of the global economic order and gave impetus to countries long browbeaten into accepting morsels from the table of the advanced industrial world. Finally, the legacy of the 1973 war breathed new life into an Arab state system that had been severely undermined by the defeat of 1967.

Nevertheless, history bears witness to the fact that the Arabs failed to build on the strategic momentum they had established during that brief period. The reasons are manifold. The two leaders of the military alliance that had showed such promise in the first few days of the war did not remain at one in the pursuance of the war as they had been in its planning and at its launch. This became apparent when the Egyptians held fast on their early gains, giving the Israelis the opportunity to single out Syria and mount a massive counterattacking onslaught on the Golan front. Egypt's attempt, several days later, to relieve the pressure on the Syrians through an ill-planned and much-delayed offensive in the Sinai backfired and set the stage for a conclusion to the war that left the Israelis in the ascendancy. This lack of battlefield coordination was further blighted by the absence of any consensus regarding the ceasefire that eventually came into effect and the stand to be taken in its aftermath. Again it was Sadat who seemed to be in a hurried, even impetuous, mood to go it alone in the reconciliation stakes as he had earlier in his conduct of the war. Still in his early and relatively untried period as leader, Assad was caught unawares in the slipstream of Sadat's zigzags, and had to adjust quickly to the new and uncomfortable realities. Another key obstacle in the consolidation of the Arabs' strategic gains was the thoroughly determined policy-making and diplomatic nous of Henry Kissinger. He played to Sadat's belief in the overwhelming power of the United States by posing as the only possible 'honest broker' who could deliver a 'just' peace. Sadat took little convincing and went along with Kissinger's step-by-step approach without much regard for the views of his Arab allies, including Assad. The result was the convening of a showpiece event in Geneva on 21 December, heralded as a peace conference, which was hosted by the United Nations and co-chaired by Kissinger and his Soviet counterpart, Andrei Gromyko. The foreign ministers of Egypt, Israel and Jordan attended, but, crucially, Syria refused to take part, citing the imprecise foundations and lack of strict terms of reference of the event. Indeed it amounted to nothing more than an arena for the repetition of platitudes on the need to carry out the fuzzy provisions of Security Council Resolution 242. The opening event remained a one-off occasion and was adjourned indefinitely. It did, however, act as cover for Kissinger to continue on what became a one-man mission to finalise, in accordance with his central objectives, the legacy of the October war. In the case of Egypt this was partly accomplished by the signing, on 18 January 1974, of a troop 'disengagement agreement' in Sinai, effectively ending any possibility of further hostilities on the Egyptian front. Assad was livid and attempted to impress upon Sadat the folly, as he saw it, of lifting the pressure on Israel at such a critical moment and without any guarantee as to the political outcome. Sadat hurried to Damascus in an attempt to assuage Assad's concerns, but his promises of continued loyalty to the common cause soon began to ring hollow. In a final blow to the Arabs' chance of strategic advancement Kissinger made one further, crucial move a few months later to defang the rising Arab beast. Backed by none other than Sadat he succeeded in persuading King Faisal to call off arguably the most important of the weapons wielded during that campaign: the oil boycott.

Assad was left with little choice but to take whatever gains he could, given the meltdown in the Arab strategic position. Kissinger, however, was not about to let Assad stew in his own juice. He appreciated the fact that a completely sidelined Assad could prove a spanner in the works of the pacified and

America-dominated Middle East he was trying to fashion. He was soon on his way to Damascus and even the taciturn Syrian leader was taken in by his wily charm. Several months of exhaustive talks took place against a backdrop of regular eruptions of heavy gunfire on the frontline – a period the Syrians then called their own 'war of attrition.' A subsequent flurry of 'shuttle diplomacy' was undertaken by Kissinger between Damascus and Tel Aviv, which resulted in the signing of a disengagement agreement between Syria and Israel on 31 May 1974. It provided for Israel to withdraw from the salient it had carved beyond the lines of 6 October, as well as a further sliver of territory that allowed the Syrians to regain the town of Quneitra, the capital of the governorate of Golan until 1967. Restrictions were put in place regarding troop levels and weapon systems. The agreement also called for the deployment of a UN force to maintain the peace. And despite its inauspicious origins the Golan disengagement agreement was to endure. Notwithstanding the turbulence and myriad wars that have swept the region since then, the Syrian-Israeli frontline has remained, until recently, an oasis of calm.[2]

Despite having agreed to the terms of the disengagement, Israel resorted to an act of crude vandalism. Before the town of Quneitra was evacuated it was bulldozed and left to the Syrians in total ruin. Nevertheless, in a gesture of heavy symbolism, Hafez Assad attended a ceremony to mark its liberation and raised the Syrian flag over what remained of the ghost town. Supported by a relentless, state-sponsored publicity campaign that painted the war and the liberation of Quneitra as supreme heroic achievements attributed to his skills as leader of the nation, Assad was elevated to a status not reached by any of Syria's modern rulers. He was riding high and was helped by the favourable press he received across the Arab world in the aftermath of the honourable showing by Syria's armed forces against an enemy that, until then, had seemed invincible. The positive outcome of the October war was not restricted to warm words of admiration. Funds started to pour into the impoverished Syrian economy as the oil-rich Arab countries, having enjoyed a windfall in soaring crude prices partly due to the war, felt duty bound to share some of their good fortune with the countries that had paid in blood for the new economic bountifulness, principally Egypt and Syria. All this meant the growth within Syria of a new breed of businessman attached directly to the state, and especially to the patronage of the president. Assad was not averse to feeding the avarice of his own immediate family and of those upon whom he relied in the military and upper security echelons as a means to oil the matrix of loyalty he was building around himself. He also had the foresight to bring into that matrix elements of the old bourgeoisie and the leaders of the souk who had been through very lean times since the Baathist takeover in the early sixties. Thus he established the early foundations of a coalition that helped him, as an Alawite, to claim to have wider and more representative support within society, and particularly among the Sunni community.

While working to broaden his power base, however, Assad's other actions, whether by intention or accident, were sowing the seeds of distrust and unease. He allowed, and obviously encouraged, the growth of a personality cult that jarred with the instincts of the population, and had not been seen since the brief, bygone days of that first dictator, Hosni Zaim, in 1949. He also gave much slack to his family members and to the feared and hydra-headed security agencies. Known collectively as *mukhabarat,* there were several such bodies competing for different patches of patronage and extra-judicial authority. Most notorious of the new powerbrokers was the president's younger brother, Rifaat, who commanded an autonomous praetorian guard, named the defence companies, that ran riot all over the country, bullying, kidnapping and terrorising as it saw fit. Known to be recruited largely from the Alawite community, these agencies of state-fostered oppression and arbitrary coercion were bound to trigger resentment among a majority already starting to feel aggrieved. This created fertile ground for those groupings, Islamist in particular, with the ability to whip up populist religious and sectarian feelings.

The challenge for Assad, as indeed for most Arab leaders who had sought their legitimacy in the fifties and sixties by riding the wave of secular nationalism which then ruled the Arab street, was overcoming the searing impact on that ideology of the apocalyptic defeat of the June 1967 war. That disaster was a gift to those who opposed the radicalism associated with Arab nationalism, chiefly the conservative circles that found themselves on the defensive as Nasserism, Baathism and other progressive forces were in the ascendancy across the region. They immediately blamed the calamity on the ideological departure from those traditional values and policies closely linked to the Saudi and Hashemite dynasties. Beyond this conservative and right-wing *Schadenfreude*, and feeding much more diligently and strategically on the general shock and despair in Arab public opinion, were the currents of political Islamism. They saw the opportunity presented to them by the perceived crash of their ideological nemesis. Many voices that had been relatively subdued for nearly two decades while Arab nationalism (and to a lesser extent left-wing proto-Marxism) held centre-stage, began to argue for a return to Islam as the answer to the bankruptcy of secular nationalism that had been so openly exposed.

A nascent Islamic insurgency had already cut its teeth in Syria by virtue of confrontations in the mid-sixties when the first Baathist leaders sought to suppress forcibly and crudely all resistance to their one-party rule. Incidents such as the storming and shelling of mosques were bound to feed into a deep reservoir of sectarian resentment. Although the coming to grief of those neo-Baathists at the hands of Hafez Assad gave the new leader a measure of true popularity, further enhanced by the accolades he received in the wake of the war of October 1973, the seismic shift in the Arab street away from the pre-1967 nationalism and towards one form or another of political Islamism was an enduring and progressing feature as the seventies advanced. This was as much the case in Syria as in other Arab lands, including Egypt. From the seventies onwards the trend in religious politics was driven to a substantial extent by the soaring rise in the flow of funds from Saudi Arabia and other oil producers – whose coffers were now brimming – towards Islamic 'causes,' such as the feverish building of mosques and religious schools. Their largesse inevitably communicated those countries' ascetic interpretation of Islamic culture and jurisprudence in contradiction to the more tolerant and open Islam that prevailed in Syria and the Levant as a whole. The nature of Assad's rule, purposely or otherwise, only fed the growing resentment of the gathering forces of Islamic reaction. His assertion of power by skewing appointments to the nerve centres in the army and security forces along sectarian lines and his turning of a blind eye to the excesses of his family and clan entourage seemed destined to provoke ire.

Assad, however, was being distracted from the turmoil brewing inside Syria by ominous developments across the border in Lebanon. There, on 13 April 1975, on the outskirts of Beirut, a bus carrying a group of Palestinians, some with arms, was attacked by Lebanese fighters belonging to the right-wing Christian Phalange Party. Many passengers died or suffered injury, and the incident went down in history as the spark that ignited the Lebanese civil war. Over previous years Lebanon had grown into a cauldron of mounting tension and violent clashes between two sharply defined camps. One was represented by an alliance of Palestinian resistance fighters (many of them displaced veterans of the previous battle of Black September in Jordan in 1970) organised under the banner of the PLO, and several nationalist and left-wing Lebanese political parties. Against it was a coalition led by the Phalange Party that brought together leading groups and figures from the Christian, mainly Maronite, establishment. The latter resented that the Palestinian armed groups, with Yasser Arafat at their helm, had established themselves as 'a state within a state' (much as they had earlier in Jordan) as they felt it constituted a grave threat to Lebanon's sovereignty. The view held by the opposing camp was that the Palestinians found themselves in Lebanon not through choice but as a result of Israeli occupation and aggression, and that it was the duty of the Lebanese – indeed of all Arabs – to tender support and protection for the resistance to the occupier and aggressor. Behind the noble words that prefaced each camp's posture were deeper issues relating to the very fabric and history of the Lebanese political landscape. The religious divide that had always been at the centre of Lebanon's sociological bipolarity grew to overshadow the left- and right-wing affiliations of political ideology. On that basis the Palestinian-leftist alliance drew much of its support from within the broader Muslim community which saw in it a force that could alter the historical political imbalance that had favoured the Christians. This was despite the fact that what was now known as the National Movement comprised a number of political parties, such as the Syrian Nationalists (SSNP) and the communists, who were fervently secular and included a substantial number of Christians in the ranks of their fighters. In fact, the grouping was led by the veteran Lebanese head of the Progressive Party, Kamal Jumblatt, the scion of a feudal Druze dynasty. They faced a bloc much more narrowly defined in its religious affiliation, whose rhetoric emphasised a vision of Lebanese nationalism coming under the threat of an armed Palestinian presence on Lebanese soil. The sub-plot in this largely Maronite call to arms was the fear that the Palestinians, overwhelmingly Muslim, would transform the demographics within Lebanon in such a way as to overwhelm the Christians and threaten the political status quo, which, since the birth of the state in 1920, had allowed the Maronites pride of place in the running of the country. Indeed, an unwritten 'national accord' of 1943 stipulated that the presidency of the country be drawn exclusively from the Maronite community.

With civil war now spreading across much of Lebanon, the Syrians faced an acute dilemma. The sympathies of the regime would have naturally leant towards the Palestinian resistance and its Lebanese allies. Yet the fear was that a triumph on that side, which seemed plausible, would lead to a last-ditch defence of the Christian enclave in Mount Lebanon and other areas to the north where Christians were concentrated, and the division of the country along sectarian lines. This was anathema to Damascus as sectarianism could so easily threaten Syria's own confessional mosaic. Also bearing on Assad's mind was the likelihood that Israel would pose as the champion of Lebanon's Christians. Indeed the latter were already starting to receive arms clandestinely from the government in Tel Aviv, while Maronite militia leaders had been travelling secretly to Israel to establish lines of communication and supply with their new allies. Alarm bells sounded loudly in Damascus, and when Jumblatt visited Assad in the spring of 1976, seeking his support for a strategic

Palestinian-National Movement thrust into the Maronite heartland, he was roundly rebuffed and warned against such a move by the Syrian leader. Undaunted, Arafat and Jumblatt went ahead with a joint offensive and seemed on the point of breaking through the Christian lines, turning the tide of war decisively in favour of the advancing forces. Assad had a vital decision to make. In early June 1976 he ordered his army to cross the frontier into Lebanon to prevent the National Movement, by force, from advancing into Christian territory. As a result he was hailed a saviour by the Christian leadership, heralding a new alliance. In the opposite camp Assad was denounced in the most venomous of terms. Syria, the historic godfather of Palestine and Arab nationalism, was siding with the enemies of nationalism and the stooges of Zionism to boot.

The shockwaves were not limited to Lebanon. Across the Arab world and indeed within Syria itself there was disbelief at this apparent reversal of decades of established attitudes that were ingrained in the political culture of the age. Official Syrian propaganda was muted in its attempts to justify the blatant turnaround. Assad, nonetheless, rose to the occasion in a speech that was greeted with a cacophony of cheers by the beleaguered Christians of Lebanon. He robustly defended the actions of his army by claiming that the aim was to prevent the division of Lebanon and thus abort the opportunity for Israel to exploit the situation to gain strategic advantage. At first it seemed he might prevail and that a Pax Syriana would establish itself over Lebanon for some time to come. But Assad was not allowed to bask in that moment of relative triumph for long. Too many other states and non-state actors of the region and the wider world had stakes in Lebanon's future. They were not prepared to tolerate a monopoly of Syrian control over the country. Very importantly, Assad had fallen foul, at least momentarily, of his main international patron: the Soviet Union. Moscow made it plain from the start that his volte-face with respect to the alignments in the Lebanese civil war was ill judged. It amounted to an attack on the 'progressive and anti-imperialist forces' and advanced the cause of the reactionary powers and their local allies that Syria had traditionally opposed. The secretary general of the Soviet Communist Party, Leonid Brezhnev, sent a clear message to Assad, calling on him to withdraw his forces from Lebanon and to re-establish his alliance with the PLO and the National Movement in that country. Assad, however, stood firm and refused to obey the request. It resulted in a coolness in the Soviet-Syrian relationship that was to last for some years. Arab leaders took turns in expressing their anger, with Sadat leading the way in breaking off relations while his foreign minister accused the Syrians of committing genocide in Lebanon. No less vituperative was the language emanating from Baghdad, the other capital of Baathism, which relished the opportunity to tarnish the image of its arch rival. Assad could hardly take solace openly from the fact that Jordan, Israel and even the United States were, at least tacitly, supportive of his strike against the PLO – an obvious kiss of death for any pretender to the Arab nationalist crown. Nonetheless it certainly assured him that he had solid backing where it mattered. Indeed, Tel Aviv had conveyed to Damascus, via Washington, that the Syrian army could carry out its mission undisturbed in Lebanon, as long as it stayed clear of the area immediately to the north of Israel bordered by the Litani river – the so-called 'red line.'

The Syrians were facing bitter opposition in the pursuit of their military campaign in Lebanon. The objective was to tame the PLO and the National Movement while protecting the territories of their newfound Christian allies. And the

Christians were not averse to using the shield now provided by the Syrian army to continue launching retributive assaults against their enemies. A number of atrocities and massacres hit the headlines and the resulting outrage was directed not only at the Christian militias but was also fully cast in the direction of Assad and his forces who were deemed to have been at least in collusion with those commanding the murderous groups. The issue of Lebanon's presidency had also arisen early in 1976. In an attempt to defuse the acrimonious political climate, the divisive presidency of Suleiman Frangieh was prematurely terminated, under Syrian pressure, and a new, ostensibly unifying personality, Elias Sarkis, was elected that spring as his replacement with the clear blessing of Damascus. By the following year the pressure on Syria to temper its policy in Lebanon reached a level that could no longer be ignored. Assad bowed to an Arab League initiative backed by Egypt and Saudi Arabia that deployed an Arab force to take charge of peacekeeping in Lebanon. The Arab Deterrent Force was a misnomer, however, as it was heavily composed of the same Syrian units already in place in Lebanon, albeit under a different flag and with token units from other Arab countries. By appearing to have responded to the calls to step back Assad gained a degree of kudos while essentially maintaining his dominant presence in the 'sister' country. That presence would continue to be a mainstay of Syria's strategic paradigm.

Before 1977 was out Syria, and the rest of the Arab world, was struck by a bolt from the blue. Egypt's president Sadat, claiming to have exhausted all other avenues in reaching a settlement of the Arab-Israeli conflict, decided to go it alone. In October he announced to a stunned audience that he was prepared to visit the den of the enemy and speak to Israel's Knesset. Nothing could so violate the political culture that had for so

long been innate to the Arabs' consciousness as this dramatic
and astonishing announcement. While much of the rest of the
world hailed the move as an act of courage and statesmanship
the broad sweep of Arab opinion – with the exception, arguably,
of a substantial segment of the Egyptian populace – was united
in denouncing Sadat's unprecedented sell-out to the bitter foe.
Sadat, however, revelled in the adulation he was receiving on
the international level, especially in America, and was adamant
in his belief in the power of his latest electric shock to deliver
what years of 'no peace, no war' had failed to do. Against all the
odds he even thought he might be able to bring his war partner,
Assad, onside and visited Damascus a few days before going to
Jerusalem in a last-ditch attempt to deflect the accusations of
acting as a renegade. Assad, predictably, would have none of it.
He desperately tried to steer Sadat off the destructive course (as
Assad saw it) that he was intent on pursuing, but to no avail.
Some hotheads in the Syrian regime were even urging Assad to
order Sadat's arrest. The Syrian leader was not about to commit
such an act of folly, and bade a formal goodbye to his wayward
guest. The two were never to meet again.

President Sadat duly visited Israel, and the Camp David
accords were the result. From that point Assad was consumed
in tireless efforts to build a solid alignment in response to
the bombshell of Sadat's signing of a peace treaty effectively
detaching Egypt from the rest of the Arab world. To that end
he found it necessary to make common cause with the rival
Baathist regime in Baghdad, leading to the formation of a
Steadfastness Front to include Algeria, Libya and the PLO.
While abiding by the general Arab consensus to ostracise
Sadat's Egypt the more moderate Arab countries, such as
Saudi Arabia and Jordan, kept their distance from the more
radical stance of the Steadfastness Front, which was seeking

to eliminate every form of engagement with Cairo. The new geopolitical landscape not only brought Syria a rapprochement with Iraq; it also imposed on Assad a marriage of convenience with the PLO and a further twist in the fluid arrangement of alliances affecting Lebanon. Christian factions were already grumbling at the increasingly heavy-handed manner in which the Syrian military and security forces were behaving in their territories and the makings were soon in place of yet another shift in the dynamics of the Lebanese conflict. After their brief honeymoon the Syrians once again found themselves at the receiving end of the hostility of the right-wing and Christian forces. So began a series of armed skirmishes that escalated at times to the level of sustained heavy bombardment by the Syrian army of Christian parts of east Beirut, as well as other areas in the Maronite mountain redoubts. On the Muslim, left-wing and Palestinian side of the Lebanese divide Yasser Arafat was in almost total command after the assassination in 1977 of the Lebanese leader Kamal Jumblatt – a victim in all probability of a Syrian hit squad. There was renewed vigour to the Syrian campaign but this time with an apparent return to the 'national cause' which they had uncharacteristically abandoned in 1976.

While deeply embroiled in dealing with the aftermath of Sadat's defection, and in navigating the vicissitudes of Lebanon's relapse into civil war, Assad had to contend with a major challenge to his rule in Syria. A festering state of resentment among large sections of the Sunni population, which had already triggered serious disturbances met by brutal repression in the mid-sixties, started to re-emerge in the mid-seventies. Assad had started his rule by posing, largely successfully, as a leader behind whom all could rally, but he had begun to lose that lustre. Those to whom he delegated power and authority, largely drawn from his inner circle, were abusing their positions, often drawing on family and Alawite affiliation with Assad to leverage their corrupt influence. By the time he was perceived to have betrayed the Muslim cause by siding with the Christians in Lebanon as a result of his own sectarian predilections the elements of cataclysmic popular protest were all but in place. The sense of grievance that was gathering such momentum was heavily exploited by a resurgent Muslim Brotherhood, which succeeded in stirring up a widespread campaign of civil disobedience as well as acts of violence and destruction. Their increasingly fierce campaign escalated into targeted assassinations of regime figures – particularly Alawites – and reached its deadly apex in June 1979 when scores of Alawite officers were gunned down at the Artillery School in Aleppo. The Muslim Brothers received varying degrees of support from Assad's regional adversaries, including Saddam Hussein and, much more covertly, Jordan's King Hussein (who was later to apologise publicly for that support).

The government's crackdown was no less brutal. Membership of the Muslim Brotherhood was declared to be punishable by death, and decrees were issued giving impunity to security and intelligence agents in the carrying out of their 'duties' (implying that they could torture and kill 'suspects' almost at will). Thousands of Muslim Brothers and presumed sympathisers were arrested – many never to be heard from again. A reign of terror seemed about to spread and, when an assassination attempt was made on Hafez Assad on 26 June 1980, a grisly retribution followed: elements of Rifaat Assad's defence companies stormed the central prison in Palmyra, where many Muslim Brothers were detained, and killed hundreds of inmates in cold blood. Assad also decided that he had had enough of the less than absolutely loyal institutions of civil society that remained and suppressed the still relatively independent professional bodies, such as the bar association and the engineering and medical unions. Their leaders were arrested and fixed elections replaced them with supine Baathists and their fellow travellers. Protests and violence continued across the country but Assad and his forces were gaining the upper hand. The fear unleashed by the regime was intimidating all but the most fanatic of opponents. Assad also proved successful in neutralising leaders of the merchant class in Aleppo and, crucially, Damascus, keeping both major cities relatively quiet. He did so partly by displaying utter ruthlessness and partly by using the carrot of economic and financial benefits to tie many of those leaders to the purveyors of largesse sitting at the top of the regime. While the urban Sunni Muslim population provided some fertile ground for the Muslim Brotherhood to gather recruits to its militancy, the case was quite different in rural areas and villages – even those with a heavy preponderance of Sunni Muslims. The Baathists accomplished much over the years, particularly after Assad came to power, in terms of transforming the infrastructure and the services available to the rural population. Roads were built and the electric grid expanded in such a way as to connect even the most outlying areas with the rest of the country. The same applied to educational and health services which were introduced for the first time to many deprived communities – those with Sunni as well as non-Sunni majorities. Assad was therefore able to rely to a significant extent on a solid base of support that was, at least in rural Syria, more identified by socioeconomic than sectarian and ethnic factors. Even where they made substantial inroads in urban areas there were many who could not swallow the message or the tactics of the Brotherhood, who were becoming increasingly associated with extreme violence and a narrow interpretation of Islam and its role in politics.

The final, blood-soaked episode of the Brotherhood's insurrection occurred in Hama in March 1982. The city had risen in a *Götterdämmerung*, with armed men, egged on from the loudspeakers of the mosques, on a wild rampage that left in its wake many victims associated with the hated Baathists. State officials and their homes and families were targeted with horrific results. The regime's revenge was of a scale never experienced in modern Syria: Hama was subjected to an assault by infantry, armour and artillery that laid waste to much of the city. The death toll will never be accurately known; sources have quoted figures of ten to thirty thousand. The story of Hama has remained ingrained in the memory of Syrians and will come back to haunt the country's Baathist rulers when they face further and fiercer challenges.

For the moment Hafez Assad could rest more easily. He had survived the most perilous defiance to his rule and his whole approach to governance was set on a new and much more coercive and totalitarian track. After giving graphic notice of just how far he was prepared to deploy the iron fist he moved on to toughening up the personality cult around his leadership. The title 'commander for eternity' (*qaiduna ila al abad*) became the Assad hallmark. Following a pattern established by Kim Il-sung in North Korea and Nicolae Ceauşescau in Romania – both regarded by Assad as useful models – large portraits and numerous statues of the president proliferated across the country, in different poses and attire as befitted his multifaceted role: commander-in-chief of the army, father of the nation, intellectual sage, receiver of the people's acclamation, and so forth. Newspapers – all state owned – and radio and television news broadcasts had to preface their bulletins by listing the president's engagements, however trivial, and headlining all the cables he had sent to or received from foreign leaders to mark this or that national day or public holiday. Nowhere could you travel in Syria without being met by that ubiquitous, stern stare. The country had indeed become, to quote a favourite Baathist rallying call, 'Assad's Syria.'

While securing absolute control of the domestic levers of power Assad was becoming freer to address the challenges and tribulations of the surrounding region, which was caught up in a spiral of events that turned the strategic certainties of decades upside down. Hot on the heels of Sadat's shocking break with the received wisdom of the Arab world's never coming to terms with the implanted state of Israel came a shattering blow to that other geostrategic certainty: a Pahlavi-ruled Iran that would act as the West's policeman in the Gulf. Suddenly the all-powerful Shah was no more and an Islamic Republic was born that dedicated itself to the complete overhaul of the policies of its imperial predecessor. Meanwhile Iraq's leader, Ahmad Hassan Al Bakr, who had engineered with Assad a process that ended the rift between their countries and was leading towards a federal state under the rule of a unified Baath Party, was pushed aside in the summer of 1979 to be replaced by the vice-president, Saddam Hussein. The new ruler had different ideas and was virulently ill-disposed towards the rival Baathists in Syria. He soon 'uncovered' a plot that he alleged was hatched in Damascus, involving 'traitor' agents within the Iraqi Baath who were loyal to the Syrian regime and aimed to seize power on their behalf. Hussein used the plot as an excuse to undertake a purge of leading Iraqi Baathists that reached into the upper echelons of the party. In a dramatic filmed account of the purge he is seen chairing a meeting of the party where the names of the accused plotters are announced from the rostrum. Those named are then made to stand and are hustled out of the meeting to be executed on the spot.

Having lost both Egypt and Iraq as bulwarks in the solid Arab front Assad believed had to be built to balance the power of Israel and its backers, he now looked to the Islamic Republic established in Tehran as a potential strategic partner. A possible basis for fraternity between the states was the religious *fatwa* Assad had obtained from the leading Shiite cleric, Musa Al Sadr (who was later to disappear in Libya, presumed liquidated at Gaddafi's behest), acknowledging the Alawite sect as a branch of Shiite Islam. Its issuing had been important for Assad at the time as the Syrian constitution required that the president of the republic be a Muslim. Even beyond the religious synergy (a fabricated one in many eyes as the Alawites' liberal lifestyle and relaxed religious observance differed markedly from the doctrinal fervour and discipline of the Iranian Shiite orthodoxy) there was much to draw Damascus and post-revolution Tehran together. Iran's leader, Ayatollah Khomeini, made pronouncements against Israel and in support of the Palestinian cause, and made the highly symbolic gesture of closing the Israeli embassy in Tehran and handing the building over to the PLO. This resonated very well in Baathist Syria, as indeed it did in many other parts of the Arab world. The joker in the pack, however, was Saddam Hussein. He understood the concern of the Gulf countries at the arrival of a revolutionary regime with a fiery, ideologically driven and potentially destabilising agent of far-reaching regional change at its helm, having replaced a long-established imperial monarch with whom they had been able do business. The bold Iraqi leader thought he could achieve easy strategic gains by a full-scale military offensive against Iran. He particularly hoped to reverse the concessions he had been obliged to agree to in a treaty signed with the Shah that recognised Iranian rights over the disputed Shatt al-Arab waterway between the two countries. He also believed he could seize the Iranian territory adjacent to Iraq long known as Arabistan by reference to the Arab origins of many of its inhabitants. Citing Iranian provocations and the call by some of Iran's new leaders for their revolution to be exported Saddam's army went into action in September 1980. So started a war that lasted for nearly eight years and cost the lives of hundreds of thousands on both sides.

While most of the Arab world, particularly the countries of the Gulf, sided to some degree or other with Saddam Hussein, Syria's Assad took a different line. His stance was partly motivated by personal venom, which characterised the relationship between the two men. But he also saw only disastrous strategic consequences of the action that had been taken. Such a reading was to prove correct since the Iraq-Iran war ultimately served no purpose but to bleed the two parties and bring comfort to Israel, as well as the new right-wing Reagan administration in Washington. These were happy to witness the equally troublesome adversaries helpfully – and hopelessly – mired in killing fields of their own making. In standing with Iran politically, and by allowing arms shipments directly from Syria or from third parties (such as Libya) to reach Iran, helping the latter to contain and ultimately withstand the Iraqi offensive, Assad invited the opprobrium of many of his erstwhile Arab allies. A descent into increasing isolation followed and the Arab Gulf money that had been so central to Syria's economic boom of the mid-seventies began to dry up. This was to cause stagnation in the Syrian economy that would last well into the 1980s.

Syria's attention was soon diverted to a vital challenge to its interests and security closer to home. In June 1982 Israel – headed by the leader of the right-wing Likud Party, Menachem

Begin – used the pretext of an assassination attempt against its ambassador to London,[3] to launch a massive attack across Lebanon's southern frontier. The so-called Peace for Galilee operation was a thinly disguised attempt to strike a fatal blow against the PLO. It contravened a ceasefire that had been agreed the year before in order to halt the clashes that had been a regular occurrence since PLO fighters established a strong foothold in that region of Lebanon in the preceding decade. With their own powerful political and military presence in the country at stake the Syrians were suddenly faced with a stark choice: come directly to the aid of the Palestinians and risk an all-out confrontation with Israel – for which they were ill-prepared – or wait and watch, hoping that the Israeli battle plan did not have the deployments of the Syrian army in its sights.

It soon became clear that Israel's war aims were much more far-reaching than they first appeared to those in Damascus or indeed in other regional and international capitals nervously eyeing the developing situation in Lebanon. Israel's leaders sought to allay any alarm by initially claiming that the mission of their forces was only to drive the Palestinian fighters back a distance of forty kilometres. Messages were even transmitted to the Syrians to the effect that their forces and positions were not under threat from the invading Israelis. It was not long, however, before Israeli formations under the direct command of the hawkish minister of defence, Ariel Sharon, were driving fast beyond the purported forty-kilometre objective and nearing Beirut. Meanwhile the Israeli air force was mounting a concerted campaign deep into Lebanon and causing widespread destruction and casualties. The Syrians now realised that their forces in and around Beirut, and their logistical and supply lines, especially the Damascus-Beirut highway, along with their vital defence concentrations in the strategic Bekaa Valley, were at grave risk. They could no longer remain on the sidelines and engaged the Israelis on a number of fronts. One of these engagements, taking place on 10 and 11 June, became known as the Battle of Sultan Yacoub. The Syrian forces halted an Israeli armoured advance on the Damascus-Beirut road, inflicting on the enemy heavy casualties and capturing several Israeli tanks in the process. However, elsewhere in the rapidly expanding confrontation it was disaster for Assad's armed forces, especially in the air. Taking full advantage of Syria's involvement in the expanding war by dint of *force majeure* Israel launched a massive air assault against Syrian positions in the Bekaa, targeting in particular the SAM anti-aircraft missile systems that the Syrians had brought in the year before. Syrian aircraft tried to intercept the much more advanced Israeli warplanes resulting in a catastrophic loss to the Syrian air force of more than a hundred fighters. Not one Israeli plane was shot down: an imbalance enormous in its poignancy. On 11 June Syria accepted a ceasefire that had been negotiated by Philip Habib, the veteran American-Lebanese envoy who had been sent to Lebanon by Washington as a mediator between the warring factions. The Syrians were now officially neutralised as a central military actor in the continuing conflict. Arafat and others in the Palestinian leadership accused Syria of betrayal as they were seemingly left alone to defend what remained of their positions.

Unmoved by calls from the UN and across the world for a halt to hostilities, the Israelis continued to advance northward, laying siege to Beirut. Arafat's PLO and the allied militias from the Lebanese National Movement found themselves surrounded by the Israelis to the south and their Lebanese Phalangist allies to the east and north. Many Syrian army units which had been cut off from their own general command were staring at the same lurid prospect. Several weeks of relentless bombardments from land, sea and air made life in Beirut unbearable for the Palestinians and their allies, for the remaining encircled Syrian troops and for the civilians trapped in the city. Leading Muslim politicians were now leaning heavily on Arafat to accept an American-sponsored plan for him and his forces to evacuate Beirut to save the city from further punishment. All parties finally agreed to the plan, and by 1 September 1982 the evacuation had been completed, with the Palestinian fighters and their leaders attempting to retain as much dignity as possible. The plan included safe passage of the Syrian troops out of Beirut and the deployment of a multinational force composed of US, French and Italian military units to oversee the evacuation. In a snub to Damascus, Arafat opted for a sea journey that took him to Greece rather than the overland journey to Damascus. The decision underlined what he and many Palestinians saw as Syria's less than wholehearted commitment to the battle that ended with a resounding humiliation – an accusation hotly rejected by the Syrian leadership who pointed to the great sacrifices endured by their armed forces and to the ferocious defensive battles, such as Sultan Yacoub, where the Syrian soldiery had exhibited considerable heroism.

Israel's moment of greatest triumph, having had an Arab capital at its mercy, also marked the beginning of a long and ultimately very costly embroilment in the tangled web of the Lebanese conflict. Sharon believed he had gained the ultimate prize when, on the back of the invasion, the leader of the Christian militias allied to Israel, Bashir Gemayel, was elected to the presidency of the country. However, on 14 September, before he could even take office, the president-elect and a number of the commanders of the Phalange Party (the backbone organisation behind the main Christian militia) fell victim to a massive blast as they held a celebratory meeting. Gemayel's assassination can be seen to have represented the beginning of a steady rollback of the Israeli juggernaut's triumphal march into Lebanon. The person who had planted the explosives was soon caught and publicly identified as belonging to the Syrian Social Nationalist Party, by now an ally of the Syrian Baathist regime. The conclusion drawn by many, later supported by evidence, was that Syrian intelligence had had a hand in planning the operation. In any case there was no doubting the severity of the blow that had struck the strategic investment that Israel, and particularly Sharon, had sought to embed in the territory to its north.

The immediate response from Israel triggered a chain reaction that shocked the world with its images of sheer horror and brutality. As soon as news of Gemayel's assassination broke the Israeli army moved into west Beirut – in violation of the agreement that had led to the evacuation of the PLO a few weeks earlier. Then, on 16 September, as Israel's surrounding armies looked on, their surrogate Christian militias entered the undefended Palestinian refugee camps of Sabra and Shatila and began an orgy of butchery that led to the deaths of some two thousand unarmed inhabitants – women, children and the elderly included. The outcry across the world was such that the Israeli public itself was shocked and General Sharon was accused of complicity in the massacre. The resulting furore led to him losing his post as minister of defence after a specially formed Israeli committee of inquiry found him responsible, albeit indirectly, for the atrocities committed by the right-wing militias. Even Israel's closest ally, the United States, joined the chorus of condemnation and successfully pressed for the prompt return to Beirut of the multinational force that had just left Lebanon believing its mission to have been accomplished with the peaceful evacuation of the Palestinian fighters and the Syrian military.

Israel's grand strategy for Lebanon was fast unravelling. Although the newly elected president, Amine Gemayel (the brother of the assassinated Bashir), tried throughout the following year to placate both Israel and Syria and adopt a far less abrasive line than Bashir, he misjudged the fury of Assad when agreeing, under American pressure, to sign a peace treaty with Israel in May 1983. The Syrians, and their now resurgent Lebanese nationalist and left-wing allies, described the treaty as a humiliating accord and vowed to abort it. A renewed civil war began in full force with Syria's allies gaining ground in the southern Druze Mountain and in southern and west Beirut. At the same time the Israeli forces of occupation were being constantly harassed by a Lebanese National Resistance composed mostly of Syrian Social Nationalist and communist fighters, as well as Shiite forces of the Amal group. The Israelis had already beaten a hasty retreat from Beirut and were continuing southward, ultimately deploying behind a unilaterally established security zone inside Lebanese territory that they would cling to until finally being forced out many years later by the Islamic Resistance – a progeny of the new and rising force of Hezbollah.

By the summer of 1983 Assad had the wind in his sails in Lebanon. He had thwarted Israel's plans, and when the Americans responded to the reversals inflicted on Amine Gemayel's Lebanese army by directly shelling the positions of Syria's allies and attacking Syrian army positions in the Bekaa Valley they suffered the humiliation of having two of their aircraft shot down by Syrian fire. An American pilot survived the attack of 4 December 1983 and was captured, only to be released after the high-profile personal intervention of the American civil rights leader, Reverend Jesse Jackson. In October the Americans had suffered one of their worst casualty tolls since the Vietnam war when a barracks outside Beirut housing US marines was truck-bombed, causing the deaths of 241 men. A similar attack the same day against the French contingent of the multinational force led to the deaths of fifty-six soldiers. Behind the attacks was the Iranian-backed group Hezbollah, marking its presence on Lebanon's stage with a loud and very deadly bang. By the beginning of 1984 the US military mission, and that of the multinational force, was in tatters: the American withdrawal from Lebanon, almost in panic, was one of the lowest moments in the history of the Marines – the pride of the US military. To cap the collapse of the Israeli master plan and the setback to Washington's Pax Americana in Lebanon, Gemayel finally surrendered to the inevitable and announced Lebanon's abrogation of the peace accord with Israel. When it was signed in May 1983 it had seemed that a second Arab country was following in the footsteps of Egypt and detaching itself from the common Arab cause, but subsequent events kept Lebanon in the fold.

For Hafez Assad 1983 represented the year in which he achieved critical successes against Israel in Lebanon and, following the withdrawal of American and UN forces, consolidated Syria's dominance in the country. However, earlier in the year the Syrian regime had been shaken to its foundations when grave health problems had beset its leader. For several weeks leading into spring a potentially explosive struggle took place among competing tsars at the head of the security and military establishments. Jumping the gun in the belief that Hafez's days were numbered was his younger brother, Rifaat, head of the powerful defence companies which had grown to rival the regular army in strength and equipment. On news of the president's descent into unconsciousness, Rifaat's men hoisted heroic portraits of him, apparently prepared in advance, with accompanying slogans anointing him as the natural successor to the leadership of the country. Other army generals with the necessary clout, such as Ali Haydar, head of the special forces, and Shafiq Fayyad, commander of the third division, were just as intent on stopping Rifaat's presumptuous takeover bid. For a brief and nerve-wracking moment Damascus held its breath as the pro- and anti-Rifaat forces squared up for what could have been a catastrophic confrontation. At the last moment, however, having recovered from his health crisis Hafez personally toured the heavily alerted troop concentrations and took charge of the situation. Having restored his authority he arranged for the would-be power-grabbers, including his brother, to be bundled onto an aeroplane and flown to Moscow for a cooling-off period. Haydar and Fayyad soon returned to Syria. Rifaat, on the other hand, was destined to remain in exile. It was not, however, to be a life of hardship. Drawing on a huge fortune of mysterious origin he began to enjoy the lap of luxury, moving between European capitals and popular resort cities such as Marbella, and acquiring upmarket properties and hotels in prime locations. In the early 1990s he founded an Arabic television news channel, which was used on occasion to further his cause as pretender to the Syrian presidency.

Hafez Assad had achieved two key objectives: the elimination of the threat from rival power centres at home, not least his own ambitious brother, and becoming the undisputed master of Lebanon. During Yuri Andropov's brief reign at the Kremlin Assad had also succeeded in ensuring a flow of new, advanced weaponry from the Soviet Union. The process not only made up for Syria's losses during the previous summer's battles with the Israelis but also amounted to a wholesale upgrading of Syria's military capabilities, including its air defence system. Assad was by then making repeated pronouncements about establishing a strategic balance with the Israeli enemy involving Syria on its own: a distinct departure from previous statements that had stressed the importance of a wider Arab front as essential for confronting the power of Israel. The new approach was largely born of Syria's newfound isolation within the region. Following the Syrian entry into Lebanon, and its decision to ally with Tehran against Baghdad, Assad began to suffer the impact of an Arab neighbourhood that was growing increasingly cold. The hostility was only compounded when Syrian forces and their allies stood against the PLO in an attempt to regain influence in Lebanon. A new and invigorated round of the feud between Assad and Arafat was taking shape and reached a peak in December 1983 when the latter decided on a Napoleon-style return from exile though the northern Lebanese port of Tripoli, only to be humiliatingly expelled by Syrian-backed forces. In the meantime Syrian intelligence had been active in supporting an internal coup within Arafat's own Fatah organisation. A grouping called Fatah Intifada, enjoying Syrian patronage, sought to recruit support for an alternative to Arafat's 'defeatist' leadership. A protracted and widely condemned assault on Palestinian refugee camps ensued. It was waged by the Shiite Amal militia, which was closely allied to Damascus. The long campaign, which caused much suffering and heaped worldwide opprobrium on both Amal and Syria, served once again to darken Assad's reputation among Arab opinion.

Syria's pariah status saw an end to the flow of capital from the oil-rich Gulf. Without these foreign funds Syria entered a period of stagnation during the mid- to late eighties that almost caused the collapse of its economy. Seeking scapegoats for the worsening situation the government turned its wrath against those committing 'economic crimes,' such as dealing in the black market or flouting currency exchange laws, and they were tried in specially created courts. Many in the business and trade communities were charged and sentenced to long periods of imprisonment, although it was noticeable that the new draconian measures were never applied to the real fat cats populating the highest echelons of state-sanctioned corruption and nepotism. The gravity of the situation was partly alleviated when sizeable areas of crude oil were discovered and created a new revenue stream for the state. This allowed the government to offset in part the significant deficit in direct foreign aid and investment.

While Syria felt the economic consequences of alienation from its Arab brothers, regional developments continued to underline that estrangement. In August 1988, having suffered a series of setbacks on the battlefield, Iran finally accepted a set of internationally negotiated proposals for a ceasefire in its war with Iraq. Until that point Ayatollah Khomeini had been holding out for a decisive victory against Saddam Hussein and he considered the decision to end the war a bitter poison that had to be swallowed. Indeed, the manner of the war's end was no less of a poison for Syria's Assad. Suddenly his bitter rival, Saddam Hussein, was claiming a victory on behalf of himself and his fellow Arabs. According to the narrative of the Baathists in Baghdad the battle they had won against the 'Persian hordes' was historically akin to the great triumph of the Islamic forces at Qadisiyyah, which opened the way to the Arabs' conquest of ancient Persia. Having backed the Iranians during the eight-year war, Assad was now distinctly on the back foot as Saddam revelled in the accolades he was receiving from across the Arab world, particularly Saudi Arabia and Kuwait. Here was the valiant hero claiming to have been the shield protecting Arabism while in his shadow cowered the Arab apostate who had betrayed his own nation. Syria's fall from grace was emphasised when a new coalition was formed in the shape of the Arab Cooperation Council. It joined Iraq, Egypt (now rehabilitated despite its peace treaty with Israel), Jordan and Yemen. It was obvious who was calling the shots in the regional rearrangement – Saddam Hussein – and who was deliberately left out of it – Assad. The elevation of Saddam to the rank of uncrowned king of the Arabs seemed complete when, in May 1990, a special Arab summit was held in Iraq as a demonstration of fealty to the all-powerful master of Baghdad.

It was not too long, however, before Saddam Hussein's folly and hubris would come to the rescue of Assad. He claimed that Kuwait was undermining Iraq's economy by flooding the market with crude oil (hence depressing its price) and stealing from an Iraqi oilfield adjacent to the common border. His solution was to order his troops to invade and occupy Iraq's small but oil-rich neighbour to the south on 1 August 1990. It was the start of one of the biggest crises to hit the international order since the Second World War. The Arab world was stunned and the shockwaves were felt around the globe. Oblivious to all demands that he withdraw his forces, and making his intentions even more emphatic by declaring the formal integration of Kuwait within Iraq, Saddam was convinced that his fait accompli would weather any attempt to have it reversed. For a short time he may have been reassured by the fact that the dazed leaders of the Arab political collective were less than decisive in taking a stand. It was a while before King Fahd of Saudi Arabia, acting on the heavy pressure being applied to him by the West, particularly the United States, agreed to host an American-led international force to deter Iraq from threatening any other, by now very jittery, Gulf neighbours, and also, eventually, to oust it from Kuwait. Eyes then turned towards Damascus and Assad.

Had Assad turned to his own people for their opinion on the position he should take on Iraq's invasion of Kuwait he would probably have found that a solid majority were, in fact, on the side of Saddam. In a sense, his actions, as brutish as they were, articulated the long-held Arab nationalist vision that rejected the boundary lines separating their states – lines drawn by colonial powers to boot. It was a vision that had been at the heart of the appeal of Baathism, in Syria as elsewhere. Every morning thousands upon thousands of Syrian students would line up in school courtyards to chant loudly in praise of 'unity' – the first of the three pillars forming the centrepiece of the party's dogma. Yet Assad understood full well that he had to circumvent the inconvenience of ideology in favour of political reality. That meant having to swallow much of the rhetoric of the past and allying himself very awkwardly with a coalition that combined the forces of Arab conservatism with those of Western countries (still bearing the stigma of a colonial past), and which was led by that arch-patron of Israel, the United States. Moreover, formed under the operational banner Desert Shield, the coalition had the clear objective of ultimately engaging Iraq in war – a sister Arab country linked with Syria by the deepest historical, demographic and cultural associations. It was a difficult mission statement but Assad succeeded in carrying it off. At an extraordinary Arab summit held in Cairo the Syrian leader challenged the gathered assembly to come up with a joint military plan that would force Saddam Hussein out of Kuwait and so trump the need for outside powers to do the job. The answer was obvious to all: no such alternative existed. Assad had made the case for the only strategy that could work, albeit with a heavy heart.

In the eyes of many Arab leaders Assad turned overnight from a villain – ironically, for having sided with Iran against Iraq – into a hero. That Syria, the historical torchbearer of Arab nationalism, should become an integral part of the effort to roll back Iraq's invasion was crucially symbolic to the Arab protagonists, such as King Fahd and Egypt's Hosni Mubarak, who had tied their fate to the American-led operation. It allowed them to present the case that standing up to Saddam was in no way to collude with Western policies and interests: it was a pan-Arab obligation that even an anti-Western regime such as that in Damascus could endorse. With that in mind the arrival of the first Syrian military units to join the multinational force in Saudi Arabia was greeted with much fanfare by the monarchy's media. When all else failed, and the attack against Iraq became inevitable, Assad made one last bid to establish at least a moral distance between himself and the Western-led coalition. In a very public announcement he addressed Saddam Hussein, urging him to spare his country and the region the devastation that inevitably lay ahead by accepting to withdraw from Kuwait, even at that late stage. Assad stressed that if that happened and the attack went ahead anyway by the gathered forces of the coalition, then Syria would stand together with Iraq against them. He would have known in his heart that there was no chance of a positive response to his appeal (Saddam, in fact, immediately and contemptuously dismissed it out of hand), but it was his way of demonstrating that Syria was no blind tool of an alliance acting against the deeply held ideals of Arab nationalists everywhere.

Only recently designated a pariah by the West, Assad had turned into a key regional player. This was established most aptly by the summit meeting held in Geneva in November 1990 between the Syrian president and President Bush. Apart from the obvious symbolism of the occasion, cementing the newly formed – albeit still delicately framed – alliance regarding Kuwait, it also proved a cornerstone moment in a process addressing the aftermath of the liberation of Kuwait. Assad spent much of the time stressing to Bush the vital importance of keeping the Arab world on side by addressing the core issue of Palestine and moving seriously and swiftly towards a resolution of the Arab-Israeli conflict through an international conference jointly chaired by the USA and the Soviet Union. The American president duly assured his Syrian counterpart of his resolve to focus on the issue once the Kuwaiti crisis was successfully concluded.

In the event Syria's role in the fighting that followed the launch of Desert Storm in January 1991 remained marginal. This reflected the embarrassment that continued to weigh on the minds of the regime in Damascus and its keenness not to be seen as too willing in their participation in the problematic venture. Nonetheless, when Kuwait was liberated a month later Assad was not averse to accepting accolades from the reinstalled emir of that country, or from the capitals of the Gulf, for having provided a useful umbrella of nationalist legitimacy to the victorious campaign. The tributes were accompanied by a very welcome flow of aid and investment into a Syrian economy that had been on its knees in the years before the crisis sparked by the Iraqi invasion. A boom was now in the offing and was to ease the strain on a government desperately in need of a revenue transfusion to maintain the services, and subsidies, it had to provide to a rapidly rising population.

Yet another windfall came Assad's way in the wake of Saddam Hussein's ill-fated adventure. The Lebanese civil war had supposedly been settled with a Saudi-sponsored agreement signed in the city of Taif in 1989. The settlement rebalanced, in favour of the Muslim majority, the sharing of power that had existed in Lebanon since 1943. It also legitimised the continued presence of Syria's forces, which had returned in strength, officially to maintain security in Beirut following Israel's retreat and the collapse of America's allies in government, with the stipulation that those forces would gradually withdraw and restrict their deployment to the Bekka Valley. However, at the end of the presidency of Amine Gemayel Lebanon had two rival governments, one pro-Syrian – led by Salim al Hoss – and another claiming to represent Christian Maronite interests and led by the head of the army, General Michel Aoun. The latter denounced the Taif agreement and launched a 'war of liberation' against the Syrian occupation. Aoun had also seized the presidential palace outside Beirut, preventing the newly elected and pro-Syrian president, Elias Hrawi, from occupying it. A standoff continued for several months, and saw levels of violence that returned Lebanon to the darkest episodes of the civil war. Aoun was receiving support from Iraq and managing to hold out as well as overcome rival Maronite leaders, such as Samir Geagea, leader of the 'Lebanese forces,' in a bid to establish sole authority as head of the resistance to 'Syrian occupation.' The fight came to an end in October 1990 when Lebanese troops loyal to President Hrawi, heavily reinforced by Syrian troops and aided by attacks from Syrian jets, stormed the palace where Aoun had been entrenched. The general was forced to flee for his life and sought refuge at the French embassy, eventually leaving for a long period of exile in France. His rebellion was over and Assad achieved a strategic aim, which, Syrian officials were ready to concede, would not have occurred so smoothly had the Syrian leader not been transformed into a useful and courted ally in Western capitals by virtue of the Kuwait crisis. Once again Syria's supremacy in Lebanon had been restored – this time with the blessings of the Arab and Western worlds, both of which were grateful for Assad having chosen the 'right' side in the conflict with Saddam.

The immediate aftermath of the Gulf War saw Assad's fortunes soar. The coffers were filled literally and also in geopolitical terms, with changes that reflected Syria's new position of influence. There was the promise of a new Arab order framed around the partnership between Egypt and Syria brought about by the war and healthy relations with the countries of the Gulf Cooperation Council (GCC), having successfully evicted the Iraqis from Kuwait. Meeting in Damascus in February 1991 the foreign ministers of the six GCC members, plus Egypt and Syria, agreed on a joint statement that foresaw a sharing of the load of responsibility for the new regional order: the Gulf countries would form the financial and economic arm, while the other two would provide military and security muscle. For a short period of time the fledgling organisation, under the name the Damascus Declaration, seemed likely to supplant the moribund Arab League as the engine of joint Arab action.

The months that followed the Gulf War also held some hope that, at long last, the international community would get to grips with that most intractable of issues: the Arab-Israeli conflict. Building on the understanding reached between presidents Bush and Assad at the Geneva summit, the Americans signalled that they were now fully engaged in being true to their word. Invitations were drafted in Washington to an international conference, chaired by the United States and the Soviet Union and overseen by the United Nations, that would pave the way for a final and comprehensive settlement in the Middle East. Much wrangling over the wording of the invitation and the shape of the putative conference was to follow, with James Baker, the American secretary of state, personally and through many a shuttle mission, driving the process forward. At that time it appeared to all that the key to progress lay very firmly in Damascus's hands as the emerging Arab powerbroker. Baker strove hard to win Assad over, and spent long and gruelling hours subjected to what he would later call 'bladder diplomacy,'[4] before it was decided that a conference be held in Madrid in October 1991. The Syrians had driven a hard bargain and extracted from the Americans their pledge, in the wording of the letter of invitation, to consider as central to peace an Israeli withdrawal from the Golan. Yet they failed to get satisfaction on a number of points. Foremost among those was the issue of Arab representation in Madrid. Syria argued strongly for a single, united Arab negotiating team to reflect a common purpose and the resolve to move jointly towards a comprehensive settlement of all issues requiring resolution. Otherwise, Damascus contended, Israel would try to play one Arab adversary against the other, as happened in the aftermath of the war of October 1973 – a process which eventually led to the controversial peace treaty between Egypt and Israel. On this point America bowed to Israel, which, led by the hard-right Likud premier, Yitzhaq Shamir, insisted on separate bilateral negotiations following the formal plenary session of the international conference. A further demand by Tel Aviv was that there be no talks with an official Palestinian delegation, only with Palestinians subsumed under a Jordanian umbrella. The Americans endorsed Israel's approach while, despite Syrian entreaties, the other Arab countries fell in line with Washington's formula. The Syrians also objected strongly to the concept of multilateral talks – or 'track two' parallel negotiations – that would involve all parties discussing regional cooperation on such issues as economic development, the environment and water. Those matters, involving the normalisation of relations between the Arabs and Israel, should come as the natural consequence of an agreed and comprehensive peace, Syrian spokesmen maintained. Discussing them any earlier would prejudice the approach to the core concerns, and the outcome, therefore, of the entire process. Again Syria's was a lone voice. The other Arab parties, with the exception of Lebanon, signed up to the track two agenda.

Despite the objections that Damascus had to swallow in defining the framework and modus operandi of the Madrid conference, the event itself, which opened on 30 October 1991, was rich in symbolism and signified a poignant, watershed moment. For the first time since the start of the Arab-Israeli conflict the leaders of the main parties were meeting openly, face to face and in joint session, to consider putting an end to one of the most intractable struggles of the past century. For the Arabs it was the moment when a great historical taboo was smashed. The single most prized weapon in their armoury – the withholding of the recognition of the usurper Israeli state (even when militarily humiliated by it) – was publicly cast aside. The enemy which for decades could not be acknowledged or openly addressed for fear of retribution from the Arab public was now to be accepted as a partner in the shaping of a peaceful Middle East. For an entire generation nurtured on, and traumatised by, the unbearable injustice of the loss of Palestine, the image of Arab and Israeli together in the chandeliered splendour of a Madrid palace was hard to stomach.

The symbolism of the Madrid conference was particularly galling to Syrians for whom Palestine was not just a sister Arab country but innate to their historical and national lore – as much a part of their country as any other province but one that had been artificially carved out of geographical Syria. Nevertheless, having crossed the Rubicon Assad and his government tried to make the best of a hand that had been weakened, as they saw it, by the machinations of others, namely the Israelis, the Americans and those Arabs who lacked the grit of national solidarity. Through the early stages of the bilateral talks that followed the launch of the Madrid 'process' Damascus held on to the hope that there would be at least a modicum of coordination between the Arab delegations as they struggled, individually, with the negotiating agenda. However, it was not long before the courses charted in Madrid ran aground. Very little progress was reported from the proceedings, either of the bilateral negotiations of track one or the multilateral forums of track two. What the majority of the participants did not know was that, behind the scenes, talks were taking place in the utmost secrecy between the Israelis and the PLO, in Norway. They resulted in the announcement in early September 1993 of an agreement between the government of Israel and the Palestine Liberation Organisation that would mean a complete upheaval of the rules of engagement as they had stood between the two adversaries. Israel would recognise the PLO as the official representative of the Palestinian people and the PLO would renounce its armed struggle, recognise Israel's legitimacy and agree to pursue its aims diplomatically within the context of bilateral Israeli-Palestinian negotiations.

The Oslo Accord was given Washington's wholehearted blessing. This was vividly epitomised in a now famous, symbolic handshake between Yasser Arafat and Yitzhak Rabin on the

White House lawn. The shock of the announcement, however, had destroyed Syria's remaining hopes of exercising control, or even serious influence, over the Palestinian leadership or of maintaining the flimsy appearance of a unified Arab stand in relation to negotiations with Israel. To make matters even worse, Jordan used the pretext of Oslo to conclude its own peace with Israel, signing a treaty on 26 October 1994. Syria was forced to acknowledge that it had been outmanoeuvred yet again. As with the war of 1973 it felt let down by the Arabs and by empty – particularly American – promises. Having reached the heights of regional and even international prestige from the stance it had taken on Iraq's invasion of Kuwait, Syria was now in danger of being marginalised once again as first Arafat and then King Hussein took central stage in Middle Eastern affairs. Assad had to confront the fact that Syria had once again been isolated and forced to act alone in trying to achieve an honourable outcome to the negotiations into which it was now locked. All was not lost, however, and it must have been clear to Assad that he still had some useful cards to play.

One of these was the fact generally acknowledged, not least by the US, that without the imprimatur of Syria there could never be a credible, stable or comprehensive peace in the region. This received wisdom was commonly expressed in the dictum: 'no war without Egypt; no peace without Syria.' Assad was also confident in his country's well-entrenched and unchallenged hegemonic presence in Lebanon. By virtue of that presence combined with its heavy influence on Hezbollah – the growing and effective resistance force in southern Lebanon – Syria was in a position to have the final say regarding the fate of Israel's volatile northern frontier. Therefore, while feeling the pressure of being left almost alone in making a deal, Damascus still had the capacity to prove at least a spoiler at the negotiating table should its interests be completely ignored. Ironically, now that the Palestinians had chosen to go it alone Assad and his negotiating team, with foreign minister Farouk Al Sharaa at its helm, sensed a freedom they had previously lacked. The issue of Palestine and its future had been the foremost consideration, while other matters, including even the Golan, were of secondary importance. After Oslo, however, Syria's stance visibly changed. Sharaa and other spokesmen were now talking openly of a bilateral deal with the Israelis, irrespective of the totemic loyalty given to the Palestinian cause. Their new motto was 'full peace for full withdrawal,' implying that a separate, bilateral peace treaty was now on offer to Israel, divorced from any Palestinian or broadly pan-Arab encumbrance. The condition was total withdrawal from the Golan Heights captured in the 1967 war and unilaterally annexed by Israel in 1981.

The remainder of the 1990s witnessed a number of serious attempts to conclude a peace agreement between Syria and Israel, and the American administration, under President Clinton, was fully committed to that end. Two summit meetings took place between Clinton and Assad in 1994, in Geneva in January and Damascus in October. Clinton arrived at the latter with what he claimed was a game changer: a verbal commitment from the Israeli Prime Minister Yitzhak Rabin that in exchange for peace and agreed security arrangements his country was prepared to withdraw fully from the Golan, to the armistice lines that formed the frontier with Syria prior to the 1967 war. Clinton assured Assad that Rabin had allowed him to hold that pledge in reserve, pending agreement on the accompanying security and political arrangements that would form the full peace treaty package. To Syrian ears this amounted to the concession they were seeking: a commitment to full withdrawal once agreement on security arrangements and timetables was reached. What became known as 'Rabin's deposit' triggered a surge of diplomatic activity, including regular talks between the Syrian ambassador in Washington, Walid Muallem (later to become foreign minister) and his Israeli counterpart, Itamar Rabinovitch. The momentum thus achieved led to high-level discussions, held under American auspices, in Washington in December 1994 between a Syrian military delegation, led by the army chief of staff, General Hikmat Shehabi, and an Israeli team led by the chief of staff, General Ehud Barak. The discussions were largely confined to the issue of the security arrangements that would accompany the peace agreement. The Syrian delegation arrived well armed with documentation and maps – proof that they were serious at reaching detailed understandings. The Israelis appeared to be caught off-guard by the degree of preparedness of the Syrian negotiators, possibly having underestimated their counterparts' sincerity in their approach to the talks. The negotiations eventually failed when the Syrians rejected the Israelis' insistence on a ground surveillance outpost, manned by their military, to remain on Syrian soil after withdrawal. Throughout the process the Syrians had felt uncomfortable at the Israelis' almost exclusive focus on the security aspects of an eventual deal and their obfuscation over the commitment to withdraw fully to the pre-1967 border.

Following the impasse the American administration continued to press for a resumption of negotiations. The secretary of state, Warren Christopher, and the head of Middle East policy at the state department, Dennis Ross, undertook repeated trips to Damascus and Tel Aviv. These renewed efforts seemed to bear fruit when agreement was reached on a key framework document concerning the 'principles and objectives' of the security arrangements that would underpin a peace settlement that both the Israelis and Syrians were now officially ready to accept. The document contained points such as demilitarised zones on both sides and limitations on force deployment, as well as early warning systems. With the aim of putting flesh on the bones of these preliminary understandings a further round of talks took place in the summer of 1995 between a Syrian delegation headed by General Shehabi and an Israeli delegation headed by General Amnon Lipkin-Shahak, who had replaced Ehud Barak as Israeli chief of staff. The two teams struggled with the devil in the detail of the framework document, particularly over questions such as the nature and positioning of the early warning systems. And the Syrians remained concerned at the Israelis' evasiveness about the issue of their full withdrawal from the Golan. Nonetheless a mood of cautious optimism took hold in the months through to the autumn of 1995, and the expectation of a breakthrough agreement was on many a mind of those involved. Indeed, Rabinovitch, who had been talking to his Syrian counterpart in Washington over a prolonged period, sounded very positive about the prospect of a deal with Syria when speaking at a meeting in London, attended by the author. There was a memorable caveat, however: a peace agreement between the Israeli and Syrian states would not mean the end of the struggle for dominance in the Levant. 'The Syrians have won in Lebanon,' he asserted, adding that that country was now 'within the Syrian patrimony;' the next battleground, as he foresaw it, was 'the Jordanian/Palestinian arena.'

Any optimism turned out to be misplaced. Events in and around Palestine and Israel were soon to bring to a grinding halt any progress in Syrian-Israeli negotiations. Tensions had been rising as a result of an increase in violent Palestinian resistance to the Israeli occupation. Suicide operations by the Islamist groups Hamas and Islamic Jihad were met with Israel's trademark ferocity. Their retaliatory attacks were often denounced as disproportionate, and collective punishment – targeting civilians – was frequently meted out. The Israeli government was now habitually in hock to minority parties with growing hawkish tendencies, and, given the hardening of the public mood, it was reluctant to take the plunge and sign a treaty with Syria that meant giving up the Golan. Rabin's Labour-led government, considered moderate within the broad spectrum of Israeli politics, was ironically hamstrung by the fact that the bulk of Israeli settlers in the Golan were Labour Party supporters, in contrast to the right-wing settlers populating the West Bank. Yet in American, and even Syrian, eyes Rabin was still considered the best chance of achieving peace with Syria. Less a politician and more a geostrategist, he understood the central importance of a peace treaty with Damascus for Israel's long-term future and its relationship with the wider Arab world.

If a moment could be singled out as having been pivotal in determining the fate of a Syrian-Israeli peace, then it was when Rabin was gunned down at a rally in Israel on 4 November 1995. The assassin, a right-wing Israeli activist, Yigal Amir, put paid to a phase of negotiations between the two parties that had achieved a good deal of progress on the path to 'full peace for full withdrawal' – the objective that could finally end the most entrenched of enmities in the region. Shimon Peres, who replaced Rabin as premier, initially seemed keen to build on the record of his predecessor and made public declarations in support of concluding a peace with Syria, which he regarded as opening the door to peace with the whole of the Arab world. Talks continued in Washington between teams headed by the two ambassadors, and Warren Christopher resumed his shuttle trips between Tel Aviv and Damascus, marking his seventeenth voyage when he arrived in Damascus in February 1996. But events on the ground were producing their own violent momentum, both in southern Lebanon, with the intensification of the Hezbollah resistance campaign, and in the Palestinian-Israeli vortex, where a series of assassinations of Hamas and Islamic Jihad leaders by Israel led to vengeful reprisals through deadly suicide bomb attacks. Amid the rising tensions Peres made the surprise announcement of early Knesset elections, adding a further element of uncertainty into the gathering doubt, as seen from Damascus, of the feasibility of a deal with a leadership in Tel Aviv unsure of its own bearings. The Americans were still pushing hard for a settlement to bolster Clinton's position ahead of the forthcoming presidential elections there. Secretary of State Christopher pressed Assad on the idea of a meeting with Peres that could provide a strong impetus to the negotiations and strengthen the hand of the latter in the Israeli elections. Assad would not budge, insisting that such a meeting could only happen once a peace treaty was agreed and signed.

The final coup de grâce to any Assad-Peres deal came in the spring of 1996 when Israel launched its Grapes of Wrath offensive in Lebanon that resulted in much bloodshed and destruction in Syria's neighbour and de facto protégé state. The fighting finally ended in an agreement known as the April Understanding, with Syria playing a leading role, along with the other parties to the accord – the United States, France, Lebanon and Israel – in establishing 'rules of engagement' for the conflict in southern Lebanon. Banning belligerents (the Israeli army and Hezbollah) from targeting civilian areas, the understanding was seen as a boost for Syria's regional influence as well as marking Hezbollah's arrival as an internationally acknowledged force to be reckoned with. Despite this significant indicator of Syrian regional power it could no longer be translated into extra muscle in the context of negotiations for a permanent peace treaty with Israel as Peres had all but given up on that front. When he lost the election that year and was replaced by the arch-hardliner Benjamin Netanyahu, leader of the Likud, any prospect for peace with Syria was firmly on ice.

Syria's domestic scene, meanwhile, was dominated by the issue of succession, as Hafez Assad became increasingly frail. It was common knowledge that his son Bashar was being carefully groomed for the top job, and the topic of familial inheritance was gaining currency despite its collision with the republican and revolutionary premises of Baathism. His elder brother having died in a car crash in 1994, Bashar was now rising swiftly through the military ranks in order to enhance his legitimacy. He also assumed the presidency of the newly formed Syrian Computer Society – a pioneering, modernising institution that spoke to the aspiring younger generation. Even more importantly Bashar was charged with overseeing the all-important 'Lebanese file,' previously in the hands of the vice-president, Abdul Halim Khaddam. The move signalled a decline in the influence of an old guard that might have held ambitions of power in a post-Hafez Syria. Throughout this period pressure was maintained on Israel through the support given to Hezbollah, both directly and by the use of Damascus as an entrepôt for Iranian logistical and military supplies on their way to southern Lebanon. Many of Syria's detractors in Lebanon, however, pointed to the sharp incongruity of Syria fuelling the flames of resistance to Israeli occupation in neighbouring Lebanon while another occupation, that of the Golan, was met with complete tranquillity. It was clearer than ever that Syria's strategy was to leverage the activities of its ally Hezbollah for its own interests in regard to the Golan but with far less risk of a direct and costly showdown with Israel. The official narrative spoke of the joining of the two tracks (Lebanon-Israel and Syria-Israel) to reflect another famous Assad refrain: 'one people within two states.'

Before the century was over a new but ultimately ephemeral attempt was made to revive the Syrian-Israeli peace talks. It followed the election in 1999 of a Labour-led government in Israel under Ehud Barak, which many interpreted as offering hope for a renewal of talks and the possibility of a more moderate approach by Tel Aviv to a peace deal. Such hopes were given a boost when Barak and Assad publicly exchanged relatively warm acknowledgements. This was a first by Assad, who had never been known to express anything but negative views of the perennial Israeli enemy. After a round of preliminary talks the stage was set for a meeting at the highest level. On 15 December 1999 an unprecedented encounter took place in Washington between a Syrian delegation led by the foreign minister, Farouk Al Sharaa, and an Israeli delegation headed by Prime Minister Ehud Barak. The Syrians were hoping that Barak would renew the commitments made by Yitzhak Rabin regarding a readiness to withdraw fully from the Golan, but neither at this round of talks nor at their resumption early in the new year was he forthcoming on this crucial point. The Syrians claimed that, while much progress was achieved at the talks on such issues as security and future relations, the major stumbling block was Israel's 'lack of seriousness' in defining the line behind which they would withdraw. The process broke down amid speculation that Barak had chosen to play it safe by stalling proceedings rather than commit to giving up the whole of the Golan in exchange for peace – and facing the wrath of his political enemies and much of Israeli opinion.

Clinton, however, had not entirely given up. Presumably aware of Assad's faltering health he made one last, desperate move to salvage that in which he had invested so much and broker the elusive deal. He contacted the Syrian president to inform him that he had some good news in his possession, which he wanted to communicate to him at a summit meeting. Believing that this could mean a breakthrough on the vexed question of Israel's full withdrawal from the Golan the Syrian leader agreed to meet Clinton in Geneva. The meeting convened on 26 March 2000 and, as the Syrian delegation listened attentively, Clinton unveiled the big news: a pledge by Barak to withdraw close to the armistice line of 4 June 1967 save for a distance of five hundred metres beyond the shores of the Sea of Galilee. This was not what Assad had hoped to hear. He had always insisted on the Syrians having territorial access to the Sea of Galilee, as had been the case prior to 1967. Indeed he was fond of recollecting that, as a youth, he used to dip his feet in that lake. Even Barak's offer to transfer territory from surrounding areas in compensation could not dissuade the Syrians from feeling that they had come to Geneva fed with false expectations. Assad decided on the spot that there was nothing on offer worth pursuing and the chapter was finally closed on a ten-year effort to achieve a Syrian-Israel peace. In a further twist Barak ordered a full Israeli withdrawal from Lebanon, without negotiation with Syria, with the aim of pulling from Syrian hands a strong card in their regional bargaining power. Of course Israel's withdrawal was conducted under duress, Hezbollah, over the years, having taken heavy toll of its forces of occupation, but the timing and method of the withdrawal also had much to do with discomfiting Assad. The Syrians hailed that event as a great victory, but the fact remained that they stood to lose ground in the geopolitical stakes as a result of yet another Arab frontline being objectively pacified while leaving the Golan high and dry.

Hafez Assad died on 10 June 2000, ten days after Israel's unilateral withdrawal from Lebanon. He had straddled Syria and the region around it like a colossus and achieved for his country a position of influence and power unprecedented in the modern age. After a quarter of a century of turmoil following its independence Syria was moulded into a new and stable shape by a leader with undoubted political and planning skills, as well as the ruthlessness to pursue a single-minded agenda. On coming to power in 1970 he ruled over a population of six million. By the time of his death thirty years later he had remained in control of over sixteen million. But it all came at a huge price: the suppression of a once flourishing political culture that placed Syria as a leading intellectual centre of the Arab world, the building of a massive bureaucratic state, with scarcely hidden, near total authority exercised by shadowy security agencies, and the silencing of all voices of dissent. Notwithstanding the important expansion of services and infrastructure into hitherto neglected rural and deprived areas, the policy of snuffing out the Syrian entrepreneurial spirit in favour of bloated and inefficient government-run establishments, combined with the growth of corruption and official nepotism, created an economic morass. The darkest of Assad's legacies, however, dates back to the mid-1970s and early 1980s when he resorted to unprecedented brutality in beating back the, albeit ruthless, Muslim Brotherhood insurgency. Whether it occurred to him at the time or not he was sowing the seeds of an inevitable sectarian conflict that would rear its ugly head in Syria's blood-soaked future. Above all, Assad tried but failed in his most determined of endeavours: to secure an 'honourable' peace that would repatriate the Golan and eradicate the shame of 1967. Once well within reach, during the last ten years of his life it was not to be. This was largely due to Israel's domestic political dynamic, which, with the possible exception of Rabin, delivered leaders in hock to extremist political parties wielding disproportionate power. Assad, meanwhile, though genuinely ready for peace, showed little appreciation of imagery in portraying that willingness. In an age of public diplomacy he ignored the potential power of words and gestures that could arguably have given a crucial boost to his mission.

Notes

1. The Egyptians attacking from the west had wanted a much later time when the sun would be shining in the face of the Israelis. The Syrians, striking in the opposite direction, had pressed for an earlier attack to favour them in the same way. The timing that was finally agreed was a compromise between the two.
2. It must be noted that this long quiescence is today under severe threat from the bitter fighting raging between various factions, including jihadists, Hezbollah and Syrian government forces.
3. The attack had in fact been the work of the Abu Nidal Organisation – a Palestinian terror group that was a sworn enemy of Arafat's PLO, whom Israel had claimed to hold responsible.
4. An allusion to Assad's habit of keeping visitors engaged in negotiations for lengthy periods without permitting a toilet break.

CHAPTER TEN

2000-2011: From Reform to Firestorm

Arising from a sincere faith in our country, in our people and in their creative capacities and vitality, and keen to interact positively with all serious initiatives for reform, [we assert that] it is vital today to establish a comprehensive dialogue between all citizens and all social classes and political forces ... in order to encourage the development of civil society – a society based on individual freedom, human rights and citizenship – and the establishment of a state of justice and rights – a state for all its people, without favour or exception ...

From the 'Statement of 1000' (referring to a thousand Syrian intellectuals, artists, writers and civil-rights activists) released on 9 January 2001.

During the last years of Hafez Assad's rule many observers were fretting over the succession. Even sworn enemies like the Israelis and many other adversaries in Lebanon, Palestine and elsewhere in the region and the wider world who had crossed swords with the 'Lion of Damascus' felt apprehensive at the prospect of a vacuum following his demise. They had got used to his obstinacy but also to his strangely comfortable presence as an assured leader with whom they could ultimately do business, and who was able to deliver a notoriously unruly country. Having so effectively – and ruthlessly – reined in the passions of a people previously steeped in apparently anarchic politics, there was much doubt over the ability of a successor to follow in his footsteps. Any apprehension was enhanced when comparison was made between the original heir apparent, the older (deceased) Basel, and the younger Bashar. The former had been extroverted and charismatic while the latter appeared ungainly and withdrawn. Impressions were rife that Bashar was being thrust into a limelight for which he was ill prepared and ill-disposed – destined to walk in the shadow of the venerated Basel.

Despite the initially guarded assessments Bashar was gradually able to forge a position of status and influence helped by the fact that in his final years his father assiduously promoted him and drove him forward. Bashar rapidly rose through the army ranks to become a major in the general staff, and by 1998 was charged with the highly prized 'Lebanese portfolio,' hitherto firmly in the hands of two future rivals to the country's top job: Vice President Abdul Halim Khaddam, and the army chief of staff, Major General Hikmat Shehabi. This gave Bashar the opportunity to launch himself as an empowered political actor on the Arab stage and even on the international scene. An early self-appointed mentor was President Chirac of France. Early in 2000 Bashar was a guest in Paris and was afforded much ceremony, including a high-profile visit to the Elysée Palace.

The other image that Bashar carefully crafted (or had crafted for him) was that of moderniser and reformer. Having spent time as a postgraduate student of ophthalmology in London, and thus being exposed to the West in a way that set him culturally apart from the closed world of his father, Bashar emerged as the champion of the digital revolution in Syria. He took over from his late brother the chairmanship of the nascent Syrian Computer Society and surrounded himself with a coterie of enthusiasts of the new electronic and Internet age. He also established close links with those advocating a more liberal economic system in an attempt to establish a network independent of the rigid ideologues of the ruling Baath Party. By the close of the twentieth century qualms about the uncertainty of the succession and the capability of the likely successor eased, with Bashar appearing surer footed in his ability to handle the challenges of leadership. Many also started to believe that he could not only maintain continuity and stability but also steer Syria in a new, open and reformed direction. Many who attended his father's funeral, such as the American secretary of state Madeleine Albright, had one eye on the formalities of the occasion but another on 'bonding' with the anointed successor.

Within Syria the transition from father to son was seamless. With hardly a murmur of dissent the rubber-stamp parliament, or people's assembly, conveniently voted unanimously and swiftly to amend the constitution: the minimum age for a president-elect was reduced from forty years to thirty-four – Bashar's exact age. Just as smoothly went the other formalities: the nomination as secretary general of the Baath Party, the promotion to the country's highest military rank of *Fariq*

(Lieutenant General) and commander-in-chief of the armed forces, and, finally, the referendum recording ninety-seven per cent in favour (slightly below the figure regularly attained by the late president). Most Syrians, it can be said, were not too disconcerted with what to outside observers must have been seen as a mockery of electoral practice. Having endured decades of hard repression but wary nonetheless of a return to the instability that had preceded it they were looking with some optimism to an orderly and managed change for the better. 'Development based on continuity' was the new mantra.

In his inaugural address that July of 2000 Bashar did not disappoint. While naturally paying fulsome tribute to his father's legacy he nevertheless pointed to the need for clear adjustments to a system that no longer met the needs of the age. He spoke of the necessity for new ideas and practices and for the toleration of alternative viewpoints. Although short of specific policy detail the speech was seen as a clear sign that reform was on the agenda. A new era seemed to be dawning and an incipient flowering of political activity soon emerged. Forums and debating clubs mushroomed all over the country while a 'petition of the hundred,' signed by leading figures from the intelligentsia, academia, literature and the arts, publicly called for major structural change in the system of government, including the lifting of martial law (in operation since the Baathist coup of 1963). Several months later a more radical document, this time bearing one thousand signatures, upped the political ante.

The Damascus Spring, as this period of socio-political enlightenment was to become known, was initially tolerated and even briefly encouraged by the young president. A sign of semi-official approval came in the form of the government-owned daily newspaper, *Al Thawra*, devoting column inches to opposition viewpoints – an unprecedented occurrence in Baathist-ruled Syria. Also, for the first time in decades, privately owned newspapers were licensed, with the renowned caricaturist Ali Ferzat granted permission to publish a satirical magazine, *Al Domari* (The Lamplighter).[1] But it was not too long before the old guard struck back. Led by such figures as the vice president, Abdul Hamid Khaddam – later, ironically, to become a defector and opponent of Bashar – a campaign was launched against those with 'foreign connections' wanting to destabilise the state and harm the 'embedded values' of country and society. 'We are in danger of becoming a second Algeria,' warned Khaddam. Independent political forums were closed down and activists hounded and arrested. The editor of *Al Thawra* was dismissed, to be replaced by a loyal apparatchik. Basing its action on a trumped-up technicality the ministry of information withdrew the licence it had granted Ferzat's magazine. From an all-too-brief breath of spring Syria returned to the long winter of political hibernation. The fact that the leopard of state repression had not changed its spots and still clung to the well-tried, brutal – and hitherto successful – method of dealing with dissent was evident in 2004 when a protest movement by the long-oppressed Kurds in the northeast of the country was violently put down by the unreconstructed and all-powerful *mukhabarat*.

Yet Bashar was still able to call on the reservoir of goodwill and high expectation that accompanied his early presidency. The population at large continued to believe in his reformist mindset, blaming the retrograde repression on the old guard, and even on the precipitate actions of some of those advocating swift reforms. They saw in Bashar's sidelining and removal of a number of figures representing the past, and the coming to prominence in his entourage of younger technocrats and innovators, a promise of gradual, if not immediate, change. However, Bashar himself was hardly enigmatic in his statements. The message was clear: political change was off the agenda; the priority had to be the economy and addressing the problem of the inefficient bureaucracy administering the state. A model of the way forward was soon being trumpeted by regime spokesmen: that of China, where radical economic reform coexisted with rigid adherence to the political status quo.

True to this doctrine steps were soon taken to introduce a measure of change to an economic system over which the state exercised a hegemonic and deeply inefficient presence. Quietly dropping the 'socialism' from its discourse the new cabinet formed by Bashar seemed eager to cosy up to a private sector which, until then, had been a reluctant partner in shoring up the ailing economy. New enterprises started to form, including a well-publicised first in the shape of a holding company through which Syrian expatriate and Saudi capital committed itself to direct investment in the private sector of the country. In June 2001 a lavish conference was held at the Dorchester Hotel in London under the banner 'Syria: a New Dawn for Investment.' Funded by leading expatriate Syrian entrepreneurs,[2] the conference hosted several Syrian cabinet ministers as well as top consultants and leaders of Syria's chambers of commerce and industry. The keynote speaker at a special gala dinner was the Syrian foreign minister, Farouk Al Sharaa. The message was that Syria was open for business and the world was being invited to take advantage of the new emerging market.

That message, which echoed round the chandeliered opulence of the Dorchester, was it turned out much overstated, as those who took it seriously and ventured to test the reality in Syria were soon to discover. Behind the slogans of a new opening was a solid wall of bureaucratic obfuscation and rampant corruption. Nevertheless there was still cause to believe that real change was on the way. For the first time in over forty years private banks were given licence to operate and the Damascus stock market was revived. Having lagged behind all of its neighbours Syria now had its own mobile phone network (the lucrative operating franchise having been controversially granted to a company owned by a cousin of the president) and a spreading Internet network. Soon to follow were measures to simplify and rationalise the foreign exchange trade and allow more convertibility for the Syrian *lira*. Another sign of the break with the past was the granting of permits to establish private universities, and a number were soon in place across the country. This process of change was driven, in part, by a liberalising guru chosen by Bashar to oversee the makeover from a socialist to a social market economy. First as head of the state planning commission and later as deputy prime minister for economic affairs, Abdullah Dardari became known as the face of the new, liberalising Syria.[3]

However, behind the scenes there was a quiet power struggle going on between Dardari and his supporters within and outside government and those within the ruling party as well as the unreconstructed state bureaucracy who were not comfortable with the new direction. Some of that discomfort arose out of genuinely held ideology and concern for the interests of the majority of the population should the process lead to cuts in welfare and state subsidies relating to the basic needs of a growing underprivileged class. Also standing in the way of reform were the barons of the state-run enterprises and state-controlled trade unions with less edifying concerns over the future of their own vested interests. For a number of years the debate over the economic future of the country was maintained. Advocates of reform and those opposed were able to engage freely through the media and other forums in the discussions – a far cry from the situation when it came to ideas for political change.

Most importantly the growing trend towards economic and financial liberation did not have the positive effect of re-establishing the vigorous, competitive and entrepreneurial middle class of the 1950s that had rendered Syria an exemplar of 'third world' indigenously led growth. Instead of directing capital into long-term productive sectors, such as industry and infrastructure, most of the new breed of investors, whether Syrian or from the Gulf, were interested in short-term and speculative ventures into real estate and forays into the new, globalised consumerism. Worse, even in those very areas that witnessed the greatest inflow of capital, corruption and nepotism were rife, giving a flagrant example of the kind of crony capitalism that plagued many an emerging market in the surrounding region. In Syria, one can even argue, that cronyism reached new heights with the circle of beneficiaries being largely restricted to the president's immediate family. Those in the military, security and intelligence nexus – the mainstay of the regime – were given the lion's share of the remaining available opportunities. As time went on, however, and with the liberation process becoming more institutionalised, the doors to the closed market started to open to a wider constituency. Nevertheless it remained the case that anyone with a promising new project in mind had not only to grease the palms of senior bureaucrats – even up to ministers on occasion – but also to have as a partner (silent or openly) a recognised member of the elite plutocratic club.

While the new president's agenda was dominated by tortuous and disjointed efforts to revamp the economy he also had to deal right from the start with urgent strategic and geopolitical challenges swarming around the country he had inherited. These were enormous for any Syrian ruler; how much more so for a yet untried young person thrust into that leadership role? The long and painstaking attempt at achieving peace with Israel and liberating the occupied Golan had collapsed a mere few months before the death of Hafez, and Bashar could conceivably have benefitted from the international goodwill that greeted his nascent presidency had he been able to revive that process. Nothing could have boosted his status locally and regionally more than delivering the peace that had eluded his father and raising the national flag over the freed territory. Unfortunately, events in Israel and the occupied territories during that first year of his presidency obviated any such option. In September Ariel Sharon, the most notoriously hawkish of Israel's politicians, made a highly provocative visit to the Haram Al Sharif in occupied East Jerusalem. The visit set off a chain of incidents culminating in a second Palestinian intifada, which in turn led to Sharon becoming the prime minister of Israel. In such an overwrought context any possibility of returning to the Syrian-Israeli negotiating track was out of the question.

The mothballing of the Syrian-Israeli peace process, apart from depriving Bashar of the kudos he could have acquired from regaining the Golan, also had the crucial effect of nullifying Washington's interest in engaging with Damascus. As the previous decade had shown the main reason the administrations of, firstly, George Bush Senior and then Bill Clinton had tried so hard to court Hafez Assad was the anticipation of his being able to reach an agreement with Israel, thereby completing the 'circle of peace' in the region, after Egypt, Jordan and the PLO had signed up. Both the Syrian and American leaderships seemed to regard any improvement in their bilateral relations as of secondary concern (Washington had officially placed Syria on the list of states sponsoring terrorism in the mid-eighties) and an outcome that could derive in future from the success of the peace process. At the turn of the century, under the new president, George W. Bush, and with that process on hold, few in the Republican administration any longer felt the need to continue a dialogue with Syria. Very early in his presidency Bashar would have sensed the new cold-shouldering mood, especially once the brazenly pro-Israel neocons were starting to call the shots in Washington and, egged on by Sharon, had in their sights a regime that, in their minds, stood in the face of their new and aggressive Middle Eastern strategy.

For a brief period following the seismic reverberations from the terror attacks of September 2001 there was a mellowing of the Damascus-Washington relationship. Bashar and other spokesmen for the Syrian government were quick to condemn the atrocity. Syrian intelligence also offered support to American counterparts in the hunt for Al Qaida operatives, leading to the saving of many American lives, as US officials would later acknowledge. Nonetheless, little serious effort was expended in building on this cooperation in the wider political and strategic spheres. The American administration was subjected to heavy pressure by Sharon to encompass within its 'war on terror' Palestinian 'terror,' as he saw it. As far as Israeli propaganda was concerned there was no difference between Al Qaida on the one hand and Hamas, Hezbollah and Islamic Jihad on the other. Needless to say, such a message resonated well with the neocons who had the ear of George W. – one more reason why any serious rapprochement with Syria remained off the agenda. Bashar himself would not, or could not, be of help; when pushed by reporters to criticise as acts of terror Palestinian suicide attacks against civilians he would not be drawn into doing so. Syria's approach was clear: acts of resistance to occupation could never be equated with those of international terror as practised by Al Qaida.

Relations with Washington became even edgier as its attention began shifting, somewhat incongruously, from the war on terror to regime change in Baghdad. There was no evidence that the Iraqi regime, albeit brutal towards its own people, had any connection to Al Qaida or the attacks of 11 September. In the build-up to the American-led invasion that became known as the second Gulf War, Syria's leaders were caught on the horns of a dilemma. On the one hand there was the bitter enmity that, until recent years, had existed between the two Baathist states. Would there be a strategic if cynical opportunity presenting itself with the toppling of Saddam even by the detested forces of the imperial West? Damascus's close ally Tehran certainly thought so and was very muted in its approach to the impending invasion of Iraq. It was planning very quietly to reap the benefit of regime change in the neighbouring country by installing its own political and sectarian allies in a future free of Saddam. However, in the early years of Bashar's rule Syria had mended a lot of its fences with Baghdad. Especially profitable for the Syrian economy was the upsurge in bilateral trade reaching into the billions of dollars. Some of that trade was legal, and Syria was well placed to make use of the 'oil for food' programme that the United Nations had put in place to alleviate the humanitarian suffering caused in Iraq by the draconian sanctions imposed in the wake of the first Gulf War. But much of it also involved illegal, sanctions-busting transactions – a market cornered by the corrupt circle that already had a stranglehold on the domestic Syrian economy. Allowing under-the-counter commercial exchange was one more method of rewarding, and maintaining, the loyalty to the government of Syria's intelligence and security barons and their associates in the docile business community. The United States voiced strong opposition to the burgeoning economic and trade ties between Damascus and Baghdad which were reported to include the opening by Syria of the Kirkuk-Banias oil pipeline which had been closed by Damascus following the rupture of its relationship with Baghdad in the 1980s. In 2001 the US secretary of state, Colin Powell, visited Damascus with the precise mission of raising the issue of the pipeline. Syria insisted that it had opened the pipeline for 'testing purposes' – an explanation dismissed by the American side.

The attitude in Damascus to the preparations for an invasion of Iraq was further influenced by the view that the successful toppling of Saddam could trigger other regime change ventures, in a domino effect, with Syria being next. By that time there was no shortage of voices in Washington upping the ante and calling for an open confrontation with the Syrian regime. The anti-Syrian lobby was led by the two major hardliners in Bush's administration: Vice President Dick Cheney and Secretary of Defence Donald Rumsfeld. Increasingly active at the same time in Washington and particularly within the congress was a growing and slick Lebanese lobby, given active support by the all-powerful Israeli lobby, that owed its allegiance to the anti-Syrian and mostly Maronite opposition starting to flex its muscle in Lebanon and calling for a withdrawal of Syrian forces from the country. The Maronite patriarch inside Lebanon, Cardinal Sfeir, and the ousted General Michel Aoun, in exile in France, were the focal points of that campaign. It ultimately led to the passing in congress in 2002 of the Syrian Accountability Act (signed into law by President Bush in 2004): a measure that imposed a wide range of sanctions and restrictions on economic and financial dealings with Syria.[4]

Given its known position and rhetoric on the march towards war on Iraq, some observers were surprised at the vote cast by Syria in favour of Resolution 1441 adopted by the UN Security Council on 8 November 2002. The strongly worded resolution demanded that Iraq cooperate fully with the international team of inspectors charged with investigating whether the country was in possession of weapons of mass destruction. It also included a thinly veiled warning of a resort to force should that cooperation not be forthcoming. Syria tried to explain its position by claiming that its vote helped avert an immediate recourse to war: a fatuous contention as, a few months later and on the basis of a dubious claim that the resolution gave them legitimacy to act, America and Britain launched their invasion of Iraq. Bashar now had to come to terms with a massive geostrategic challenge that required the shrewdest of handling. Instead of playing a waiting game as other players were doing – especially, as noted earlier, in the case of Iran – the Syrian president decided to play to his own gallery and wider Arab public opinion by loudly denouncing the imperialist aggression on a sister Arab country, promising, through his official spokesmen, to help defeat it. Soon reports were spreading of fighters – including many jihadists – assembling in Syria and being provided access across the frontier into Iraqi territory. American spokesmen, most forcefully Donald Rumsfeld, rushed to accuse Syria of complicity not only in allowing fighters across the border but in sending arms to support the incipient insurgency. Other allegations related to Syria giving safe haven to leading Iraqi Baathists and even of hiding on its territory smuggled weapons of mass destruction that the invading allies, to their extreme embarrassment, were unable to find in Iraq. Further charges included the transfer of much of the reserves of the fallen Iraqi regime into the Syrian coffers.

The cacophony of sabre-rattling emanating from Washington certainly rattled the nerves of Syria's leaders who started to sound more subdued in their public pronouncements regarding the war being waged against their neighbour. Having counted on Iraq's army being able to put up a long fight, thus giving second thoughts to those in Washington banking on a quick-fix regime change, they saw the early collapse of Saddam's rule as encouragement for those who now wanted to go for Syria. As a result the calls exhorting defiance and support to the heroic struggle against the US-led invasion gradually began to be replaced by disclaimers of any Syrian involvement with the armed resistance that had begun to grow in its eastern neighbour. There were now repeated assurances by spokesmen that the country was doing all it could to seal off its border with Iraq – a task rendered particularly difficult by the length of the border and the many easily accessible crossing points. These Syrian assertions of the right desire but limited capability did not cut much ice with the Americans. In May 2003 the US secretary of state, Colin Powell, visited Damascus again and by all accounts had an unfriendly encounter with President Bashar and his team. Powell was very explicit and stern in his demands: Syria should seal off its border and stop the flow of foreign fighters into Iraq as well as closing the offices in Damascus of Palestinian 'terror groups,' such as Hamas and Islamic Jihad. Having previously expressed some optimism over the impact of the visit the Syrians did not hide their resentment at what they regarded as a menacing tone adopted by Powell. Nonetheless, attempts were made to appear to respond to the American pressure, for example by persuading Palestinian operatives to lay low temporarily or declaring that their offices were mere information bureaux, as well as repeating the line that all was being done to stop any fighters from reaching Iraq. Yet it was all to no avail in halting a rise in American-Syrian tension that would continue through the years to come.

Relations with other major Western powers saw different and fluctuating trajectories. In the case of the United Kingdom, an encounter in Damascus between President Assad and Prime Minister Tony Blair following the attacks of 11 September received very bad press in Britain. Blair was pictured as the victim of a public humiliation by a haranguing Syrian president who had warned against military retaliation. A much better mood prevailed in December 2002 when Bashar, with his new wife – the glamorous, British-born Asma – paid an official visit to Britain. The couple were received by Queen Elizabeth in Buckingham Palace, and the media were generally positive in their reporting of the visit – the first by a serving Syrian president. Many observers believed at the time that it could prove to be a harbinger of a general qualitative lift in what had been a low-key and dormant relationship. Not long later this mood was reinforced by the announcement of the formation of the British Syrian Society (BSS). Chaired by Dr. Fawaz Akhras, the father-in-law of the Syrian president, and with leading figures from the Syrian community, as well as representatives from the British political establishment, chosen as directors, the BSS became a useful, unofficial vehicle, which, with the encouragement of both governments, helped to promote political, economic and cultural links between Britain and Syria. In Syria itself the BSS played the role of a pressure group, pushing for internal reforms in line with the stated objectives of the new president. Although there was much denunciation in Syria of Britain's role in the invasion of Iraq, the desire to improve relations with Britain overcame that hurdle and the appointment of a high-profile ambassador to London in 2004 was indicative of the importance that Damascus placed on its UK connection.[5]

But while the Damascus-London axis was showing signs of steady improvement the opposite was occurring on the Damascus-Paris engagement track. By the summer of 2004 the French president, Jacques Chirac, an early cheerleader for Bashar Assad, had grown averse to the Syrian leader. The reasons were complex and manifold: some observers pointed to Chirac having felt snubbed by promises of French political and economic eminence in the new Syria being forged by Bashar that were never upheld. More credibly, though, it was the influence being brought to bear on Chirac by the developments in Lebanon that turned him against Assad. New elections for a Lebanese president were due to be held later that year; yet in the face of strong protest by the Maronite establishment and a scarcely concealed negative reaction from the powerful Saudi- and French-backed Sunni prime minister, Rafic Hariri, Syria insisted on extending the presidency of its chosen protégé in Beirut, Emile Lahoud. In effect, Assad bluntly resorted to the instruments of control he could wield in Lebanon to bring about a constitutional amendment in the country's parliament that allowed for the forcing through of a three-year extension to Lahoud's term in office. The die had been cast and Bashar's gambit – an early demonstration of his headstrong judgement – would soon come back to haunt him. Meanwhile, Chirac and Bush, who had fallen out over the American-led invasion of Iraq, now found common cause in turning the screws on Assad. In a move that was said to have had Hariri's blessing, a joint French-American-sponsored resolution (number 1557) was adopted by the Security Council of the United Nations, demanding the withdrawal of Syrian forces from Lebanon.

The Syrians, and their allies in Lebanon, denounced the resolution. Assad spoke publicly and defiantly of a plot that stretched beyond the issue of Lahoud's presidency and went to the heart of the lofty national principles that defined Syria's role in Lebanon. In the latter itself a sharp cleavage had developed among supporters and opponents of Resolution 1557. Despite Hariri, and his supporters, having voted – under presumed duress – to extend Lahoud's presidency, he was widely seen as having been the secret driving force behind the resolution – a tag that many suspected would render him a doomed target. On Valentine's Day 2005 an explosion ripped through Hariri's motorcade as it was making its way through the streets of West Beirut, killing him and slaying and injuring many of his entourage. It was a cataclysmic moment in the modern history of Lebanon and its reverberations would be felt far and wide. Almost immediately fingers pointed in the direction of Damascus. No operation of this scale, level of sophistication and degree of planning, it was forcefully argued by Syria's opponents in Lebanon, could have been carried out without at least the tacit knowledge of the pervasive Syrian intelligence apparatus that directly or through its Lebanese surrogates was in effective command of internal security in the Lebanese capital. The loud voices of anger directed at Syria and its leader, Bashar, reached a crescendo. Beirut's main square filled with multitudes of protesters, heralding the dawn of the Cedar Revolution.

Although the Syrian government swiftly denied any responsibility for Hariri's murder, it was noticeable that no announcement of official condolences from the presidency was forthcoming. However, the Syrian vice president, Abdul Halim Khaddam, a known friend of Hariri, arrived in Beirut in a personal capacity to offer sympathy, and was subjected to some abuse from the ranks of the gathered crowd.[6] In the days and weeks that followed much was revealed (or claimed) about the background to Hariri's assassination – in particular concerning the final rancorous encounters that he had had with Bashar Assad in Damascus. The Lebanese leader, it was said, was subjected to a verbal bludgeoning, and to threats of Lebanon's being 'flattened' should he not go along with the decision taken by Bashar to extend the presidential term of Emile Lahoud.

The clamour became too much for the Syrian leader. In April he ordered a complete withdrawal of Syrian forces from Lebanon – a humiliation that no amount of window-dressing from official Syrian spokesmen could conceal. Syria's relations with the outside world also suffered, with the United States and France withdrawing their ambassadors from Damascus, and the European Union putting on hold any strengthening of ties. This was Bashar's worst moment since he had taken office, and criticism of his bad judgement in handling the situation in Lebanon, particularly in his dealings with Hariri, who had become the leading symbol of its Sunni community, appeared even among his supporters. The holding of the Baath Party's long-awaited 'regional' (i.e. country-specific) conference in Damascus early that summer was useful in its timing. It enabled Assad to project the promise of future reform and to rid the party of some of the old guard, who, in light of the recent debacle in Lebanon, would have been comparing his faltering policies with the much surer-footed performance of the father whom they had so loyally served. Also to the rescue of Assad came his main Lebanese ally, Hezbollah. The Party of God was quick to plant itself in opposition to the Cedar Revolution as far back as 8 March when it had succeeded in mobilising hundreds of thousands of its supporters and allies to mass in the streets of Beirut to thank Syria for the support it had given the people of Lebanon. That mass rally triggered a counter rally less than a week later by the proponents of the

Cedar Revolution, which resulted in the country splitting into '8 March' and '14 March' rival coalitions – a Lebanese political divide that remains until today.

Despite still being able to call on substantial support within Lebanon, Bashar and his government continued to feel the heat of the lasting and growing impact of Hariri's assassination. Strong momentum was developing behind a call to investigate and uncover the truth surrounding it, and the UN Security Council decided to set up a special commission of inquiry for the purpose. That autumn the preliminary report of the commission named leading figures in Syria, including Bashar's brother and commander of the elite fourth army division, Maher Assad, and his brother-in-law and head of intelligence, Assef Shawkat, as likely culprits in the planning of the operation to kill the Lebanese leader. The fortunes of Bashar and his leadership seemed at their lowest ebb. There were even hints of panic as the Syrian authorities, through the embassy in London, sought the urgent advice of British lawyers in an attempt to defend against what appeared to be inevitable criminal charges with grave political and strategic ramifications. Meanwhile inside Syria the regime was once again being challenged by the re-emergence of civil society movements. Several leading advocates of political and constitutional change united with human rights activists behind a programme named the Damascus Proclamation. The government reacted in typical fashion by denouncing it and accusing its supporters of following a foreign agenda. Several of the leaders were arrested in a clampdown reminiscent of the earlier quashing of the Damascus Spring.

The state of apprehension persisted well into the new year and questions continued to be raised as to the ability of the regime to withstand the pressure being applied to it by the West, as well as by Arab countries such as Saudi Arabia (the major patron, with the French president, Chirac, of the late Hariri). But a sudden event was to come to Bashar's rescue. In mid-July 2006 a group of Hezbollah fighters crossed into Israeli-held territory. They attacked and killed a number of Israeli soldiers and took two of the troops prisoner. The operation was bound to provoke a response, and it came with a vengeance. For the next three weeks Lebanon became engulfed in a mini-war that ravaged the country but also caused Israel to suffer if not defeat, at least a battlefield standoff – a complete break with the history of Arab-Israeli wars. Although more than a thousand Lebanese were killed and part of Lebanon's infrastructure devastated, Hezbollah could claim that, for once, an Arab force had stood up to the full fury of Israel's war machine and inflicted heavy losses, while fighting it to an honourable standstill. The party's leader, Hassan Nasrallah, certainly permitted an element of triumphalism to emerge as he proclaimed a victory ordained by the divine; yet even his adversaries within Lebanon found themselves grudgingly joining the chorus of plaudits. And it was not only in Lebanon. Across the Arab world Hezbollah, and especially its leader, became overnight heroes, with Nasrallah's portrait appearing in many streets and households. Remarkably, the fact that Hezbollah was patently Shiite, and resolutely pro-Iranian to boot, did little to dampen the enthusiasm of the mostly Sunni multitudes who now spoke of him almost as fervently as they had of Gamal Abdul Nasser in the past.

The Syrian president was not slow to bask in the glory being afforded to him through the success achieved by his close ally. From a state of near isolation he could now – with a good deal of credibility – claim credit for having been a strategic supporter of Hezbollah and the main conduit for the arms and resources that made its 'victory' possible. He had behind him the Arab street and could face down those Arab rulers who had sought to diminish and discredit him in the wake of Hariri's assassination. Some of those rulers, in particular the Saudi monarchy, had had the temerity, he declared, to voice criticism of Hezbollah at the height of the battles in Lebanon for its act of rashness in provoking the Israelis and bringing such retribution upon the Lebanese. Bashar decided that it was payback time and he relished the occasion. In a speech intended to pay tribute to the achievements of the Lebanese resistance he launched into a sharp invective against those Arab rulers who had timidly stood aside – indeed even taken the enemy's side – during the conflict that had just ended. In an affront that was to have the widest of resonance he accused those rulers of 'lacking manhood.' There was no hiding the fact that this was primarily intended as a reference to the King of Saudi Arabia. The outburst, another example of Bashar's precipitate approach to policy, would produce far-reaching repercussions as it set Syria's relations with the Saudis on a deep and lasting hostile course.

For the moment, however, Bashar was looking a winner. In his mind he had weathered the storm once again. The fallout from the Hariri affair was starting to recede and slowly but surely the regime was regaining its balance. By the time a referendum on a second presidential term was held in July 2007 (duly won by the usual ninety-nine per cent or so figure) the road to Damascus was once again being trodden by Western delegations. One such visit, organised by the British Syrian Society, gave a large parliamentary group from Britain the opportunity to meet the Syrian president. He was well on his way to full rehabilitation and that process was crowned by the hosting in Damascus of an Arab League summit in March 2008. In July that year Assad was a feted guest of the French president, Nicolas Sarkozy, at a parade marking Bastille Day. The following September Sarkozy in turn went to Damascus on an official visit, followed in November by the British foreign secretary, David Miliband. From America senior figures in congress started to arrive and the American government officially invited Syria to participate in the Annapolis Conference, which was intended to revive the Middle East peace process. Adding to the new, refurbished image of Bashar was the growing publicity surrounding Syria's first lady, Asma. Seen, especially by the British media, as holding deeply Western attributes and exerting a strong, modernising influence on her husband, she began to attain international celebrity status. She used it to good effect, not only to enhance the regime's portrayal but also to make improvements in the country that the doctrinaire Baathist regime would have found hard to swallow. This was especially the case in her championing of civil society and non-governmental bodies outside the framework of official authority. Although the new organisations – promoting Syrian culture as well as innovative approaches to rural social and educational life – steered clear of any attempt at political change, they represented a departure from long years of the state being the near sole purveyor of social and cultural services to the masses.

In contrast to the vicissitudes in the relationship between Bashar and the West, and some of his Arab neighbours, through the first decade of his rule one regional connection remained continually on the rise: that linking Syria with Turkey to the north. A process which had started with Hafez Assad in the late 1990s grew by leaps and bounds, on strategic, political and especially economic levels. Assad and the new Islamic-inclined Turkish leaders moved at a rapid pace to cement those links. While the process helped Syria through some of its worst periods of international isolation, it was not without a price.

Syrian industry, in particular, suffered as a result of its stronger and more advanced Turkish counterpart capturing heavy slices of the Syrian consumer market. Ignoring the lop-sided nature of the burgeoning economic relationship, Bashar exuded confidence as he spoke of Syria as the new hub of a multifaceted industrial, trade and energy vortex – the so-called 'region of the five seas,' drawing together Turkey, Iran, the Fertile Crescent and Arabia, as well as other bordering countries, to form a new economic space. The high level of trust and cooperation between Ankara and Damascus was further highlighted through an attempt to revive the moribund Syrian-Israeli negotiations, this time brokered by the Turks and taking place in Turkey itself. In 2008 the talks gave rise to some hope of progress but were finally abandoned when Israel launched its massive war on Gaza at the end of that year.

As the first decade of the twenty-first century drew to a close Bashar could certainly look back with satisfaction at an albeit turbulent period, during which – against many expectations and despite the scoring of a number of own goals – he not only survived his father's intimidating legacy but was emerging as a leader in his own right, comfortably straddling the regional and international stages. Success in foreign affairs, however, proved in the end to be a poisoned chalice. It blinded him to what was brewing beneath the tranquil surface at home. Bashar failed to appreciate the extent to which elements were gathering that needed only a spark to burst into a storm. Even as warnings emanated from other countries embroiled in the upheavals of what came to be called the Arab Spring he revealed himself to be utterly cocooned from reality. The degree of his complacency was demonstrated in a now notorious interview given to the *Wall Street Journal* and published on 31 January 2011. He denied any similarity between that month's revolution in Tunisia, and the beginnings of the same in Egypt, with the situation in his own country and dismissed the idea of such occurrences in Syria. Stating that the leaders of those countries were paying the price for being out of touch with the sentiments of their people, he claimed he was a different kind of ruler: 'We have more difficult circumstances than most of the Arab countries, but in spite of that Syria is stable. Why? Because you have to be very closely linked to the beliefs of the people. This is the core issue. When there is divergence between your policy and the people's beliefs and interests you will have this vacuum that creates disturbances.' Those words would soon return to haunt the Syrian president as they became the curtain raiser to an almighty tempest.

Notes

1. Shortly after the uprising of 2011 Ferzat was assaulted and kidnapped by suspected government agents. The fingers of one hand were broken before he was released. He is today in exile and continues to publish cartoons sharply critical of Bashar and his rule.
2. The main sponsor of the event was Wafic Saïd – a high-profile Syrian businessman and investor.
3. Dardari was to become an early casualty of the 2011 uprising. Scapegoated by the ruling authorities for his liberal policies, which they saw as having fed the socioeconomic underpinnings of the protests, he left the government and took up a senior UN post in Beirut.
4. President Bush's executive order relating to the act stated that Syria posed 'an unusual and extraordinary threat to the national security, foreign policy, and economy of the United States,' requiring a 'national emergency to deal with that threat.'

5. The appointed ambassador, Dr. Sami Khiyami, was not a career Baathist diplomat, and held independent and even outspoken views that jarred with the official message. He was also a specialist in information technology. As a leading figure in the Syrian Computer Society he worked closely with Bashar in the drive to bring Syria into the age of the Internet.

6. At the end of the year Khaddam openly declared his defection and placed himself in opposition to Bashar from exile in Paris. The fact that he was a stalwart of the regime and implicated by decades of loyalty to it blunted much of his critique; nonetheless the defection, and its timing, were clearly unnerving to the Syrian president and his entourage.

EPILOGUE

On 17 December 2010 Mohamed Bouazizi, a young Tunisian, set fire to himself. His act of ultimate despair resulted from the conditions of deprivation he had been enduring, which had culminated in being stopped by police from selling on the street to earn a living. Tunisians rose in protest and in a few weeks one of the most entrenched Arab dictatorial regimes was overthrown with its head fleeing into exile. The message from Tunisia reverberated throughout the Arab world. The international political scene and media were transfixed by the completely unforeseen awakening of the sleepy Arab street that for long decades had been dismissed as a supine appendage to the despots in charge of their societies. The term 'Arab Spring' was soon coined and applied to all manifestations of unrest and protest that erupted, in varying degrees of gravity, across almost the whole expanse of the Arab region. The most serious of these occurred in Egypt, followed by Libya, Bahrain and Yemen. By the spring of 2011 many pundits were busy listing Arab regimes in a descending order of probability of falling victim to the tsunami battering their shores. Most placed a country as closed as Saudi Arabia or as rich as the United Arab Emirates in the 'least probable' category. But many also regarded Syria as almost certainly immune to the unleashed force of popular power. Much of that belief was based on knowledge of the iron grip of the regime in Damascus and of the long history and experience of that regime in dealing ruthlessly with dissent. Also, despite having inherited the mantle of totalitarian rule from his father, Bashar Assad had succeeded in projecting an image of himself as a reformer, enjoying much popular support (there was no doubting the genuine nature of the latter, if not the former claim).

The president, as we saw at the end of the last chapter, was convinced that his rule was invulnerable. His spokespeople were soon to engage with the Arab Spring phenomenon by disingenuously claiming that the angry masses that had overthrown Ben Ali in Tunisia and Mubarak in Egypt had been motivated by anger at their rulers' 'soft line' on combating Israel. Early signs of the soundness of the confidence of Syria's rulers emerged when calls by activists through social media networks for street demonstrations seemed to fall on deaf ears. For example, a day of action announced for 4 February never materialised. However, even while the dominant mood remained one of assurance, the government was sufficiently concerned by the idea of fallout from Tunisia and elsewhere suddenly to ordain a sharp hike in state salaries. It was the same resort to bribery as that chosen by, for example, Saudi Arabia in answer to the Arab Spring.

Despite the prognosis to the contrary, Syria's 'Bouazizi moment' was not long in coming. It arrived on 6 March 2011 in the town of Daraa, to the south of Damascus. Mimicking what they had heard on television broadcasts from the streets of Tunisia and Egypt, some children scrawled the message 'the people demand the fall of the regime' on a wall in the town. The authorities immediately rounded up the 'guilty' youth and reportedly subjected them to abuse and torture, refusing pleas for their release from anxious parents and relatives. The anger of those families soon grew into street protests and on 18 March a large-scale demonstration followed Friday prayers. Until that moment almost all the disturbances had been centred on Daraa. However, news quickly spread of a violent reaction by the police and security forces to what many believed were justified actions on the part of an aggrieved community, and of the first spilling of the blood of unarmed protesters. In towns and cities across Syria people poured into the streets in a show of solidarity with Daraa. Starting as small groups, the crowds soon became larger but, rather than reflecting a mood for radical, revolutionary change, most of their slogans and demands displayed a yearning for simple freedom: 'hurriyeh ... hurriyeh.' Another common rallying call was that for Syrian unity: 'wahid ... wahid ... al shaab al Suri wahid' (one ... one ... the Syrian people are one). This message was meant as a retort to the government's warnings that the protests risked drawing Syria into a spiral of sectarian strife.

Two weeks after that fateful date of 18 March President Bashar was due to address Syria's parliament, the people's assembly. The whole of Syria, and much of the outside world, waited in anticipation for what he would be declaring. Indeed, the signs on the eve of that speech encouraged those who held on to the belief that Bashar, unlike his father, was going to be conciliatory and responsive to the demands of the protesters. Both the vice president, Farouk Al Sharaa, and the presidential adviser, Dr. Buthaina Shaaban, publicly declared that the president's announcements would be decisive, and pleasing to those demanding change. However, as soon as he began his speech on 30 March Bashar adopted a defiant tone. Instead of reaching out to the protesters he launched into a tirade against the 'conspirators' who were bent on delivering the country to its foreign enemies. Syria, he claimed, was being targeted for its stand in opposition to imperial and Zionist designs, and he vowed to confront and confound the plotters who were behind the seditious elements threatening the country's security. As for the demands for reform he dismissed them in mocking terms, insisting that he had always been in favour of reform but that circumstances of grave national import, meaning the pressure of regional geopolitical challenges, had not allowed the opportunity to implement domestic change. By the time he eventually fell silent, having made no apparent concession to, or even having acknowledged, the new reality taking shape around him observers were stunned. Inside parliament, however, the faithful were in full adulatory and applauding mode: one over-enthusiastic 'representative of the people' hailed Bashar as president not just of Syria but 'the whole world.'

Bashar's speech was the latest and most pivotal lost opportunity to forge for himself and his country a hopeful path away from the apocalyptic course that was set in train . Earlier in his rule he had spurned the chance of riding rather than confronting the Damascus Spring of 2000-01. Later on, after successfully weathering the storms of, first, the American invasion of Iraq and second, the aftermath of Hariri's assassination, and seeing his leadership endorsed both locally and internationally, he failed to build on that solid base by engaging seriously with the reforms for which the country was crying out. Once again, 30 March 2011 presented him with a golden chance to embrace the largely modest demands of the protesters – which did not, at that stage, target him personally – to become the very open champion of managed change. Instead he chose to throw down the soon-to-become-bloodied gauntlet. Up to the eve of that fateful speech reliable reports from sources very close to Bashar point to another text being considered for delivery – one that would have charted a different destiny for the country. If that was the case, then what caused the last-minute volte-face? The most persuasive of theories is that a family caucus stepped in to warn Bashar of the consequences of being seen to bow to the protesters' demands. Pointers to the recent fates of Ben Ali in Tunisia and Mubarak in Egypt, both ultimately overthrown despite having publicly offered concessions, were presented with urgency to a ruffled president caught on the horns of a dilemma. What he failed to appreciate sufficiently by accepting that argument, if this theory holds true, is that, in contrast to Ben Ali and Mubarak, he could have relied on a strong reserve of personal popularity had he decided to make those concessions. Rather than a sign of weakness such a move would arguably have projected an image of a leader in tune with his people and raised his popularity to greater heights. Had he chosen to set himself against a discredited 'regime' he would very likely have been painted as a hero. Unfortunately he had neither the imagination nor the will to consider such a course and the consequence proved to be an unmitigated disaster.

The events that followed are now the stuff of contemporary and unfolding history and it is beyond the scope of this book to chronicle them in detail. As Syria today faces the most existential threat to its very being the guilty parties – the vultures that hover above in the hope of a slice of the spoils – are many. Those presuming to entertain the highest ideals in pursuing their stake in the Syrian conflict are contributing in one way or another to that country's tragedy. All parties to what has become a pitiless conflict, taking such a toll in lives and destruction, as well as rendering millions destitute and now being dubbed the greatest human tragedy for a generation, share in that guilt.

Starting with the Syrian regime its culpability is evident and beyond dispute. By responding so brutally to those who set out as largely peaceful demonstrators, and targeting in particular secular and civil rights leaders and activists, the government and its security agencies made sure that the protests would gradually take on a religious and sectarian dynamic. At the same time as seizing those who could have steered the uprising in the direction of democratic and secular change the authorities released hardened jihadists from prison in full knowledge of the role they would play in skewing the course of the rebellion.

The opposition, in its many manifestations, is no less guilty of betraying the initial trust of the protesters. Instead of holding fast to the principles of a democratic, non-sectarian struggle, and avoiding at all costs falling into the trap of 'Islamising' the uprising, it allowed populist slogans to imbue the movement with a largely sectarian (Sunni) agenda. The result was devastating and alienated the bulk of opinion within sectors of the population identified as minorities (chiefly Alawites and Christians). It also helped to drive away many other Syrians – initial sympathisers with the uprising – who had inherited a culture of non-sectarian inclusiveness and felt unhappy at the path down which the uprising was being pushed. That direction was being pursued with energy by a major component of the Turkey-based official opposition – the Muslim Brotherhood.

'Outside' parties are all playing their destructive role whether wittingly or unwittingly. The West, and the United States administration in particular, having maintained during the first few months of the protests that Bashar Assad could still 'rise to the occasion' and lead a reform programme, changed its tune by the summer and by August President Obama was asserting that Assad had 'lost his legitimacy.' Many protesters read that as meaning that an intervention on the scale witnessed in Libya was forthcoming, feeding the illusion that 'the world' would come to their rescue. When that did not happen and the regime resorted to a full military offensive the effect was to turn a substantial section of the protest movement towards armed struggle, helped along by defections from the official army. Thus was born a vicious cycle of killing and destruction, and the mutations in the fighting forces that eventually brought the world the monster that is Daesh. All the parties that have used the Syrian conflict to pursue their narrow interests have, at one point or another, used Daesh to leverage those interests even as they heaped opprobrium on the barbaric entity that straddles Syria and Iraq. For the West Daesh was a useful and ever-present reminder to local powers of their need for stronger security ties and regular concomitant sales of military hardware available from their post-imperial protectors. For Russia Daesh is a convenient alibi for the real purpose of their intervention in Syria: to prop up its ally in Damascus and secure its strategic interests in the region. For Turkey Daesh is a good cover for mounting attacks on the more 'immediate' enemy: the Kurdish PYD party affiliated to the PKK. For Iran and its appendages in the Lebanese Hezbollah militia and the other Iraqi and Afghan Shiite forces doing battle in Syria Daesh is the perfect personification of the evil of Sunni *takfir* (the charge of religious heresy directed at others), helping to stoke even further the fires of Shia revanchism. For Saudi Arabia – and Qatar – Daesh might be an eventual existential enemy but it momentarily serves the purpose of keeping the hated Iranians and their Shiite proxies in check in both Syria and Iraq. So did the Daesh phenomenon insert whole new levels of complexity into an already hydra-headed conflict.

At the time of writing, and further especially to the terrorist attacks of 13 November 2015 in Paris and the downing a few days earlier of the Russian airliner over Sinai (claimed by Daesh), a certain urgency is growing over the need to deal decisively with the terror 'state' with its capital in Raqqa. Only time will tell whether the emotional outrage will be matched by cohesive action that will override the game-playing referred to above. Even more important is the attention now seeming to be paid to the need to get at the fundamental causes of Daesh's strength – its ability to exploit to the full the conflict inside Syria (and Iraq). Syria stands out as exactly the kind of failed state, fuelling ethno-sectarian passions, that provides oxygen for Daesh and feeds its appeal. An international initiative, arising from a meeting in Vienna of all parties with a stake in the Syrian conflict – including, for the first time, Iran – has mapped out a pathway to a political settlement in Syria. The odds, however, are stacked against the success of that initiative, given the differences still outstanding over key issues, particularly the fate of the Syrian president. Yet, should diplomatic efforts fail, no military strategy, however coordinated or fully resourced with firepower, could overcome Daesh or any successor to its mantle. The inescapable truth is that Daesh is a symptom and all efforts to deal with it independently of Syria's sickness are doomed to failure.

A singularly dispiriting fact is that the frenetic mood of international activity over Daesh, together with the many voices from the outside bearing on Syria's destiny, has smothered the voices of the Syrians themselves. These are the real victims of the relentless carnage, and on their shoulders must rest the ultimate responsibility for determining the shape and nature of their ancient homeland's future. The historian Tom Holland recently wrote that 'when, in due course, the killing stops, the blood dries and the Syrian people attempt to refashion something out the rubble to which their land has been reduced they will need symbols.' These symbols are there in the pages of Syria's rich history. They are to be found in the heritage that created the first alphabet, in the soil from which the first human-sown produce was reaped, in the welcoming, melting-pot tradition of its society, in providing the territorial platform for the spread into the world of the great religions of Christianity and Islam, in the bravery of Zenobia, Saladin and Youssef Al Azmah, in the splendour of the Ummayads of Damascus and Andalusia, in the rich tapestry of political and cultural life that rendered Syria a pioneer of the Arab national awakening, in its victorious stand against colonial rule, in the vibrant, inclusive, metropolitan life of Aleppo, in the stubborn resistance to attempts (notably by the French in the twenties and thirties) to establish walls of separation between the pluralistic composites that form a unique and historically resilient feature of Syrian society. These and many others are the very symbols that will see Syria through the bleakness and devastation of today, and, when the guns fall silent, they will surely be the cornerstones upon which its future will be built.

FURTHER READING

FURTHER READING

ENGLISH LANGUAGE

Antonius, George, THE ARAB AWAKENING, Khayat's, Beirut, 1955

Armanazi, Ghayth, 'Bouncing Back' (Syria's New Confidence) article in THE WORLD TODAY, Royal Institute of International Affairs, May 2006

I

Armanazi, Ghayth, 'Syrian Foreign Policy at the Crossroads', article in Youssef M Choueri ed., STATE AND SOCIETY IN SYRIA AND LEBANON, University of Exeter Press, 1993

Clark, Peter, DAMASCUS DIARIES, Gilgamesh Publishing, London, 2015

Everett, Flynt, INHERITING SYRIA: BASHAR'S TRIAL BY FIRE, Brookings Institution Press, Washington DC, 2005

Fromkin, David, A PEACE TO END ALL PEACE: CREATING THE MODERN MIDDLE EAST 1914-1922, Penguin Books, London, 1991

George, Alan, SYRIA: NEITHER BREAD NOR FREEDOM, Zed Books, London, 2003

Hitti, Philip, HISTORY OF SYRIA INCLUDING LEBANON AND PALESTINE, MacMillan, London,1951

Lesch, David W, SYRIA: THE FALL OF THE HOUSE OF ASSAD, Yale University Press, 2013

Longrigg, Stephen Helmsley, SYRIA AND LEBANON UNDER FRENCH MANDATE, Oxford University Press, 1958

Louis, William Roger, THE BRITISH EMPIRE IN THE MIDDLE EAST 1945-1951, Clarendon Press, Oxford, 1984

Ma'oz, Moshe, ASAD: THE SPHINX OF DAMASCUS, Weidenfeld and Nicholson, London, 1988

Ma'oz, Moshe; Ginat, Joseph; Winckler, Onn eds. MODERN SYRIA, Sussex Academic Press, Brighton, 1999

Mardam Bey, Salma, SYRIA'S QUEST FOR INDEPENDENCE, Ithaca Press, Reading, 1994

McHugo, John, SYRIA: A RECENT HISTORY, Saqi Books, 2014

Rabinovitch, Itamar, THE ROAD NOT TAKEN, Oxford University Press, 1991

Scheller, Bente, THE WISDOM OF SYRIA'S WAITING GAME: SYRIAN FOREIGN POLICY UNDER THE ASSADS, Hurst and Company, London, 2013

Seale, Patrick, ASAD: THE STRUGGLE FOR THE MIDDLE EAST, I.B. Tauris, London, 1988

Seale, Patrick, THE STRUGGLE FOR SYRIA, Yale University Press, London, 1987

Spears, Edward, FULFILMENT OF A MISSION: SYRIA AND LEBANON 1941-1944, Leo Cooper, London, 1977

Wieland, Carsten; Almvqvist, Adam; Nassif, Helena, THE SYRIAN UPRISING, University of St. Andrews Centre for Syrian Studies, 2013

Yasmin-Kassab, Robin and Al-Shami, Leila, BURNING COUNTRY: SYRIANS IN REVOLUTION AND WAR, Pluto Press, 2016

Zeine, Zeine N, THE STRUGGLE FOR ARAB INDEPENDENCE, Khayat's, Beirut, 1960

ARABIC LANGUAGE

Armanazi, Najib, ASHR SANAWAT FI AL DIPLOMASIA (Ten Years in Diplomacy), Dar Al Kitab Al Jadid, Beirut, 1963

Armanazi, Najib, SOURIA MIN AL IHTILAL HATTA AL JALAA (Syria from Occupation to Independence), Dar Al Kitab Al Jadid, Beirut, 1973

Al Azmeh, Abdelaziz, MIRAAT AL SHAM (Mirror of Syria) Riad El-Rayyes Books, London, 1987

Babil, Nasouh, SAHAFA WA SIYASA (Journalism and Politics: Syria in the 20th Century), Riad El-Rayyes Books, London, 1987

Bashour, Amal Mikhael, DIRASA FI TARIKH SOURIA AL SIYASI AL MOUASSIR (A Study of Syrian Contemporary Political History) Undated private publication

Butros, Antoine, QISSAT MUHAKAMET ANTUN SAADEH (The Story of the Trial of Antun Saadeh), Manrikh Publishers, Beirut, 2002

Hanna, Abdullah, ABDUL RAHMAN AL SHAHBANDAR, Al Ahali Publishers, Damascus, 2000

Husain, Louai ed. HIWARAT FI AL WATANIA AL SOURISH (Syrian National Dialogues), Petra Publishers, Beirut, 2005

Shaaban, Buthaina, 'ASHR A'WAM MA HAFEZ AL ASSAD (Ten Years with Hafez Assad), Centre for the Study of Arab Unity, Beirut, 2015

Al Sharaa, Farouk, AL RIWAYA AL MAFQOUDA (The Lost Story), Arab Centre for Research and Policy Studies, Beirut, 2015

INDEX

INDEX

A

Abbasid Caliphate, 20-22
Abdul Aziz, 85
Abdul Hamid (Sultan), 30
Abdullah, (King), 85
Abdullah, Emir, 83
Abu Nidal, 232
Aflaq, Michel, 80, 89, 116, 143, 145, 147, 153, Plate 12
Africa Corps, 68
Ain Jalout, 22
Akhras, Fawaz, 247
Akkadian Empire, 15
Al Ahd, 32-33, 36
Al Ahram, 159
Al Ali, Sheikh Saleh, 51
Al Aqsa Mosque, 178
Al Assifa, 152
Al Atassi, Brigadier Luay, 148
Al Atassi, Hashem, 59-60, 63, 94-95, 99
Al Atassi, Nur Al Din, 154, Plate 13
Al Azmah, Youssef, 47, 266, Plate 2
Al Azmeh, Bashar, 4
Al Bakr, Ahmad Hassan, 201
Al Barazi, Mohsen, 92, 93
Al Domari, 237
Al Faranjah, 21
Al Hafez, Brigadier Amine, Plate 11
Al Hinnawi, Brigadier Sami, 92

Al Horani, Akram, 81, 85, 93, 100, 110, 116, 123, 131, 133, 173, Plate 7
Al Ikha Al Arabi, 30
al Jabiri, Saad Allah, 71
Al Jazaifri, Abdul Qader, 25
Al Jazeera, 125, 127
Al Jundi, Captain Abd Al Karim, 139
Al Khouri, Faris, 71-72, 86
Al Kudsi, Nadem, Plate 10
Al Malek Al Zaher Baibars (Sultan), 22
Al Mazraa, 54
Al Mir, Major Ahmad, 138
Al Muntada Al Adabi, 31
Al Qaida, 242-243
Al Qawukji, Fawzi, 85
Al Qudsi, Nazem, 134, 138
Al Quwatly, Shukri, 71, 76, 83, 86-87, 99, 106, 108, 114, Plate 6 & 12
Al Rashid, Caliph Harun, 20
Al Sadr, Musa, 202
Al Said, Nuri, 83, 119
Al Saiqa, 165
Al Sarraj, Abdul Hamid, 102, 115, Plate 11
Al Sharaa, Farouk, 223, 229, 238, 260
Al Shishakli, Adib, 85, 93, Plate 8
Al Thawra, 236-237
Al Walid, Khaled Ibn, 19-20

Al Zaim, Brigadier Husni, 87, 89
Albright, Madeleine, 235
Ali, Ben, 259, 262
Allenby, General, 37, 39
Allied Supreme Council, 46
Alwan, Jassim, 140, 146
Amal Movement, 211
Amer, Hakim, 123
Amer, Marshal Abdul Hakim,
    123, 126, 130
Amir, Yigal, 226
Andalusia, 20
Andrews Centre, 269
Andropov, Yuri, 210
Annapolis Conference, 254
Aoun, General Michel, 217, 244
Arab Centre, 270
Arab Congress, 32
Arab Cooperation Council, 213
Arab League, 84, 140, 195,
    218, 253
Arab Liberation Movement, 95, 97
Arab Nationalist Movement, 103,
    141, 146, 164
Arab Socialist Party, 81, 133
Arafat, Yasser, 163, 168, 191,
    197, 221
Aref, Abdul Salam, 119, 142, 147
Armanazi, Ali, 5, 36, Plate 1
Armanazi, Najib, 5, 75, Plate 6
Assad, Bashar, 248, 250, 259, 263,
    Plate 14
Assad, Bassel, Plate 14
Assad, Hafez, 7, 138, 154, 165,
    167, 171, 173, 175, 177, 179,
    181, 183, 185, 187, 189-191,

193, 195, 197-201, 203, 205,
    207, 209-211, 213, 215, 217,
    219, 221, 224, 225, 227-229,
    231, 234, 241, 246, 254, 270,
    Plate 13 & 15
Assad, Maher, 251
Assad, Rifaat, 198
Augustus, Emperor, 17
Australian Light Horse
    Brigage, 38
Azm, Khaled, 100, 104, 108,
    110-111, 114, 133, 141
Azmeh, Bashir, 138-139

B

Baath, 81, 89, 144
Baghdad Pact, 100-103, 109
Baker, James, 171, 219
Barak, Ehud, 224, 225, 229
Barazi, Mohsen, 93
Bekaa Valley, 205, 208
Bikdash, Khaled, 81, 100, 111
Bilad Al Sham, 13, 76
Bitar, Salah Eldin, 123, 131, 133,
    143, 148
Bizri, General Afif, 109, 111, 115
Blair, Tony, 247
Bouazizi, Mohamed, 258
Brezhnev, Leonid, 194
Britain, 40, 74
British Syrian Society, 247, 253
Broumana High School, 26
Bush, George (Senior), 216, 241,
    244, 256
Bustani, Butrus, 27

C

Cairo Radio, 113, 132
Camp David, 196
Campbell, Menzies, 8
Catroux, General, 69
Cedar Revolution, 251
Chamoun, Camille, 75, 118
Cheney, Dick, 244
Chirac, Jacques, 234, 248
Christian Phalange Party, 91, 190
Churchill, Winston, 48, 74
Clemenceau, Georges, 41
Clinton, Bill, 223, 241, Plate 15
Communist Party, 81, 120, 173
Constantinople, 23
Cooper, Leo, 269
Crane, Charles, 43, 52

D

Dardari, Abdullah, 239
Dawalibi, Maarouf, 134
Dayan, Moshe, 160
De Gaulle, Charles, 71
Dentz, General, 68
Druze Mountain, 52, 54-55,
   57, 97, 208

E

Eban, Abba, 159
Ebla, 14, 15
Eden, Anthony, 75, 106
Edinburgh, Duke of, Plate 4
Erishum, (Akkadian King), 15

F

Fahd, King, 213, 215
Faisal, Emir, 33, 37, 39, 40, 44,
   45, 47, 51, 178, 186, Plate 2
Faisal, King, the First, Plate 2
Farouk, King, 85, 91, 95
Fatah Intifada, 211
Fatimids 21
Fayyad, Shafiq, 210
Ferzat, Ali, 237
Frangieh, Suleiman, 195

G

Gaddafi, Colonel, 175
Gamelin, General, 55
Gemayel, Amine, 217
Gemayel, Bashir, 206
General Syrian Congress, 45
George, Lloyd, 41-42, 46
Glubb Pasha, 106
Gouraud, General, 46-48, 51-52,
   73, Plate 3
Gromyko, Andrei, 186
Gulf Cooperation Counci
   (GCC), 218

H

Habash, George, 164
Habib, Philip, 205
Hafiz, Brigadier Amine, 148, 150,
   152-153
Hanano, Ibrahim, 50-51, 63
Haram Al Sharif, 241

Hariri, Major Ziad, 143, 145
Hariri, Rafic, 248
Hasani, Sheikh Taj al-Din, 58
Haydar, Ali, 210
Helou, Farajallah, 116
Hezbollah, 264
Hinnawi, Brigadier Sami, 92
Hrawi, Elias, 217
Hussein, Grand Sharif, 35, 48
Hussein, King, 33, 38, 42, 106,
    121, 151, 156, 168, 177,
    198, 222
Hussein, Preident Saddam, 198,
    201-203, 212-215, 217

I

Ibn Marwan, Abd Al Malik 20
Ibrahim Pasha, 25

J

Jackson, Reverend Jesse, 209
Jadid, Major Salah, 138, 154,
    165, 167, Plate 12
Jamal, Pasha, 37-38
Jamiat Al Fatat Al Arabiya, 31
Jerusalem, East, 151, 155, 159,
    178, 241
Johnson, President Lindon, 159
Jumblatt, Kamal 192, 197

K

Khaddam, Abdul Halim, 228,
    234, 237, 249
Khiyami, Sami, 257, Plate 15
Khleifawi, Abdul Rahman, 174

Khomeini, Ayatollah, 202, 212
Kissinger, Henry, 175, 185
Kuzbari, Colonel Haydar,
    134, 136

L

Labour Party, 226
Lahoud, Emile, 248, 250
Lawrence, Y.E., Plate 2
Lebanese National Day, 71
Lebanon, 51, 71
Lebanon, Mount, 26-27, 51, 192
Likud Party, 203
Lipkin, General Amnon, 225
Literary Club, The 31

M

Machiavelli, 41-42, 44, 46
Madrid Peace Conference, 171
Makhos, Ibrahim, 154
Malki, Colonel Adnan, 102
Mardam Bey, 268
Mardam Bey, Prime Minister Jamil,
    Plate 5
Marj, Dabeq, 40
McMahon, Sir Henry Arthur, 35
Meir, Golda, 85
Miliband, David, 254
Mubarak, Hosni, 215
Muhammad Ali Pasha, 25
Murphy, Robert, 121

N

Nahlawi, Major Abdul Karim, 136
Nasrallah, Hassan, 252

Nasser, Gamal Abdul, 95, 104,
113, 114, 252, Plate 9 & 12
Netanyahu, Benjamin, 228
North Africa, 20, 24, 77, 117
North Korea, 200

O

Omran, Lieutenant Colonel
Mohammad, 138, 154
Ottoman Empire, 24-25, 30, 33,
35, 38

P

Palestine 268
Palestine Liberation Organisation
(PLO), 151, 221
Palestine Salvation Army, 85
Palmerston, Lord, 25
Paris Peace Conference, 42, 44
Pasha Al Atrash, Sultan, 54-55, 57,
Plate 3
Peres, Shimon, 226
Phalange Party, 191, 205, 206
Picot, Georges, 36
Ponsot, Henri, 57, 60
Powell, Colin, 244, 246
Progressive Party, 192
Puaux, Gabriel, 67

Q

Qassem, Abdul Karim, 119,
135, 142
Qudsi, President Nazim, 135
Queen Elizabeth, 247

R

Rabin, Prime Minister Yitzhak,
221, 223, 229
Rabin, Yitzhak, 221, 229
Rabinovich, Itamar, 90, 224
Razzaz, Munif, 153
Red Sea, 37
Roman Empire, 18
Rommel, General, 68
Ross, Dennis, 224
Rumsfeld, Donald, 244-5

S

Saadeh, Antun, 80, 91, 270,
Plate 5
Sadat, President Anwar, 110, 175,
196, Plate 14
Salim, Sultan, 23
San Francisco, 72
San Stefano, 28
Sarkis, Elias, 195
Sarkozy, Nicolas, 253
Sarrail, General, 53-56
Saudi Arabia, 72, 83, 90, 104, 117,
121, 177-178, 180, 184, 190,
195-196, 213, 215, 251, 253,
259
Security Council Resolution, 186
Seleucid Empire, 16-17
Selo, Brigadier Fawzi, 95
Sfeir, Cardinal, 244
Shaaban, Buthaina, 260
Shahbandar, Abdulrahman, 61,
Plate 4
Shamir, Yitzhaq, 219

Sharm El-Sheikh, 158
Sharon, General Ariel, 183, 204, 207, 241
Shawkat, Assef, 251
Shawqi, Ahmad, 49
Shehab, President Fouad, 139, 121
Shehabi, General Hikmat, 234, 224-5
Shehabi, Major General Hikmat, 224, 234
Shuqairi, Ahmad, 151, 163
Sinai Peninsula, 34, 157
Sourya, Nafir, 27
Suez Canal, 105, 169, 177, 179, 182, 184
Sultan Yacoub , Battle of 205-206
Sykes, Sir Mark, 36
Syrian Communist Party, 81, 100
Syrian Computer Society, 228, 235, 257
Syrian Protestant College, 26
Syrian Social Nationalist, 80, 91, 207-208, Plate 5

T

Tel Aviv, 155, 159, 176, 178, 187, 192, 194, 219, 224, 227, 229
Tito, President, 101
Twain, Mark, 13

U

United Arab Emirates (UAE), 259
United Arab Republic (UAR), 7, 111, 113-115, 117, 119, 121, 123, 125, 127, 129, 131, 137, 145, Plate 12

United Kingdom (UK), 100, 166, 247
United Nations (UN), 72, 158, 186, 218, 243, 248
United Nations Security Council, 86
United States (US), 44, 70, 72, 74, 83, 90, 157, 160, 168, 175-176, 181, 185, 194, 207, 213-214, 218, 227, 244, 250, 256, 263

V

Versailles Peace Conference, 41

W

Wall Street Journal, 255
Warren, Christopher, 224, 226
Weygand, General, 53
Wilson President Woodrow, 41, 44
Wingate, Sir Reginald, 38
World War I, 32-33
World War II, 9, 66, 213

Y

Yazigi, Nassif, 27
Yom Kippur, 179

Z

Zaher Baibars, 22
Zahreddin, General Abdul Karim, 119, 137
Zaim, Field Marshal Hosni, Plate 7
Zengi, Nur ad-Din, 21
Zuaiyin, Prime Minister Yusef, 154